A History of the Royal Air Force
in the Far East
1945 — 1972

MINISTRY OF DEFENCE AIR HISTORICAL BRANCH (RAF)

EASTWARD

A History of the Royal Air Force
in the Far East
1945 — 1972

Air Chief Marshal Sir David Lee GBE CB

LONDON: HER MAJESTY'S STATIONERY OFFICE

ISBN 0 11 772354 1*

THE AIR HISTORICAL BRANCH (RAF)

The Air Historical Branch is located within the Air Force Department of the Ministry of Defence. The tasks include the preservation of the historical archive of the Royal Air Force, the answering of historical enquiries, and research and writing. Since the official documents of the years up to and including World War II are now available at the Public Record Office, the Air Historical Branch now concentrates its work largely on the history of the Royal Air Force since 1945. A number of post-war studies have already been completed for official use, and this volume by Sir David Lee is the second to be placed on public sale. It is hoped that more will follow in due course.

The author has been given full access to official documents. He alone is responsible for the statements made and the views expressed.

HER MAJESTY'S STATIONERY OFFICE

Government Bookshops

49 High Holborn, London WC1V 6HB
13a Castle Street, Edinburgh EH2 3AR
Brazennose Street, Manchester M60 8AS
Southey House, Wine Street, Bristol BS1 2BQ
258 Broad Street, Birmingham B1 2HE
80 Chichester Street, Belfast BT1 4JY

Government publications are also available
through booksellers

Contents

Illustrations

Maps

Diagrams

Note by the author

A number of place names in this book changed during the period covered, eg Batavia has become Djakarta, Siam is now Thailand.

The spelling used is in accordance with the time described, and may differ from that found in modern documents and maps.

Foreword

by Marshal of the Royal Air Force Sir John Grandy GCB KBE DSO

The Far East has a special fascination for me. I first flew there in 1944 ferrying a Beaufighter Mark X from Cairo West on appointment to the Combat Cargo Task Force; the Burma Campaign was building up to full momentum. I remained until a posting home came some little time after the Japanese surrender.

I returned in 1965 as Commander British Forces Far East (CINCFE), and sensed once more that magic attraction of the Orient with its myriad peoples, mystery and colour so graphically recaptured in this book.

Primarily the tale Sir David Lee has to tell concerns the almost continuous series of campaigns in which the Royal Air Force took part during the post-war years until the final withdrawal. He starts by describing the immediate clearing-up problems including a difficult and involved operation (in which we both took part) in the Netherlands East Indies. Not so long after this comes the Malayan Emergency, a campaign that was to last for twelve long years for three of which the Korean War was also in progress. After a comparatively quiet pause there follows Confrontation with Indonesia, and then the return home.

In describing the role of the Royal Air Force in these distant activities Sir David writes vividly of the men and women concerned, the conditions under which they lived and operated and the aircraft which they flew and maintained. Working closely with the Navy and Army and the Air Forces of our Commonwealth partners, the Royal Air Force had to contend with some of the most challenging operating conditions in the world. And it must be remembered that they did so without those sophisticated electronic and other aids to navigation, communications and maintenance which are the commonplace today.

This is an important book. I commend it to all interested in Service history, particularly those who served in the Far East. It is a striking record of the Royal Air Force contribution to that peace and freedom upon which the stability and prosperity now enjoyed by Malaysia and Singapore have subsequently been built.

Acknowledgements

The writing of this history necessitated a great deal of research into archives, and consultation with many individuals and authorities who were involved in the campaigns and incidents described herein. The RAF material has been drawn largely from official documents, Operations Record Books, Air Staff files and associated papers made available to me by the Air Historical Branch (RAF). Air Commodore H A Probert MBE MA RAF (RETD), the Head of the Air Historical Branch, and his staff have assisted me in every possible way, and it would not have been possible to write this book without their unstinted help, notably that of Mr D C Bateman whose work in copy editing the text, compiling the Index and helping to select the illustrations I greatly appreciated.

My thanks go to Marshal of the Royal Air Force Sir John Grandy GCB KBE DSO, sometime Commander-in-Chief, Far East, upon whose experience I was able to draw, and who has kindly written the Foreword. My thanks also to Wing Commanders J R Dowling MBE DFC AFC and P R A Austin AFC who provided much of the information on helicopter operations from their own wide experience.

I received many valuable comments from Dr Peter Lowe, of Manchester University, who took a great interest in the political aspects of developments in the Far East. The work of Squadron Leaders T C Chivers, F W J Davies and S H Grey must be acknowledged for the brief but excellent staff narrative of the Malayan Emergency which they compiled and which has been extensively quoted in the appropriate chapters.

The work of preparing the maps was undertaken at short notice by the Royal Air Force Staff College, and my thanks go to the Commandant for making available the facilities of his Drawing Office under the direction of Mr M P Root, who ably produced the maps, often from the most inadequate information.

Production of the book and design of the cover and jacket were undertaken by Her Majesty's Stationery Office to whom I am indebted.

D J P L

Acknowledgements

Introduction
Setting the Scene

We have left Singapore and Malaya, Burma and Borneo. We have left India and Ceylon and even relinquished the island staging post of Gan. We have retained a foothold in Hong Kong, and that is all that remains of the powerful military presence which Britain maintained throughout the vast area of the Indian Ocean and South-East Asia which we have always called the Far East.

The narrative in this book deals essentially with the relatively short period of twenty-seven years—from 1945 to 1972—at the beginning of which Britain either returned to her old possessions or temporarily occupied those of her allies while the debris left by World War II was being cleared away. It was a period of immense change: country after country came to independence and threw off the yoke of colonialism. In the military field the development of air power, which had been given such impetus during the war, continued at an even greater pace and in no theatre was the immense versatility of aircraft better demonstrated than in the Far East. Had their true potential been understood during the decade preceding 1941, the defences of Singapore in particular might have been more realistically organised and our Far Eastern empire might not have been so catastrophically overwhelmed by Japan.

Some brief description of Britain's role in the theatre prior to 1939, and of the part played by the Royal Air Force, will help the reader to visualise the extent of the area which Britain and her allies in World War II were compelled to relinquish and which it fell to Britain to reoccupy after the Japanese capitulation in 1945. From the Maldivian island of Gan in the Indian Ocean it stretched to the east as far as Hong Kong and from Burma in the north to the southernmost part of the Netherlands East Indies (see Map 1).

Prior to the 1920s Hong Kong was regarded as the base for British forces. The difficulties of defending the Colony against a determined attack were fully realised but a modest naval base and army garrison were considered adequate at that time to safeguard the trading activities in the colonial possessions and to secure the sea route through to Australia and New Zealand. A handful of airmen were pioneering an air route across India and down the west coast of Burma, Siam and Malaya to Singapore but air transportation was in its infancy and, at that time, posed no threat to the great ocean liners of the P&O Company and others which dominated the sea routes to the Far East.

Japan was, however, showing increasing signs of expansionist activity, notably towards China. Her navy was the third largest in the world after those of Britain and the United States. Being concentrated in the mid Pacific area, in contrast to the navies of Britain and of the United States which tended to be dissipated by world wide commitments, it posed a powerful threat to Japan's neighbours. Under these circumstances it was understandable that Britain should have her earlier doubts about the adequacy of her Hong Kong base reinforced. It was too small and it was too far to the east of the centre of gravity of Britain's Far Eastern interests and responsibilities. Consequently, on 16 June 1921, the British Government decided to establish a naval base at Singapore. After much discussion a site was selected on the Johore Strait to the north of the island in preference to Keppel Harbour on the exposed southern side close to Singapore Town.

It was one thing to decide upon this project, but quite another to implement the decision. Changes of Government and political vacillation caused the construction of the naval base to be stopped, resumed, and stopped again with the result that more than a decade passed before a final decision to complete it was taken. The decision was made no easier by the growth of air power during this period. It had always been assumed that the dense Malayan jungle would preclude any threat to Singapore from an overland advance, and that the only significant threat lay from the sea: hence the decision to protect the naval base with heavy coastal artillery sited to fire seawards with a restricted arc of fire. This was anathema to the protagonists of air power who mounted an increasingly powerful lobby to include aircraft in the Singapore defences. A further factor which created delay and favoured those who opposed construction of the base was the "ten year rule", a strange Cabinet dictum introduced after World War I, when Britain's enemies had been routed and there was no likelihood of her involvement in a major war in the foreseeable future. The rule assumed annually that there would be no major conflict for a further ten years. Under the changing circumstances of the late 1920s and early 1930s this was a stupid and unrealistic perpetuation which only the insistence of the Chiefs of Staff caused to be dropped in 1932.

Despite the short sighted view taken by many in Whitehall of the potential of air power, a decision to develop an airfield and a seaplane base at Seletar, in association with the naval base, was pressed through. The first RAF aircraft to land on the Johore Strait was a Fairy IIID seaplane from *HMS Pegasus*, on 20 April 1924. From that moment work went ahead slowly to develop the air base on a 600 acre site of undulating, tree and scrub covered land rising from the foreshore alongside the seaplane base at Seletar. The work of preparing the airfield was arduous and technically difficult. Great credit goes to Mr C E Woods, the Principal Works and Buildings Officer, RAF Far East, for constructing what many airmen subsequently described as the finest airfield they had ever seen. In view of the torrential monsoon rains which affect Singapore at certain times of the year, the drainage of this grass airfield was all important. It was constructed as an oval inverted saucer with monsoon drains located every few yards around its circumference. So accurate were the gradients that, after a heavy storm, every drain could be seen to be filling to capacity, so that within half an hour, what had been a lake several inches deep, was again a hard green surface.

Almost two years before the airfield was completed and opened officially on 1 January 1930, four Southampton flying boats were despatched to Singapore and carried out a magnificent pioneering flight from the United Kingdom to Seletar, via Australia and Hong Kong, where they became the Far East Flight, subsequently renamed 205 Squadron. They were followed, when the airfield was usable, by 36 Squadron, equipped with the Horsley torpedo bomber. The role of these two early maritime squadrons illustrated the obsession that Singapore could only be attacked from the sea. That thinking was, however, soon to change.

In 1933 both Germany and Japan withdrew from the League of Nations, an action which caused Britain not only to accelerate the completion of the Singapore base, but also to initiate a general programme of rearmament. Events then moved comparatively rapidly when a committee under Stanley Baldwin succeeded in breaking down the obsession with the seaward defence of Singapore by recommending that its defences should be organised on a basis of co-operation between the three Services, the gun retaining its place as the main deterrent against naval attack, and the air force acting as a valuable addition to the fixed defences as well as providing an offensive capability. Accordingly the RAF was to participate in all aspects of the defence of the base, including fighter defence and offensive action against ships.

By this time 100 Squadron had joined 36 Squadron at Seletar and both squadrons were equipped with the Vildebeeste torpedo bomber. It was a busy time for the station, largely because it had to be used by the increasing number of civil aircraft flying down the route which had been developed from Europe to the Far East and on to Australia and New Zealand. Imperial Airways, KLM, Air France and QANTAS led the way in pioneering these long distance routes. The pressure on Seletar was relieved by the opening of a civil airport at Kallang close to Singapore harbour and, in addition, the decision was taken to start work on a second RAF airfield at Tengah, well to the west of Seletar.

This modest growth in the RAF presence called for the establishment of a Headquarters to control, not only those stations and units in Singapore, but also any RAF activities or facilities in Burma, Malaya and Hong Kong. Headquarters, Royal Air Force, Far East was therefore constituted, initially at Seletar and moving subsequently to Union Buildings in Singapore town. The first Air Officer Commanding was Air Commodore A W Tedder, later to become the Chief of the Air Staff. Under his command the construction of a number of up-country airfields on the mainland of Malaya was undertaken. Such landing grounds as existed were situated along the west coast, having been developed largely for civil aviation. Although the RAF was welcome to use these, and indeed did, the lack of landing grounds on the east coast of Malaya was keenly felt. It was here that the new construction took place, notably at Kota Bharu, Kuantan and Kahang. They were not, however, well sited for the defence of the approaches to Singapore, which was still thought to be vulnerable only from the sea.

The potential of air power was, however, beginning to be realised and attitudes towards it were changing. The rapid expansion of the RAF to combat the increasing threat from a resurgent German Air Force and the equally rapid growth of Japan's air force began to have their effect on strategic thinking with the result that, in 1938, the General Officer Commanding, Malaya, admitted in a strategic appreciation that invasion of the east coast of Malaya was indeed possible and the dense Malayan jungle was not impassable to infantry. He concluded that the defence of Singapore and its naval base had become dependent upon the security of north Malaya.

This was indeed a change of heart, coming as it did at a time when the situation in Europe was deteriorating rapidly despite the brief respite afforded by the Munich Agreement. It would take seventy days for a British fleet to reach Singapore from home waters and it had always been considered, at least by the Government, that Singapore's defences could hold out until the fleet arrived. By 1939, however, there was doubt whether it would be possible to spare an adequate fleet when the security of the United Kingdom was threatened. In view of this uncertainty, it was decided to strengthen both land and air forces in the Far East. Plans to reinforce Singapore with bomber squadrons from India had existed, and had been practised, for several years. These plans were now implemented and 11 and 39 Squadrons, each equipped with twelve Blenheims, were despatched from the North West Frontier stations in India. Hardly had they arrived when war in Europe broke out. The news reached the Far East during dinner at RAF Seletar, whereupon the Station Commander, Wing Commander G M Bryer, rose at the table and announced, "Gentlemen, we are at war". Within two weeks, two more Blenheim squadrons, Nos 34 and 62 with 16 aircraft apiece, reached the island from the United Kingdom, resulting in an order of battle of two flying boat squadrons, two of obsolescent Vildebeestes and four of Blenheims.

The story of the wartime years is fully chronicled in the five volumes of the official history series 'The War against Japan', and the RAF contribution is also well covered in Volumes II and III of Denis Richards' 'The Royal Air Force 1939–45'[1]. The briefest summary will therefore suffice here.

The war did not, of course, come to the Far East until December 1941, and Britain's failure to provide adequate defences in South-East Asia must be viewed in the context of the battle for survival that was being fought in Europe. As Sir Maurice Dean comments on the fall of Singapore in 'The Royal Air Force and Two World Wars'[2]

---

[1] HMSO, 1975
[2] Cassell, 1979

Britain was at no time capable of taking on Germany and Japan simultaneously. It must nevertheless be said, with the benefit of hindsight, that the failure to appreciate that air power in the support of land forces had made Singapore vulnerable from mainland Malaya was regrettable. Only in July 1940 did the Chiefs of Staff officially accept that Britain must endeavour to hold the whole of Malaya, and there can be little doubt that the efficacy of the Japanese air force in China since 1937 had never been adequately assessed. In particular the performance of the Zero fighter should have given cause for alarm. Even in Singapore in 1940 there was disagreement between the Army and RAF about the manner in which the land/air defences should be strengthened. Much too little and much too late must be the conclusion of any historian reviewing Britain's Far Eastern defences prior to the Japanese attack.

The attack itself found the RAF with only 158 front line aircraft in Singapore and Malaya, mostly obsolescent and spread across some 26 airfields, many of them far from adequate in both siting and facilities. Yet in October 1940, the number of aircraft required for successful defence had been estimated as 566. The two month campaign witnessed a number of gallant actions against overwhelming odds but by early February the remnants of the RAF squadrons had been evacuated to Sumatra and Java, where the Japanese again very quickly caught up with them, the few survivors eventually making their way to Australia or Ceylon. In Burma, too, a pathetically small force of aircraft did its best to support the Army but to no avail, and by March 1942 India, Ceylon and Australia were virtually in the front line.

The next two years saw little by way of offensive activity. Not only could Britain and the USA spare too few resources from the war in Europe—and, from the American point of view, the battles of the Pacific—but without proper base facilities no effective operations could ever be mounted. Consequently every effort was devoted to developing India as the main base for the Army and the RAF. Previously the RAF in India had been concerned mainly with the defence of the North-West Frontier, together with a certain amount of training; now, with the main battles to be fought in the East, there had to be a complete reorientation. The task entailed building well over 200 airfields, and bringing in from overseas not only the personnel and aircraft but also most of the fuel and the support engineering—a mammoth undertaking when set alongside the needs of the Army, the problems of transportation, the difficulties of the climate, and the local political situation.

Gradually the work was done, and under the direction of Air Chief Marshal Sir Richard Peirse, Air Command South-East Asia was built up. This was a combined RAF/USAAF force, with some Indian Air Force squadrons contained within it; its main RAF components were 221 Group, which provided the tactical support for the 14th Army; 224 Group, covering the Arakan and Bay of Bengal area; and 222 Group, based in Ceylon and engaged in the maritime role. Other Groups in the complex organisation covered the bomber and transport roles, the defence of India, and the many supporting functions.

The changeover from defence to offence took place gradually during 1943 and 1944, with battles on the Arakan front, the Chindit operations in Central Burma, and the great fight to contain the Japanese attack on Imphal and Kohima. Crucial to these operations was the achievement and maintenance of air superiority which made possible a very high standard of tactical air support, and the air supply operations which, in the absence of surface transportation, were so essential. By the end of 1944 there was hardly any Japanese air opposition, and the reconquest of Burma in 1945 was supported by the full weight of the Allied air forces in a classic example of land/air cooperation. These victories were won in a far distant part of the world at a time when public attention was concentrated on the final stages of the war in Europe, and the Forgotten Army and Air Force have never had the recognition they so richly deserved. Had the war continued and the planned invasion of Malaya and Singapore taken place, far more attention would have been attracted, but mercifully that was not to be.

1

Transition from War to Peace

The only day upon which a postwar history of the Royal Air Force in the Far East can logically start is 14 August 1945. It was a memorable day, the day when Japan capitulated after almost six years of a war which had spread throughout the world, involving almost every nation to a greater or lesser degree. The unconditional surrender of Japan came as no great surprise in the corridors of power, but it was an unexpected shock to the thousands of airmen scattered throughout India, Ceylon and Burma who, after a brief respite from years of gruelling fighting to liberate Burma, were girding themselves alongside their Navy and Army comrades for a final onslaught to recapture Malaya and Singapore. All the way down the east coast of India from Calcutta to Ceylon, ports were packed with invasion fleets, some of the ships already assault loaded, and airfields crowded with those RAF squadrons detailed to support the invasion of the west coast of Malaya.

So well had the secret of the atom bomb been kept that it took some time for these men, waiting to participate in ZIPPER as the operation was called, to understand what had brought about this sudden end to the war. It seemed inconceivable that two bombs on Hiroshima and Nagasaki, coming on top of increasingly heavy conventional bombing, could effectively cause Japan to surrender within a few days. They did not know at the time that the first of the two bombs had destroyed four square miles of the centre of Hiroshima and killed more than 78,000 people. The second bomb, coming only three days later, caused similar devastation and casualties in Nagasaki. As it was assumed by the Japanese Government that more would follow, and there were no effective measures they could take to prevent them, unconditional surrender was accepted.

Unlike VE Day, to which there had been a lengthy build-up, VJ Day arrived so unexpectedly that a stunned silence fell upon the RAF for about 24 hours while the news percolated around stations and units and the full implications sank in. It did not take long for every unit to arrange its own victory celebration. Aircraft were left standing at dispersal, tools were downed and offices were locked while parties and sports programmes were held throughout the length and breadth of South-East Asia Command (SEAC). Firework displays, often using surplus Verey cartridges and various dangerous devices invented by Armaments Sections, lit up the night sky. On one station inland from Madras, a Verey light falling on the Sergeants' Mess burned it to the ground in a matter of minutes, its roofing of palm leaves burning at a rate of 30 feet per minute. Nobody worried. The war was over and everybody would soon be able to throw away their sweat-stained jungle green battledress and Burma hats, and return to the comforts of home and the good jobs which a grateful country would provide.

This was the euphoric atmosphere in which the VJ Day celebrations were held but, unfortunately, it lacked reality. As in Europe, the war against Japan had left a trail of destruction and chaos across the vast area of South-East Asia and the Pacific. Tens of thousands of British and Allied prisoners-of-war were existing under appalling conditions in Siam, Indo-China, Malaya, Singapore, Java and Sumatra. They had to be succoured and rescued quickly before many more died as the result of the terrible hardships which had been inflicted upon them. Moreover, Japanese forces had to be disarmed and civilian populations helped to reconstitute their shattered countries. Individual airmen did not, and could not be expected to realise the magnitude of the task which lay ahead before many of them could hope to be repatriated.

Inevitably, when the few days of celebration were over, anti-climax set in. Even if Headquarters South-East Asia Command had felt that Japan would not hold out much longer, the suddenness of the capitulation was unexpected, with the result that plans for the immediate postwar period were far from complete and some weeks were to elapse before all the ZIPPER squadrons and supporting units could learn what lay before them.

The Boundaries of South-East Asia Command

Almost coincidental with Japan's surrender, it had been decided by the Combined Chiefs of Staff to extend the boundaries of South-East Asia Command and to transfer to it a large area of the South-West

Pacific, hitherto controlled by United States forces under the command of General MacArthur. The Supreme Allied Commander South-East Asia (SACSEA), Lord Mountbatten, arrived back at his headquarters in Kandy from a visit to London only the day before the capitulation with a new directive in his pocket, and it is little wonder that few plans for the occupation of his expanded command had been finalised.

For the duration of the war, South-East Asia Command had comprised India and Ceylon, Burma, Siam, Malaya and Sumatra, an area of approximately one million square miles. After a number of high level discussions in mid 1945, a final decision was reached and a directive handed to SACSEA on 13 August 1945 which increased the area of his command to one and a half million square miles by the addition of Borneo, Java, the Celebes and that part of Indo-China lying below the 16th Parallel (see Map 1). A further part of the South-West Pacific including New Guinea, the Solomons and other island groups was to be controlled by Australia. Control of the extended area of SEAC was to take effect from the date of the Japanese surrender, coming as it did with unexpected suddenness on the following day. The area of the Command would then contain 128 million people, but perhaps of greater significance, no less than 750,000 Japanese of whom about 630,000 were armed troops. There would also be some 123,000 Allied prisoners-of-war and internees scattered in camps throughout the theatre. Furthermore no reliable civil police forces existed and, except for Siam, there was no civil government which had even the shadow of an independent administration. The problems facing SEAC in bringing this vast area back to peacetime normality were indeed formidable and VJ Day, welcome though it was, signalled no relaxation for the many thousands of airmen in the Command.

The Immediate Task

Important though it was to re-occupy the Japanese-held territories, disarm the Japanese forces and provide stable conditions for the resumption of normal life, one task stood out above all others as demanding the highest priority. That was the release and rehabilitation of the Allied prisoners-of-war and civilian internees. Their numbers and locations were not accurately known as the Japanese had never responded to the requirement of the Geneva Convention to make known the whereabouts and the occupants of their POW camps.

Allied intelligence had however built up some sort of estimate during the previous three years and, when the war ended, there were thought to be about 55,000 prisoners-of-war and internees in the original SEAC, and a further 70,000 mostly in Java. Estimates of the numbers of camps varied between 225 and 250.

As early as 3 February 1945, the War Office had charged Mountbatten with responsibility for planning the recovery of all those unfortunates who were known to be suffering terrible privations, particularly in the construction of the Burma-Siam railway, in Singapore's notorious Changi Jail, and in camps in central Java. Before the atom bomb brought swift capitulation, it had been expected that POW camps would be liberated as the Allies progressed from country to country. In the event, Mountbatten was faced with the impossible task of freeing all the prisoners and internees at once. Even if it were possible to locate and reach all the camps simultaneously, there would not be adequate means of transporting the inmates to safety.

On 16 August the Supreme Commander set up a Co-ordination Committee at his headquarters for the Recovery of Allied Prisoners-of-War and Internees (RAPWI) and decided to treat the task as an 'operation of war', thus instilling into it the necessary sense of urgency. Three distinct phases of the operation were planned. The first phase entailed dropping leaflets, in both Japanese and English, on all known camps, main towns and concentrations of Japanese troops, partly to inform camp guards and the civilian population of the surrender and partly to instruct POWs to remain in their camps until help arrived. The second phase, following shortly after the leaflets, involved dropping medical and food supplies with Red Cross relief teams carrying wireless sets and operators into all known camps. The final phase, which would clearly take many weeks and even months, was the evacuation of the prisoners by whatever means could be arranged. The first two phases and much of the third would fall to the Royal Air Force as the quickest and, in most cases, the only means of bringing succour to the widely dispersed camps.

The preliminary document of surrender was signed in Rangoon on 28 August, allowing the first phase (BIRDCAGE) to commence on the following morning. Liberator squadrons with experience of clandestine operations took off on the long range tasks, concentrating on the camps in distant areas, whose whereabouts were not precisely known and which were difficult to find. Thunderbolts, Dakotas, Lysanders and any other aircraft which could be pressed into service undertook the short range tasks. Camps in Malaya and Sumatra were covered by aircraft from Ceylon and the Cocos Islands, those in western Siam from Rangoon, and eastern Siam and French Indo-China were visited by aircraft flying from Jessore (north-east of Calcutta). Weather conditions were bad as the monsoon had broken in the northern regions of SEAC. This made the location of camps even more difficult but, nevertheless, BIRDCAGE was completed as far as the available intelligence allowed in three days, with the dropping of 150 tons of leaflets on 58 sorties. As was subsequently discovered, by no means all the existing camps were found and visited: some of them, deep in the central regions of Java where the occupants had been particularly badly treated, were not located for some considerable time, largely due to the dangerous political situation which developed there, and which will be described later.

Without awaiting the completion of BIRDCAGE, the second phase (MASTIFF) of the operation began in the safer regions of Burma, Siam and northern Malaya. By 5 September extensive areas in Malaya, Siam, French Indo-China and Sumatra had been covered and control teams had parachuted in to contact the senior Allied officer in each camp, with food and other necessities being dropped from Dakotas and Liberators. In spite of the unknown situation in Java, a team went in by parachute on 7 September followed by a MASTIFF drop on the following day. Meeting with a hostile Indonesian reception, however, it was unable to make much progress until supported later by the arrival of British forces by sea.

Meanwhile the third phase was proceeding apace and it speaks highly for the RAPWI operation that 53,700 prisoners and internees had been evacuated from South-East Asia by the end of September, mostly by sea through Singapore. This total reached 71,000 by the end of October, after which the speed of recovery slowed down as the more difficult areas came to be liberated.

Redeployment of ACSEA Forces

While the immediate task of succouring the prisoners-of-war and internees was in progress during the weeks following VJ Day, plans for the rapid re-occupation of all the Japanese-held countries in the Command were formulated, and a complicated and formidable task it proved to be.

The total air forces of ACSEA, which had been built up after the victory in Europe on the assumption that the war against Japan would continue for a considerable period while the enemy was driven slowly and painfully out of country after country, were neither needed nor available for occupation duties after the sudden capitulation. In the Command were some 12 Groups containing 73 squadrons and a large number of specialised independent flights: while most units were RAF, the air forces of India, Canada, South Africa, the Netherlands and the United States were strongly represented. Just as the end of the war in Europe had brought an urgent demand for rapid repatriation and demobilisation, the pressure from those serving in South-East Asia was no less great and the problems associated with it will be dealt with later in this chapter.

Broadly speaking Mountbatten had available for occupation duties the air forces which had remained in Burma, under command of RAF Burma, and those which had been assembled for operation ZIPPER. RAF Burma controlled some 28 squadrons while the Order of Battle for ZIPPER contained $21\frac{1}{2}$ squadrons plus at least 50 individual and specialised aircraft for such diverse tasks as DDT spraying, jungle rescue and light communications duties. Although basically these were the air forces available, many adjustments had to be made, partly because the aircraft types were not in all cases what were needed for the various occupation tasks, and partly because personnel had to be sorted out to ensure that the repatriation and demobilisation plans could continue with all speed, permitting the longest serving airmen and those in the highest priority classes for release to leave the Command first. Both of these adjustments were immensely complicated and gave rise to much criticism and dissatisfaction as will be seen later.

Each of the territories to be liberated presented a different problem. Burma, for example, was relatively straightforward, much of it having already been recaptured. Rangoon had been freed three months prior to VJ Day and provided a ready base, not only for those forces required to clear the prison camps in Burma and set the country on its feet, but also for many of the forces required to move on into Siam and Indo-China. The Netherlands East Indies, on the other hand, created an immense problem as it became apparent from the moment that the first RAPWI team dropped into Java that the Japanese, sensing defeat, had permitted an Indonesian Government to be established some weeks before VJ Day, with the result that

1. A Vildebeeste torpedo bomber of 36 Squadron being refuelled at Kuala Lumpur, 1937

2. Singapore III flying boat from Seletar over the Malayan jungle

3. The pierced steel plank runway constructed at Changi by Japanese labour in 1946

4. The Supreme Allied Commander (Lord Louis Mountbatten) and Air Chief Marshal
Sir Keith Park (Allied Air Commander-in-Chief) at HQ SEAC, Kandy

fierce resistance could be expected to any Allied occupation force. Clearly the NEI, with its many islands and dense jungle, was a perfect area for guerilla activity and would have to be handled with extreme caution if heavy casualties were to be avoided.

But the highest priority set, not only by Mountbatten but by the British Government and Chiefs of Staff, was to re-occupy Malaya and, in particular, Singapore. The loss of this important area of the Commonwealth had been a profound blow to British prestige which had continued to rumble throughout the war. Its re-occupation would also be a prelude to assembling and preparing whatever forces were needed to tackle the problem of the NEI.

It will be recalled that ZIPPER forces were already being assembled when the war ended. A vast fleet of ships and landing craft was loading in ports all along the eastern seaboard of India from Calcutta to Madras. The plan involved assault landings on the beaches of Western Malaya in the vicinity of Port Swettenham and Port Dickson. Certain airfields were to be captured, whereupon a number of squadrons of 224 Group would be called forward from the airfields on which they had been positioned in the general area of Rangoon. Thereafter an advance southward would begin with the ultimate object of liberating Malaya and capturing Singapore. So far advanced were preparations for this operation that it was within a month of being launched when VJ Day intervened. To have unscrambled it and reallocated the forces to meet the new situation would have been a time-consuming project—at a moment when time was vitally important if immediate succour was to be brought to the occupied countries.

Mountbatten therefore decided to continue with ZIPPER and to land the forces as planned over the Malayan beaches but, of course, unopposed, and then to move swiftly down to Singapore. This was seen to be the quickest and most efficient way of introducing the large numbers of troops, vehicles and supplies into the mainland of Malaya. In the meantime, as opposition no longer existed, a naval task force, supported by RAF aircraft, would be despatched to Singapore in advance of the more cumbersome ZIPPER forces.

These then were the broad plans for occupying the various territories of South-East Asia and each will be described in the next chapters with particular emphasis on the part played by the Royal Air Force. But the problems confronting the ACSEA staff were not confined to sorting out and despatching appropriate units to various areas of the

Command. An entirely different problem, and a particularly worrying one, reared its head as soon as the euphoria which followed VJ Day had subsided. It was a problem which continued to cause anxiety until well into 1946.

Disaffection in the Ranks

It is difficult to say what proportion of the tens of thousands of airmen serving in South-East Asia at the end of the war consisted of men and women serving on regular engagements, but it cannot have been higher than 10%. At least 90% were on hostilities only terms of service, and many of these, who considered that the war in Europe should have brought their active service to an end, were highly disgruntled at being moved on to the Far East to continue the fight against Japan shortly after VE Day. In addition there were thousands who had completed overlong and often excessively arduous tours of duty in the Far East and looked forward anxiously to repatriation and demobilisation. Willing, if not happy, though these RAF personnel were to play their part in finishing a war which had all but brought defeat to their country, they were far from content to carry on for a further indefinite period, 7,000 miles from home, to clear up the debris and mess that remained afterwards. Visons of men at home demobilised and obtaining the best civilian jobs haunted them constantly, creating a situation which was ripe for disaffection, particularly when encouraged by the hardcore of troublemakers which was always present and ready to take advantage of such circumstances.

A repatriation scheme (PYTHON) had been inaugurated during the early part of 1945 based upon a tour length of three years and eight months. After Germany had been defeated and when the war against Japan looked certain to end in the near future, political pressure to shorten the length of the tour in SEAC mounted. Despite Mountbatten's strong objections, a decision was taken in Whitehall on 6 June 1945 to reduce all tours to three years and four months. This decision, based entirely on political grounds, proved to be most unwise and events showed that insufficient Allied sea and air transportation existed to carry out ZIPPER and to satisfy PYTHON at the same time—even if the longer tour of duty were retained. It must be remembered that Allied shipping losses in the Atlantic and elsewhere had been immense and long range (transport) aircraft suitable for trooping from the Far East were relatively scarce. Lancasters, Halifaxes and Wellingtons were diverted to the transport role but their capacity was limited and the discomfort to the passengers considerable; not that a few more days of hardship mattered to troops who had borne so much in Burma and were on their way home. Commanders and Movement staffs performed miracles in getting men away but, nevertheless, the resources were inadequate and during the months following VJ Day PYTHON fell far behind schedule.

Towards the end of 1945, as the first Christmas since the end of the war approached, the dissatisfaction of the airmen with their conditions increased and there is no doubt that a small number of politically motivated agitators in the ranks exacerbated the situation. The first serious outbreak of trouble came at the beginning of 1946, at Mauripur in Karachi. At this time it was well known from the American forces broadcasting programme, which was popular and widely heard in SEAC, that US Forces in Germany were holding mass parades to demand speedier demobilisation. The publicity given to these demonstrations had a harmful, if not subversive effect on ACSEA personnel with the result that a similar demonstration took place at Mauripur on 22 January 1946. This, and similar demonstrations which were to follow, were alluded to as 'strikes'. As the airmen involved were still on active service, these actions could have been regarded as mutinous, but the authorities wisely decided against that interpretation which could clearly have led to most far-reaching results and severe punishments. For the first time in its history the prestige of the Royal Air Force was sadly besmirched by these actions instigated by a handful of trouble makers.

Had Mauripur been an isolated incident it could perhaps have been excused and attributed to poor leadership or some other local cause, but Mauripur was not an isolated incident. Within a few days the trouble spread to Ceylon and refusal to carry out the servicing of aircraft and other duties occurred at Negombo, Koggala, Colombo and Ratmalana. On the whole, the airmen were well behaved and respectful to their officers but were adamant that their complaints should be handled expeditiously. As most of these complaints were such that they could be dealt with only at Government or Air Ministry level, commanders on the spot could do little to rectify them and could only refer them back to London, which was done with the utmost despatch. The Inspector-General of the Royal Air Force, Air Chief Marshal Sir Arthur Barratt, was on a tour of the Far East at this time. He interviewed and addressed many airmen but, on his own admission, was nonplussed by these widespread examples of

insubordination and could do little more than reiterate official demobilisation policy and promise to represent the airmen's problems to the
Air Council.

Far from signalling the end of the disturbances, those in Ceylon were
but the introduction. They spread throughout India with stoppages of
work at Palam, Dum-Dum, Poona, Cawnpore and Vizagapatam. Most
were of short duration, orderly and respectful but, nevertheless,
determined. To make matters worse personnel of the Royal Indian
Air Force were infected and there were many demonstrations on
RIAF stations.

From India the disaffection spread on to Singapore, which had
been so recently reoccupied, and at Seletar a mass parade was
addressed by the Commander-in-Chief himself, Air Chief Marshal Sir
Keith Park. The most vocal agitators, who refused to accept the Air
Ministry facts and figures on release, were those who had been sent
out to SEAC after VJ Day and were deeply resentful. A further
incident at Kallang resulted in a certain LAC Cymbalist being caught
redhanded inciting his colleagues to "come out on strike" in sympathy
with the Seletar airmen. He was arrested and court-martialled, being
given a long sentence of imprisonment which was subsequently
reduced to a nominal period.

Nor did the RAF in Burma escape this insidious disease and the
airmen of 194 Squadron stopped work on 29 January. In this case
the complaints were concerned more with local conditions, poor food
and the introduction of peacetime 'bull'. The somewhat unsatisfactory
solution of disbanding 194 Squadron earlier than was originally
planned was decided upon and no disciplinary action was taken.

There were no more major instances of disaffection in the Command
but the grumblings continued and several months were to elapse,
during which a high level enquiry presided over by the Inspector-
General looked into the affair, before the progress of PYTHON resulted
in the trouble makers leaving the Command. While the Court of
Enquiry was in progress, firm instructions were issued to all Commanding Officers by the Commander-in-Chief to ensure that the closest
personal contact was maintained between officers and airmen; that
the latter were kept constantly aware of the latest information on
demobilisation; that mass meetings were to be avoided and that all
complaints were to be transmitted without delay to the Air Ministry.
As the political situation in India was extremely sensitive, bearing in
mind that these occurrences preceded the granting of independence

to India by no more than a year, he made arrangements for the RAF in India to be reinforced in an emergency with squadrons from outside the country. Sir Keith's instructions concluded with the following injunction:—

"1946 is going to be the most severe test of the abilities of an officer to command, and leadership and team work are even more important than during active operations".

The situation slowly returned to normal during the year, but the experience had been as unpleasant as it had been unexpected. It is easy to feel, with hindsight, that it should have been foreseen. But when it is appreciated that only the most senior officers and a handful of senior NCOs were regulars, and that the remainder had received little leadership training, it is perhaps understandable that their handling of thousands of restless 'civilian' airmen, who had been willing enough to play their part during a long and difficult war, lacked experience and the understanding which was needed when that war abruptly ceased.

This catalogue of disaffection has carried the narrative well beyond the events which took place in the various countries of South-East Asia to be liberated, but it was desirable to present the whole picture of the 'strikes' through to its conclusion. It is now time to return to the significant part played by the Royal Air Force in the occupation duties which followed VJ Day.

2

Re-occupation of Burma, Siam, French Indo-China and Hong Kong

By 27 August 1945, some thirteen days after the capitulation, it had become clear to Mountbatten that the Japanese forces scattered throughout SEAC would obey his instructions. He decided that a certain risk must be taken as neither the forces nor the transport at his disposal were adequate to carry out his priority tasks of securing the speedy and orderly establishment of civil governments, the evacuation of at least 100,000 Allied prisoners-of-war and internees, the disarming and round-up of three quarters of a million Japanese and the disposal of millions of tons of explosives, munitions and weapons. The risk which Mountbatten took was to preserve temporarily the Japanese chain of command, making their Supreme Commander responsible for maintaining law and order in the areas in which they had operated prior to the termination of hostilities. Distasteful though this policy was in many respects, there was no alternative in view of the vast area to be occupied and the opposition which was likely to be met from the indigenous population in certain of the territories. With a few minor exceptions the Japanese forces were both correct and helpful, which greatly facilitated what proved to be, even with their co-operation, a lengthy and dangerous occupation task.

Burma

It will be recalled that Rangoon had fallen to the Allies some three months before the Japanese surrender and Burma was, therefore, already largely occupied by Allied forces. Headquarters, Royal Air Force, Burma, under the command of Air Marshal Sir Hugh Saunders KBE CB MC DFC, had already been established in Rangoon, and was to have been the base from which many of the squadrons participating in operation ZIPPER against Malaya and Singapore would be despatched and controlled. What was more natural than that this base should be used under the new situation produced by the capitulation? RAF Burma controlled some 28 squadrons on VJ Day but this became a constantly changing force as some squadrons were despatched to other areas, and some were disbanded to maintain the flow of airmen for repatriation. In addition many American aircraft which the RAF had received under the Lend/Lease agreement were either returned to the United States or 'cannibalised' to provide spares for those remaining in service.

Understandably, transport aircraft were in the greatest demand, and in particular, that great maid of all work, the Dakota. At the beginning of September there were nine Dakota squadrons, each of 24 aircraft, in the Command, controlled by HQ 232 Group and distributed between Mingaladon (Rangoon), Hmawbi and Chittagong. These squadrons had been operating intensively for many months past and the position became precarious as the supply of new aircraft from the United States ceased and the repair and supply organisation ran into increasing difficulties in keeping the squadrons up to strength. In spite of these problems and the monsoon conditions, which are always at their most severe in August and September, the Dakota squadrons continued to fly at intensive rates to meet the many demands upon them. These demands consisted mainly of continuing to supply the British 12th Army in its sweep through those parts of Burma still in Japanese control, the supply and evacuation of Allied prisoners-of-war and, finally, the feeding of the civil population whose plight had become serious due to lack of the staple foodstuff, rice.

In addition to the Dakota squadrons, RAF Burma which, on 20 September 1945, was reduced from the status of a Command to that of an Air Headquarters, officially redesignated 'Air Headquarters, Burma', retained three Spitfire squadrons including one PR squadron, two P47 Thunderbolt squadrons, a Mosquito light bomber squadron and sundry specialised units for DDT spraying, jungle rescue, special duties and meteorological flights. All of these squadrons were able to assist the Dakotas in such tasks as identifying POW camps, dropping leaflets and medical supplies and, of course, in photography which was of inestimable value to the ground forces amid the dense jungle of central and eastern Burma.

While the urgent military and humanitarian tasks were under way, the problems concerned with the political future of Burma were being pursued. Even before the war came to South-East Asia, Burma had been subject to internal communal strife between Burmese, Karens,

Indians and Chinese, while a number of hill tribes had virtually
maintained an independence of their own. When war came the
Burmese had been encouraged to side with the Japanese. This
encouragement created even greater internal dissension between those
elements which remained loyal to the Commonwealth and those
which, under the leadership of Aung San, formed the Burma National
Army and fought against the Allies from 1942 to 1944. After the
Japanese retreat from Imphal, however, Aung San and his followers
sought an opportunity to change sides. This eventually resulted in
the Burma National Army being renamed the Patriotic Burmese
Forces (PBF), whereupon they proceeded to harrass the retreating
Japanese.

The situation was further complicated by the creation of an independent movement by the youth of Burma, the Anti-Fascist Peoples'
Freedom League (AFPFL) which soon proved to be stronger in
numbers than the PBF and represented a political unity hitherto
unknown in the country. Stronger in numbers the AFPFL might be,
but the PBF was well equipped with both British and Japanese arms
and was thus able to dominate the new youthful force. Understandably
the original Burmese regular forces, the Karens, and other elements
which had fought alongside the Allies throughout were far from
pleased at these political developments and showed considerable
concern over the future.

Mountbatten decided upon the creation of a new Burma Army and
to hold Aung San responsible for the behaviour of his troops; in so
doing offering him a commission in the new force on condition that
he abstained from politics. He refused the commission but agreed to
the formation of the Burma Army. This was the situation on 17
October 1945, when Rangoon welcomed HE the Governor of Burma,
the Rt Hon Sir Reginald Dorman-Smith PC GBE, as he came ashore
from *HMS Cleopatra* to be greeted by a fly-past of eight Spitfires of
No 8 (Indian) Squadron, dipping in salute as he landed. No 2942
Squadron of the RAF Regiment mounted a guard of honour and
Rangoon prepared to cast off memories of the war and tackle the
huge problem of resettlement. Subsequent developments in Burma
are described later in this chapter.

Siam

The political situation in Siam was more stable than that in either
Burma or Indo-China. Nevertheless there were many problems to be
faced as the Japanese had made Siam their main base from which to

support their forces in Burma and Malaya. As these forces were pushed back in Burma they had retreated eastwards across the Sittang and Salween rivers in an effort to regroup in Siam. Attempting to shorten the long supply route by sea round Singapore and Malaya to Burma, they had employed thousands of prisoners-of-war in building a Siam-Burma railway. The appalling conditions under which these unfortunate men laboured is well known, and the location and release of the survivors was the very highest priority task.

Although Britain had been technically at war with Siam, the Government which had declared war against the Allies was overthrown on the surrender of the Japanese and the declaration of war withdrawn on 16 August 1945. This paved the way for Mountbatten to negotiate with the Regent and the King of Siam was able to return to his country from Switzerland on 5 September, whereupon SEAC forces were flown into Bangkok and warmly welcomed.

The Bangkok airfield (Don Muang) was found to be fully serviceable and capable of accepting up to 100 Dakota sorties a day. This permitted five of Burma's Dakota squadrons to be allocated to the supply task and, on the basis that monsoon weather would allow flying on two days out of three, the fly-in of Army, RAF and RAPWI Control personnel began. No 909 Wing, a Thunderbolt fighter wing stationed in Burma, was detailed to form the headquarters of the RAF force in Siam, but without its Thunderbolt squadrons which, with their long range and heavy fire power, were assigned to more appropriate tasks in Malaya and the NEI. Under the command of Group Captain D O Finlay DFC AFC, 909 Wing moved into Don Muang on 9 September and changed its title to Air Headquarters, Siam.

The first task was to set up on the airfield all the technical and administrative facilities of a staging post, not only to receive and turn round the Dakotas bringing in the occupation troops and taking out POWs but also to pass transit aircraft on to Indo-China. Within a few days the first of AHQ Siam's new squadrons flew in, 17 pilots and the same number of Spitfire VIIIs of 20 Squadron being the first to take up residence in the somewhat basic accommodation at Don Muang which, like that of most other Japanese-occupied airfields in SEAC, had been gravely neglected.

No 211 Squadron equipped with Mosquito VI aircraft, joined 20 Squadron during October. There was little operational activity for either squadron and their flying mainly comprised resumption of

training and various reconnaissances at the request of the Navy and
Army to locate and identify Japanese units and establishments. The
opportunity was however taken, as elsewhere, to up-date photographic
survey records by sending in a small detachment of 685 Squadron.
In addition to the survey work, the PR Mosquitos proved their value
in locating and photographing some of the more isolated POW camps,
and directing relief to them.

The security of Don Muang posed a considerable problem for
2945 RAF Regiment Squadron. The attraction of widely dispersed
ammunition and fuel dumps together with stocks of food and clothing
held in the flimsy buildings was too tempting for the half starved
natives in the vicinity. Thieving was rife and the protection of all
these valuable stores stretched the single Regiment squadron to its
limits. There were nightly exchanges of fire resulting in many Siamese
being arrested or injured with, fortunately, few RAF casualties.

The evacuation of APWI and the rounding up of Japanese forces
continued. The King returned to his capital and the port of Bangkok
was cleared of mines and reopened. This latter event brought immense
relief to the Dakota squadrons which had borne the brunt of both
supply and personnel movement. By Christmas the country had
settled down to a point at which the withdrawal of British forces
could begin, and shortly afterwards 20 Squadron left for its new
home at Mingaladon and 211 Squadron was disbanded leaving only
a few PR Mosquitos of 684 Squadron at Don Muang to complete
their survey work. The staging post remained but, by the end of
January, 1946, the RAF presence in Bangkok had been reduced to
about 150 personnel, and as had been expected, the occupation of
Siam had caused fewer problems than any other area of the Command.

Indo-China

It will be recalled that the only part of French Indo-China to be
included in SEAC when the Command boundaries were extended
was that which lay below the 16th Parallel. This area contained the
capital, Saigon. The northern part of the country remained the
responsibilty of the Chinese under Generalissimo Chiang Kai-Shek,
and Mountbatten's object was to hand the whole country back to the
French as soon as the APWI had been evacuated and French forces
could be made available.

The arbitrary division of the country at the 16th Parallel created
certain political problems. Moreover, there were 'too many fingers in

the pie'—Chinese, British, released French prisoners-of-war and armed Annamites. There was no great enthusiasm among certain factions for Indo-China to revert to French colonial control and, in particular, the Annamites caused serious trouble within a few days of the arrival of the occupation forces. As will be seen later in the case of the Netherlands East Indies, British forces tended to be the meat in the sandwich, endeavouring to fulfil their humanitarian role but popular with nobody. Under the circumstances which arose, Mountbatten was compelled to use the Japanese forces temporarily to assist in maintaining control.

The first moves were the dropping of leaflets over Saigon by Thunderbolts and Mosquitos from Burma. They contained a warning that Allied forces were about to be landed. On 8 September an advance party of engineers and medical reconnaissance personnel arrived by Dakota at Tan Son Nhut airfield near Saigon. This airfield, with two runways of 1700 yards and 1250 yards (in process of extension to 2000 yards), was found to be usable, with hard standings for up to seventy Dakotas which greatly facilitated the subsequent fly-in of 20 Division. The monsoon weather was particularly bad at this time and the Dakota crews had to contend with flying conditions which were as arduous as their worst moments in the Burma campaign. Furthermore it was a long flight from the Rangoon area. The build-up was slow and it was 26 September before all the personnel, vehicles and equipment of 20 Division reached Saigon.

Fortunately there were considerably fewer APWI in Indo-China than in other SEAC countries. Estimates vary but a figure of less than 5,000 is generally agreed. Contact with them was made with little delay and they were speedily evacuated to Rangoon, mostly by returning Dakotas.

As in the case of Siam, a small Air Headquarters was established in Saigon, under the command of Air Commodore W G Cheshire, with 273 Spitfire Squadron placed under its control at Tan Son Nhut as well as 684 Squadron with its PR Mosquitos to undertake the reconnaissance and survey tasks in both Indo-China and Siam. HQ ACSEA deserves much credit for the speed with which it took every opportunity to bring up-to-date the photographic surveys of all the countries in the Command during the brief periods of occupation, and the work of the Mosquito and Spitfire PR Squadrons at this time provided material of immense value in later years. It must be remembered that photographic survey had been in its infancy before

World War II and the mapping of many countries in the Far East was extremely inaccurate. The wartime needs of the European theatre had produced astonishing progress in photographic and survey techniques, not to mention the production of specialised Spitfires and Mosquitos with very long range and high performance, of which full advantage was taken.

The desire of Mountbatten and the British Government to avoid confrontation and deep involvement in Indo-China looked, at one time, as if it would not be fulfilled. The Annamite Independence Movement (Viet Minh) was both active and hostile, particularly in northern Indo-China, and there was some extension of this hostility below the 16th Parallel before the build-up of 20 Division was anything like complete. It was clearly imperative that French forces take over rapidly if Britain was to avoid serious involvement. Thanks to a powerful proclamation by Lieutenant-General Gracey, the British Commander in Saigon—and it was a proclamation which he would have had some difficulty in implementing with his few available forces—the situation was temporarily contained. Although British/Indian troops were attacked on more than one occasion, French forces began to reach the country during October and the situation did not immediately deteriorate to a point at which the Spitfires of 273 Squadron were required to take offensive action. By 30 October the position, although far from stable, was judged suitable for a French High Commissioner to take over control in Saigon.

The build-up of French forces which now began to arrive in increasing numbers created an additional problem for the hard pressed Dakota squadrons, namely, a daily commitment of 48 tons of rations and other essential supplies during the first two weeks of November. Coming at a moment when the AOC Burma had promised his Dakota crews some much needed relaxation, this was a most unwelcome extra task. The lift required 18 Dakota sorties per day which, as the round flight from Rangoon to Saigon occupied two days, locked up 36 Dakotas without making any allowance for essential servicing. The commitment was met but only by according to it the highest priority at the expense of carrying food in the form of rice to many hard pressed areas of Burma and Siam where evidence of starvation was beginning to be seen.

A number of French Air Force personnel reached Saigon with the land forces in November but, although many of them had belonged to a French Spitfire Wing in Europe, they were without aircraft on arrival. ACSEA, however, possessed a small quantity of Spitfire VIIIs which were intended to re-equip some of the squadrons in the Command, and Sir Keith Park decided to make these available to the French, thus relieving 273 Squadron at Tan Son Nhut. On 12 December 12 Spitfire VIIIs were handed over with spares backing for two months on the understanding that these were on loan and their future would be negotiated later. The wisdom of this transfer was shown by the fact that, before the French squadron could become operational, 273 Squadron was called upon to support the French garrison at Banme Thuet which came under attack from Annamite forces. Warning leaflets were dropped and the Spitfires of 273 Squadron attacked with cannon fire three targets indicated by the French; little activity was seen but buildings and road junctions were strafed. This was a development which the RAF had been anxious to avoid, and every effort was made to assist the French to become operational on their own Spitfires as quickly as possible.

On 1 December, Mountbatten visited Saigon in person and addressed all RAF personnel. He praised their work under difficult circumstances and had particular regard for the PR work of the Mosquitos of 684 Sqn and for the men of 1307 Wing of the RAF Regiment who handled all the security arrangements for a ceremony at which the swords of senior Japanese officers were handed over. The sword of Count Terauchi, the Japanese Supreme Commander in the area, was handed to Mountbatten who revealed that it would be presented to His Majesty King George VI. In a moving ceremony a number of other swords were handed to RAF officers with the hope that they would be tended with care as, to Japanese officers, the sword was a sacred possession.

As the French Air Force gained in strength, the RAF was able to begin its withdrawal. No 273 Squadron was destined for disbandment and was finally withdrawn from Saigon on 31 January 1946. Two weeks later the Air Headquarters was disestablished, having completed its tasks of rescuing all the APWI in the country and handing its responsibilities for disarming the Japanese over to the French authorities. A small RAF station headquarters with 2963 RAF Regiment Squadron and No 2 Staging Post was then all that remained for a further few months. These elements were essential to handle the modest flow of RAF aircraft through Saigon which continued to assist the French in their extremely difficult and sensitive occupation role. The political situation remained so tense in Indo-China that it was an immense relief to Mountbatten to be able to withdraw his forces from this area which had become a British post-war responsibility only by an arbitrary boundary-drawing decision.

Hong Kong

It will be seen from Map 1 that Hong Kong lay outside the boundaries of SEAC as re-drawn immediately before the Japanese surrender. However, being a valuable and important British colony which had suffered a humiliating occupation, it was rightly left to the British to re-occupy it and re-establish the civil administration as rapidly as possible. It was considered important that the Japanese surrender in Hong Kong should be accepted by a British officer and also that the RAF element of the forces sent there should be mounted on British aircraft.

Rear Admiral C H J Harcourt, Flag Officer 11th Aircraft Carrier Squadron of the British Pacific Fleet, was the nearest British commander, being based at Luzon (see Map 1). He was allotted an RAF Airfield Construction Unit of 3,000 airmen who, at the time of surrender, were on passage across the Pacific to construct airfields on Okinawa for Tiger Force, the RAF bombers to be used in the final assault on Japan. With this force Harcourt reached Hong Kong on 29 August, sending an emissary in to Kai Tak airfield in a naval Avenger escorted by Hellcats from *HMS Indomitable*. Apart from some sniping in Victoria, and the threat of suicide attacks from craft anchored off Lamma Island, which were destroyed by air attack, the Japanese offered no resistance and Hong Kong was occupied on 1 September. An interim civil administration had already been set up by a number of British internees and, within hours of landing, the Airfield Construction airmen could be directed to repairing public utilities and services which had been totally neglected by the Japanese. This work was quite foreign to these airmen, who were specialists in constructing airfields, but such was their versatility that they brought the essential services back into use in a very short time. The former Airfield Construction Branch of the RAF has never received due credit for many feats of construction world wide both during and after World War II, and the Hong Kong effort must go down as one of its best and most unusual achievements.

Twelve days later the first convoy sailed into Hong Kong carrying 3 RM Commando Brigade and No 4 RAPWI Control Staff. It was accompanied by the aircraft carrier *Smiter* with 132 Spitfire Squadron aboard. Since this was one of the smaller carriers, the RAF squadron was not entirely happy about flying off. The Spitfires could not be catapult launched but they managed the take off successfully with half full fuel tanks, no ammunition and with *Smiter* steaming into a stiff breeze at full speed. Within a few minutes the whole squadron had landed safely at Kai Tak and the RAF had resumed its interrupted air defence of the colony.

Headquarters, Royal Air Force, Hong Kong was immediately established under the command of Air Commodore W A D Brook CBE. The single Spitfire VIII squadron proved adequate for the initial purpose of 'showing the British flag' above the Colony once again, but the newly established Headquarters contained a balanced force of technical and administrative units suitable to reactivate the Kai Tak base and to assist with the task of restoring the communications and services which had fallen into disrepair under the Japanese. It was noticeable here and in every country in SEAC that the Japanese had totally neglected to maintain public utilities, such as water, power, sewage disposal and telephones; so great was this neglect in some areas that it almost looked as though they had a premonition that their stay would be short.

One particular task which the RAF undertook without delay was the preparation of a flying boat base with its associated moorings and slipways, as it was fully intended that a Sunderland squadron should eventually be located in Hong Kong after the main Far Eastern flying boat base at Seletar, in Singapore, had been rehabilitated. The immense coastal periphery of SEAC made it particularly suitable for boats of the Sunderland and Catalina type and, of course, BOAC was anxious to re-establish its Empire flying boat routes with as little delay as possible. It was as clear in Hong Kong as elsewhere that the reactivation of civil air routes would initially depend almost entirely upon the assistance which the RAF could give from its world wide chain of staging posts.

The teeming population of Hong Kong had been seriously affected by shortages of rice and other staple food. As soon as Kai Tak was operating again, as many sorties as could be spared from the other hard-pressed areas of the Command were flown by Dakotas to bring much needed relief and to bear away the APWI who had been held in Hong Kong in considerable numbers. As the port had suffered no great damage, it was not long before shipping could relieve the RAF of the supply task, allowing the Colony to return to normal in a relatively short time.

Developments in Burma

With the return of the Governor to Burma on 17 October 1945, it was hoped that transition from military to civil administration would be speedy and smooth, but this was not to be. Although Burma was promised independence with Dominion status in the Commonwealth as soon as feasible, the political intransigence, particularly of Aung San and his AFPFL, continued to make great difficulties for the administration. Fortunately, however, the Burmese people showed little or no hostility towards the RAF, which had very many humanitarian commitments to feed the people, extract the APWI and support the forces in neighbouring countries, not to mention round up and disarm the remaining Japanese.

During the last quarter of 1945 the RAF began to concentrate its rapidly diminishing units upon a few airfields with good facilities, and gradually to close down most of the rough, hastily prepared landing grounds and strips with which Burma abounded as a result of the war. Mingaladon, Hmawbi and Pegu, all in the general area of Rangoon, became main airfields with Meiktila in the north continuing to be fully used as an important staging post and forward airfield.

The Dakota squadrons which, with disbandment, cannibalisation of aircraft and spares, and shortages of manpower, gradually reduced to five in number—namely Nos 62, 194, 267, 52 and 96 Squadrons— were controlled by 341 (Transport) Wing from Mingaladon and Hmawbi. The latter airfield also housed 10 (Spitfire) Squadron, while 20 Squadron eventually flew its Spitfires back from its temporary stay in Bangkok to Mingaladon. This left Pegu with various detachments from specialised Liberator and Lancaster squadrons based elsewhere in ACSEA. By the end of the year RAF Burma had slimmed down to this basic force but that by no means represented all that was under its control at any one moment. Geographically Burma lay at the crossroads of the West to East route from Europe through India and Siam to Hong Kong and the North to South route from India to Singapore and the Netherlands East Indies. In consequence there was a constant movement of units, too numerous to mention, through Burma for which adequate facilities of all kinds had to be provided. The same facilities had also to be provided by AHQ Burma for BOAC, KLM and QANTAS civil airlines which were quick to reactivate the Far East routes that had been interrupted by the war. Indeed, as early as 14 October British Overseas Airways inaugurated their Empire Air Route with a Sunderland flying boat which landed on the Rangoon river and was greeted by the Air Officer Commanding.

Air/Jungle Rescue

One of the essential facilities which had been provided throughout the war, and which it was necessary to continue to provide, was Air/Jungle Rescue. This service was peculiar to SEAC: nowhere else in the world had the RAF been required to provide it, but the wartime dependence of the Burma theatre upon air supply in flying conditions which were often extremely hazardous made the need for specialised rescue squadrons and flights paramount. A variety of aircraft had been used during the war years, combining Air/Sea with Air/Jungle rescue operations where appropriate. Long range Liberators, capable of carrying airborne lifeboats to distant sea areas, were employed at one end of the scale while short range Lysanders, Beaufighters and various light aircraft were used for jungle rescue at the other end. Many of the units were either disbanded or moved down through Malaya with the occupation forces. No 27 Squadron however remained with its Beaufighters in Burma under the control of the Air/Jungle Rescue Co-ordination Centre at Rangoon.

The intensity of operations by the ageing Dakotas during the last quarter of 1945 resulted inevitably in an increase in engine failure followed by forced landings in the jungle. No 27 Squadron was kept busy and its work greatly increased by the failure of some aircrews to report their positions accurately during cross-country flights. A notable exception occurred on 15 December 1945, when a Dakota of 267 Squadron crash-landed after an engine failure. So accurate and frequent had been the course, height and position reports right up to the time of landing that the aircraft was found within a few hours. All the passengers were uninjured and supplies were dropped before rescue parties could reach the scene. Unhappily there were many incidents with less successful conclusions. For example, a Mosquito crashed in transit across Burma at about this time and no less than 50 flying hours were spent in a fruitless search. Neither the aircraft nor its crew was ever found. In this case accurate position reporting would probably have resulted in the wreck being successfully located. Eventually, in order to improve the rescue services, five Lancasters,

which had been modified in the UK for Air/Sea Rescue duties, were
sent out to re-equip 1348 Flight and to combine the sea and jungle
rescue roles. The Liberators which 1348 Flight had been operating
for several years were in any case due to be returned to the United
States after their long and successful service in Burma. The Lancasters, painted blue and each carrying an airborne lifeboat below the
fuselage, were extremely well equipped and versatile replacements
which aroused much interest and, indeed, confidence among the
aircrew.

Over 'The Hump'

A few words are necessary here about another special operation that
involved the RAF in Burma at this time. 'The Hump' route from
north-east India to China had been inaugurated when the Japanese
cut the Burma Road, the original land route with China, in 1942.
'The Hump' was flown during the final years of the war by a
combination of USAAF and RAF transport aircraft, specifically to
supply the force of USAAF bombers and fighters operating in the
Chungking area of China. As, however, the tonnage carried over 'The
Hump' greatly exceeded that which could have been taken over the
old land route, and as it also exceeded the needs of the American
force in China, a useful surplus was available for Chiang Kai-Shek's
own forces.

It was a hazardous route, necessitating flying at heights up to
17,000 feet in bad monsoon weather at certain times of the year, and
with little hope of rescue in the event of a forced landing. USAAF
aircraft were withdrawn from the route in September, 1945 but the
RAF Dakota squadrons, which had been participating since July
1944, continued for two more months. In particular, 52 Squadron
had flown continuously for eighteen months with the loss of only
one Dakota, and had the distinction of flying the last sortie on the
last day of December 1945. Latterly the withdrawal of Japanese forces
to the south had permitted a more southerly route to be flown so
that the Dakotas could clear the highest peaks safely at 13,000 feet.

The dangers of 'The Hump' are admirably illustrated by one pilot
who had climbed in cloud to a height which his instruments told
him was 32,000 feet. He emerged from cloud to find himself only
just above the mountains below—and he swore that he was nowhere
near Everest! The Operations Record Book of AHQ Burma for
December 1945 describes the route as the worst air journey in any

part of the world. To those accustomed to jet aircraft and pressurised cabins, it may not sound all that hazardous, but to the pilot of a heavily laden twin-engined Dakota with no pressurisation and unreliable navigation aids, it was an immense challenge. Among other squadrons, 52 Squadron deserves the highest praise for its determination and efficiency in bringing a successful conclusion to one of the most remarkable examples of air supply which World War II produced.

By the end of 1945 the immediate postwar tasks in Burma were virtually complete. The APWI had been rescued from their prison camps, Japanese forces had been rounded up and disarmed, and the southern part of the country had been freed from the fear of starvation. But the political situation was far from stable. Dacoity was widespread and it was essential to retain military control until April 1946, when the Governor considered that the situation justified a handover to civil administration. The main task which the RAF was called upon to carry out during the early part of the New Year was the ferrying of rice to the hill tribes in northern Burma. The combination of Japanese depredations and an exceptionally poor rice crop produced near starvation conditions which could only be alleviated by air supply and once again the remaining Dakotas were called upon for help. Nos 96, 62 and 267 Squadrons were those remaining from the force of nine squadrons which had borne the brunt of the immediate postwar tasks. A number of 10 Squadron Dakotas from India also assisted with HUNGER II, as the rice-dropping operation was named. Many hundreds of tons were delivered to the Karens and other northern tribes, earning the gratitude of the tribesmen who, over the years, had come to understand the difficult nature of these operations. Many complimentary messages of thanks were relayed through to the squadrons.

Burma was moving slowly towards independence and 1946 saw a steady reduction in RAF operations which were mainly concerned with carrying supplies to the civil population. It was not, however, until Burma's independence a year later that the RAF finally left the country, an event which will be described in a later chapter.

3

Return to Malaya and Singapore

It had always been the intention of the British Government to recapture Malaya and Singapore at the earliest possible moment after the fall of Rangoon, and while mopping-up operations in the remainder of Burma continued. The sudden end to the war on 14 August 1945 only sufficed to increase the desire to re-occupy these two important parts of the Commonwealth without delay and to release the thousands of British prisoners-of-war who were languishing in Changi Jail and elsewhere throughout the area.

Consequently Mountbatten decided to send a Naval Task Force directly into Singapore and, at the same time, launch operation ZIPPER over the beaches on the west coast of Malaya as originally planned, but now in order to occupy Malaya without opposition. The ZIPPER forces would then move rapidly down through Malaya to Singapore and join up with the Naval Task Force which had preceded them. Some slight delay was occasioned by the insistence of General MacArthur that no territory should be occupied until a surrender document had been signed. In the case of Malaya and Singapore, this was an essential safeguard to ensure that the Japanese disclosed the position of their many minefields in the Strait of Malacca and in the confined waters around Singapore Island.

Entry into Singapore

Purely by accident, it fell to the crew of a Mosquito to be the first Britishers to return to Singapore some days before the surrender document was signed. On the morning of 31 August a PR Mosquito of 684 Squadron took off from the Cocos Islands to photograph parts of southern Malaya. Before the task was completed, one of the constant speed units developed a fault which could not be cured in flight, leaving the pilot with the prospect of a long open sea flight back to the Cocos on one engine.

After much thought he decided to land at Kallang, the airfield alongside Singapore harbour. It was a decision which worried him but he reasoned that the war had been over for a fortnight and he should get a polite if not friendly reception. He circled Kallang slowly. The runway was unobstructed and so, after firing a red Verey light, he came in to land over the harbour wall and turned in towards the control tower. His arrival caused much excitement but he was courteously received by the Japanese airmen who went to the trouble of finding an RAF engineer officer and a fitter, both of whom had been prisoners-of-war in Changi Jail. Between them they rectified the faults in the constant speed unit, a fitting which neither of them had ever seen before. They naturally wanted to know how much longer it would be before British forces arrived to release them. On the following morning a second Mosquito appeared overhead, circled the airfield and landed after getting a 'thumbs up' signal from the first crew. Somewhat fortuitously the RAF had stolen the limelight by being the first to return to the island—but only by a few days.

While this unrehearsed event was taking place, the Naval Task Force destined for Singapore had paused at the head of the Malacca Strait, off northern Sumatra and Penang, awaiting disclosure by the Japanese of the location of their minefields. On 2 September, a surrender document was signed at Penang and the island was occupied by the Royal Marines on the following morning. Immediately—indeed on the same day—152 and 155 Spitfire Squadrons, followed by 84 and 100 Mosquito Squadrons, flew in from Rangoon, this being the first stage of their journey to Singapore. They found Penang airfield usable with care, but suffering from the same neglect that was evident on every airfield which the Japanese had occupied. No attempt had been made to sabotage the installations but, nevertheless, no risks were taken with Japanese aviation fuel, most of which was downgraded for MT use.

The Naval Task Force got under way once more on 3 September, preceded by three minesweeping flotillas, and reached Singapore that same day, followed within hours by a convoy carrying the leading occupation troops and 3 Commando Brigade. The formal surrender of Singapore and Johore took place on board *HMS Sussex* on 4 September when the strength of Japanese forces was given as 50,118 army and air force personnel and 26,872 naval personnel.

Perhaps the most heartening sight for the Allied prisoners-of-war who, although still in their camps, were now under the command of their own officers, was the sight of the four RAF squadrons from Penang flying in formation as they arrived over the island on 6 September. Parties of airmen had been rushed from the first troop convoy to Tengah and Seletar and were ready to receive the four squadrons as they landed.

Four days later six Sunderland flying boats landed at the old seaplane base at Seletar. Five were from 209 Squadron and one from No 205, having flown direct from Ceylon led by Group Captain G Francis DSO DFC. He stepped ashore on 12 September to accept the formal surrender of the Japanese at an impressive ceremony during which the six Sunderlands led a fly-past of all the aircraft which had so far reached the island.

Back to Malaya

While the liberation of Singapore was in progress the return to Malaya got under way. Operation ZIPPER could not be greatly accelerated, partly owing to its complexity and partly because many of the forces were already being assault-loaded in various Indian ports when the war ended. In addition, some modification to the original plan was needed in view of the lack of opposition and changed circumstances. For example, air support for the initial landings had previously been required from naval aviation until such time as the RAF could be established ashore. The Fleet Air Arm cover could now be cancelled.

Headquarters, 224 Group, under the command of Air Vice-Marshal The Earl of Bandon CB DSO continued as the controlling formation of the tactical air force units supporting XXXIV Corps for the revised operation. However, the number of squadrons and supporting units in the Group was reduced to enable some to be directed to other areas in SEAC, notably to the Netherlands East Indies. In broad terms the alterations to his order of battle left the AOC 224 Group with the following forces for the revised ZIPPER:—

902 Wing (Spitfires)
903 Wing (P47 Thunderbolts)
905 Wing (P47 Thunderbolts)
185 Wing (Spitfires)

The distance from the main bases in India to the Malayan airfields was too great to permit the squadrons to fly with safety directly across the Bay of Bengal when their destination airfields had been occupied. With the exception of two squadrons of Spitfires, which were to fly in from aircraft carriers, the aircraft were to fly round the head of the Bay of Bengal and position themselves in Burma ready to be called forward. Some of the Thunderbolt squadrons had left for their Burma locations immediately after VJ day, where they waited with some impatience to fly in to Malaya.

The Earl of Bandon and the advance elements of 224 Group sailed in 'D Day' convoys, as planned, from Bombay and Madras, with ground parties of airmen from those squadrons scheduled to fly in as soon as the first airfields had been occupied. The full story of the landings over the beaches in the Port Swettenham and Port Dickson areas does not belong to this narrative: it has been well chronicled in the official history *The War Against Japan*,[1] but it must be said that it proved to be a difficult and dangerous operation with some loss of vehicles and landing craft due, not to any opposition, but to the unsatisfactory nature of the selected beaches. Had ZIPPER been launched against determined Japanese opposition, there can be little doubt that heavy Allied casualties would have been inevitable.

The RAF parties in the D-Day convoys took their share of the delays and misfortunes which occurred, but eventually went ashore on 9–10 September and set up the Advanced 224 Group Headquarters on the airfield at Kalanang. Without further delay the Spitfires of 11 and 17 Squadrons flew off the two escort carriers, *HMS Smiter* and *HMS Trumpeter*, and landed at Kalanang. This part of the operation caused some concern. The decks of the carriers were small and the Spitfires were not adapted in any way for carrier operations. Nevertheless a number of trials off the coast of India near Madras had established that the risks were acceptable. When the time came for the aircraft to fly off, there was virtually no wind and conditions were far from favourable. However, all the Spitfires, with half-full tanks and no ammunition, completed the take off safely, but it was far from being the 'piece of cake' attributed to one pilot of 11 Squadron. With 24 Spitfires established at Kalanang a measure of air protection was now available for the troops pouring over the beaches and fanning out into Malaya. Also in the carriers were the Austers of 656 AOP Squadron. They were destined for the Kuala Lumpur airfield, but finding it temporarily unusable they landed and set up their headquarters on the golf course nearby.

[1]History of the Second World War. The War Against Japan, Vol V, Chapter XXV. HMSO, 1969

Owing to the unexpected difficulty of landing vehicles over the beaches, many of the airmen had to footslog with their packs to their airfield destinations which, in some cases, were many miles inland. In due course Headquarters 905 Wing, whose Thunderbolt squadrons were waiting at Rangoon, occupied Port Swettenham airfield and was able to call its squadrons forward. On 20 September, 131, 258, 60 and 81 Squadrons flew in direct from Rangoon with long range tanks on their Thunderbolts. Apart from an Air/Jungle Rescue detachment of Beaufighters of 27 Squadron from Burma, which went into Penang on 1 October, this completed the revised built-up of 224 Group in Malaya.

From this point the movement of formations and units into and through Malaya became frequent and highly complicated. In effect Malaya became something of a transit area for squadrons and other units on their way to Singapore, the Netherlands East Indies and Hong Kong. To catalogue all these movements would be tedious and we are more concerned with the build-up at the final destinations. The fortunes of 224 Group itself, however, need to be followed as that was the controlling formation throughout this phase of occupational transition.

After a few days of intense discomfort at Kalanang airfield, the Advanced Headquarters personnel moved inland on 14 September to Telok Datok and then on again to Kuala Lumpur on the 18th. For the first time since leaving India the staff were able to find some reasonable accommodation and to rescue baggage and clothing, much of which had been landed at the wrong beaches. The Headquarters settled into the former Federated Malay State Volunteer Force building and took over a series of bungalows in the residential area of the city. This 'Utopia', however, was anything but permanent and, at very short notice, HQ ACSEA decreed that 224 Group should press on to Singapore by road. Some vehicles took an inland route while others travelled by a coastal route through Malacca. Everywhere the convoys were greeted by cheering crowds of Malays and Chinese with the villages bedecked with flags and triumphal arches of exotic flowers and foliage. Malay was 'en fete' during the rapid movement of British forces down towards Singapore.

When at last the convoys drove across the causeway on to Singapore Island the end of 224 Group's travels was in sight. Accommodation was initially found in Raffles Square and the staff spent several days foraging for office equipment, furniture and somewhere for the officers and airmen to live. At last some stability had been achieved, but it signalled the end of 224 Group as such. On 30 September the Group became Air Headquarters, Royal Air Force, Malaya.

No 224 Group had completed a long and distinguished operational career. From Calcutta in the uncertain days of 1942 it had moved to the Bengali port of Chittagong. Then, as the Japanese advanced through Burma, the Headquarters as well as its stations came under frequent and heavy air attack. It moved to Cox's Bazaar to support the Arakan offensive and thence to Akyab on 1 March 1945. Its squadrons took part in the final assault on Rangoon, which fell to the Allies on 2 May 1945. Withdrawal to a tented site outside Bangalore in India followed the fall of Rangoon and, from this pleasant location, the build-up of its units for ZIPPER took place. By the time the Group reached Singapore, the feet of its staff had hardly touched the ground since 1942. It had always been a highly flexible and versatile formation consisting entirely of mobile wings and squadrons. When the time came to dispense with mobility and to convert 902, 903 and 905 Wings into RAF Stations Tengah, Kallang and Kuala Lumpur respectively, it was appropriate that the Group should assume the more static title of AHQ Malaya.

It was also time for that great AOC, Air Vice-Marshal The Earl of Bandon, to return to the United Kingdom. Usually known either as 'Paddy' or 'The Abandoned Earl', he was greatly loved and respected, having led 224 Group through all its vicissitudes from the beginning of the 1944 Burma campaign. In a nostalgic and moving farewell Order of the Day,[2] he said, inter alia:—

"You worked at top pressure all the way, and the result was achieved by your individual efforts, and I cannot speak too highly of your endeavours. Your loyalty to me and your devotion to duty I have not seen surpassed during my service in the Royal Air Force ......"

He was succeeded on 2 October 1945 by Air Vice-Marshal J D Breakey CB DFC, who thus became the first postwar AOC of RAF Malaya. The squadrons which then came under his command are listed in Figure 1.

---

[2] AHQ Malaya Operations Record Book for October 1945

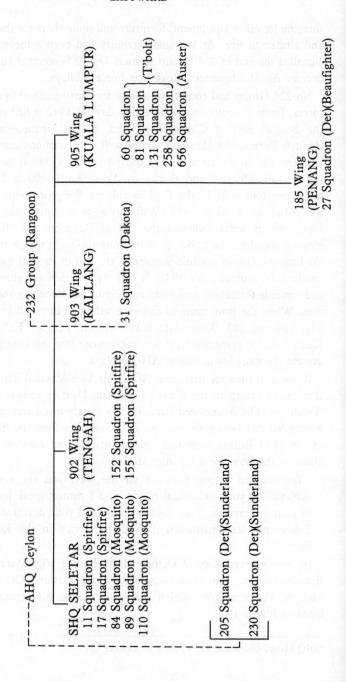

Figure I

Order of Battle of Air Headquarters, RAF Malaya on 1 October 1945

The First Weeks in Singapore

First impressions of Singapore were of a city of boarded shops, public buildings stripped of fittings and empty bungalows in overgrown gardens. The shadow of the torture chambers of the Kempeitai, built in their Headquarters at the YMCA building, had not lifted. APWI personnel were crowding through Singapore—emaciated civilian internees from the Changi and Sime Road camps, British, Indian and Australian prisoners-of-war released from the forced labour camps along the Burma-Siam railway and haggard Dutch families from Java. Airfields were littered with Japanese aircraft, most of them deliberately wrecked. The whole island presented a scene of chaos and neglect but there was a great feeling of release from bondage and a determination to clear away the wreckage, repair the damage and resume normal life as quickly as possible. Shops began to open with remarkable displays of prewar British goods which had somehow survived the occupation. As was to be expected, a black market, particularly in cigarettes and NAAFI goods, sprang up and had to be checked immediately. So short were food supplies that for some time British troops were forbidden to buy cooked food anywhere away from their messes and canteens.

The four airfields on the island, although usable, were in a sorry state due mainly to the total neglect of the domestic and administrative buildings and facilities. Tengah was probably in the best condition and was taken over as the home of two of the Spitfire squadrons, 152 and 155, thus inaugurating a main RAF operational base which continued as such throughout the postwar years. It had fine, unobstructed approaches and a good, if somewhat undulating runway. The old circular grass airfield at Seletar was small for the new generation of aircraft which initially were deployed there—Mosquitos and the remaining Spitfires. The prospects for further runway construction were severely limited as the single tarmac runway which had been built was restricted by the Johore Strait at one end and steeply sloping ground at the other. Seletar was no longer suitable for full operational use and eventually it was to become the main maintenance base in the Far East. This in no way affected the flying boat base which continued to be fully used for as long as Sunderlands remained in the theatre.

Kallang, Changi and Sembawang, the other three airfields, were in a thoroughly unsatisfactory condition. Kallang was the Singapore civil airport with a relatively short runway, approached over a low harbour wall at one end and a main road at the other. It had a grass and sand surface but, unlike Seletar, was badly drained. Changi was even worse, having been built on marshy ground by the Japanese with prisoner-of-war labour. Many of the labourers were British and they had endeavoured, with some success, to sabotage the construction as they toiled on the two runways.

As both Kallang and Changi were urgently needed by the RAF, it was decided to lay PSP on the runways at both airfields, and this was rapidly carried out by a Japanese labour force during late 1945 and early 1946. When completed, Kallang was used for a while by the Dakotas of 31 Squadron but it tended to revert to its original role as a civil airport in spite of the fact that it was never popular with the operators of the larger civil aircraft such as Skymasters and Lancastrians.

Even when the east/west runway at Changi had been covered with PSP[3], it was highly unsatisfactory. The marshy subsoil caused it to wrinkle with the result that, during every landing by a heavy aircraft, a bow wave of PSP several inches in height could be seen running ahead of the aircraft. It was necessary to close Changi for three days in every week to enable this surface to be tightened and straightened. Not only was this constant maintenance expensive but it placed almost unacceptable restrictions on Changi's use until it was rebuilt several years later. It may be some small satisfaction to those prisoners-of-war who were forced to work at Changi that their efforts at sabotage were certainly successful even if, in the event, they caused more trouble to the RAF than to the Japanese!

The Situation after Two Months

In many respects the occupation of Malaya and Singapore created fewer problems than were encountered elsewhere in SEAC, and certainly in the Netherlands East Indies, an area which is dealt with in the next chapter. Probably the biggest problem with which Mountbatten was faced was the repatriation of the Japanese surrendered personnel. It has to be remembered that there was virtually no Allied shipping to spare beyond the needs of his own forces and the essential commitment to feed the occupied territories and repatriate APWI. The best calculations that could be made indicated some

---

[3]Pierced Steel Planking

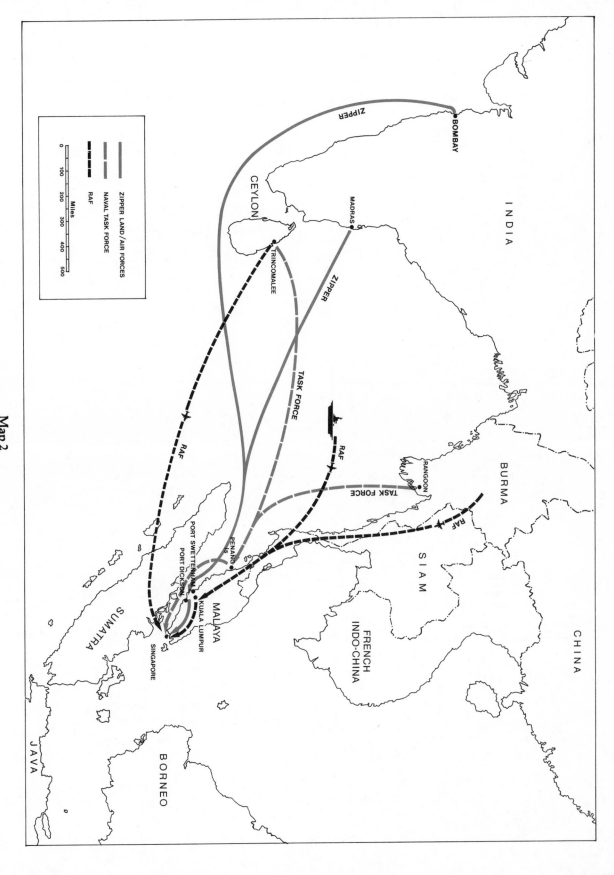

Map 2
Re-occupation of Malaya and Singapore
Operation ZIPPER

680,000 Japanese within the Command, of whom 125,000 were in Malaya and Singapore. Even if all the ships which Japan could at that time produce were used, it would take many years to send this huge total home. This was clearly an unacceptable situation.

For a while, of course, there was plenty of work for them to do. As the dreadful neglect of roads, canals, railways and public utilities of every kind came to light, it was possible to form large numbers of Japanese into labour contingents, and make them repair much of the damage they had caused. Those not so employed were moved by small coastal shipping, junks and fishing boats to Rempang Island at the eastern end of the Strait of Malacca where they could be economically fed and guarded until means of repatriating them could be found. Thus, by the end of 1945, some semblance of order had been achieved as far as the immediate disposal of Japanese forces was concerned.

The repatriation of APWI, on the other hand, created no great problem as rightly it was given the very highest priority. In all about 39,000 were found in Singapore and on the mainland. Some were flown home by long range transport aircraft, some went to India and Australia by Dakota and Sunderland, but most were shipped from Singapore. So well organised was the RAPWI operation that no less than 2,000 a day left by one means or another which quickly brought this humanitarian task to an end.

As the euphoria of being liberated began to fade, the inevitable political problems arose and towards the end of the year bitter fighting broke out between former Malayan and Chinese resistance forces on the mainland. It was sporadic and did not involve British forces, but it was an indication of troubles to come. The fighting died down after a short time but it was replaced by a great increase in armed robbery, particularly along the Malaya-Siam border. In Singapore itself, this breakdown of law and order took the form of serious strikes, accompanied by demands for higher wages, better food and living conditions.

During the years of occupation the Japanese, although they had encouraged nationalistic feelings among Indians and Malays, had not, in any way, encouraged demands for Malayan independence but there was no doubt that, during those years, a new degree of political consciousness had developed; something quite unknown during the prewar days of colonial rule. Much of the interior came under the control of resistance and guerilla forces who were as determined to resist a resumption of colonial rule as they had been to fight Japanese domination. It became all too clear that it was going to be extremely difficult to establish a civil administration which could gain control of these politically motivated factions. And so, after a mere four months of re-occupation, a situation which had initially seemed simple compared with that found in other areas of SEAC looked to be fraught with future problems.

The RAF was involved in these developments only to the extent that widespread strikes and disruption of civilian labour, upon which the stations depended heavily, delayed the rehabilitation of many of their facilities. As there was no operational activity beyond photographic and visual reconnaissance, the effects were confined to interruptions of training and maintenance. Support of RAF units in the Netherlands East Indies and Hong Kong was not greatly affected and the development of Singapore as the main RAF base in the Far East progressed steadily.

Certain changes in RAF organisation took place during this period in accordance with plans which had been drawn up in advance. Mountbatten's headquarters and those of his three Service commanders were no longer suitably located at Kandy in Ceylon, being too far removed from the active areas of the Command. Towards the end of the year the Supreme Headquarters and those of the Army and RAF therefore moved across to Singapore. Air Chief Marshal Sir Keith Park and his ACSEA staff were established on the island during November, a move which greatly facilitated control of the now widely spread stations and squadrons which extended from Burma to Soerabaya in Java and from Ceylon to Hong Kong.

This organisation affected AHQ Malaya which once again found itself on the move; this time returning to Kuala Lumpur which it had vacated, as 224 Group, only two months earlier. Still under the command of Air Vice-Marshal Breakey, the headquarters returned to its old accommodation on 25 November 1945. In so doing its responsibilities changed somewhat. Just as its mobile Wings had been converted into static station headquarters, the Air Headquarters itself lost its mobile role, becoming responsible for the main stations at Butterworth and Kuala Lumpur on the mainland, for Tengah and also for control of the Spitfire and Mosquito squadrons at Seletar in Singapore. AHQ Malaya thus became the operational Group in the area while most technical and administrative support was controlled directly from HQ ACSEA.

Four months had been sufficient to re-occupy the whole of Malaya and Singapore, and to settle the pattern of RAF organisation for the future. Although normality was slowly returning, life for the airmen was full of discomfort and uncertainty. The dissension and 'strikes' which spread through the ranks have been described in Chapter 1, and these affected the Singapore stations particularly. There were undoubted signs of political unrest among the mainland Chinese and Malays, fostered by communist influence, and the future looked anything but stable.

But while Malaya and Singapore were settling down albeit most uneasily, the RAF in the Netherlands East Indies was actively engaged in what amounted to a virtual extension of the war which was thought to have been finished on 14 August. The next chapter will deal with this prolongation of activity.

4

Occupation of the Netherlands East Indies

There must have been many occasions upon which Lord Mountbatten regretted the addition of the Netherlands East Indies to his already extensive Command. The complexities, hazards and indeed the casualties suffered by his forces in Java alone far exceeded those in all the other territories put together, and more than a year was to pass before he could extricate British sailors, soldiers and airmen from the East Indies. It is no exaggeration to say that the war continued for this length of time, but against a different enemy, and many more British soldiers and airmen lost their lives when they could reasonably have expected to be repatriated.

Background to Indonesian Independence

It needs to be remembered that the boundaries of SEAC were extended a matter of days only before the Japanese capitulation. Because of this, no up-to-date intelligence about conditions in the Netherlands East Indies was available in Kandy. It was known that an Indonesian Independence Movement had existed before the war and that it had been supported by prominent intellectuals, some of whom had been banished for their involvement in political propaganda.[1] No information was available as to the fate of the Movement during the Japanese occupation and there was no reason to suppose that re-occupation would present any operational problem other than rounding up the Japanese forces and extricating prisoners-of-war and internees. In the light of subsequent events this may seem to have been a naive appreciation but, nevertheless, it was so, and not even the Dutch Government was aware of the true situation in its former colonies.

---

[1] See Report to Combined Chiefs of Staff by SACSEA, Section D, p. 269. (AIR 23/2083).

As soon as the first RAPWI control team parachuted into Java and met with an unfriendly, if not actively hostile reception, the facts began to emerge. The Japanese, seeing that their defeat was inevitable and hoping to create as much difficulty as possible for any Allied occupation force, encouraged the Indonesians in their desire for independence. Consequently a Republic of Indonesia was proclaimed by Dr Soekarno on 17 August 1945, a mere three days after the capitulation. Furthermore, the tens of thousands of Japanese forces in Java and Sumatra handed over their weapons to the Indonesians and quietly retired into self-imposed internment to await developments. When a representative of the Dutch Government arrived in Batavia to take control, on 15 September, Dr Soekarno had had a month in which to organise his Government and a 'fait accompli' faced the Allied occupation forces.

The intention of the Dutch Government—an intention which had been agreed with HM Government—was to resume control of the East Indies as they had left it in 1942. If there was any underlying intention to introduce liberal reforms, no intimation of this had been made known to the people prior to the arrival of SEAC forces. In consequence the attitude of the new Indonesian Government towards the Dutch was openly hostile and towards the British forces deeply suspicious. It was understandably thought that the role of the latter was to hand back the East Indies to Dutch control as soon as RAPWI had completed its work and Japanese forces had been removed. Political confusion was complete and it was under these highly dangerous conditions that the work of the occupation forces had to commence.

The Entry into Java

On 15 September *HMS Cumberland*, flying the flag of Rear Admiral W R Patterson, reached Batavia carrying No 6 RAPWI Control Staff. No sooner had the cruiser docked at Tandjoeng Priok than the leader of the small team which had earlier parachuted into Java came aboard and gave the Admiral a clear but intensely disturbing report of the military, economic and political situation. The country was clearly in chaos with little transportation, severe food shortages and extreme danger to the tens of thousands of internees who, if any signs of Dutch militancy became apparent, were liable to be used as hostages with great risk to their lives. The political negotiations which followed have been well covered in the official history[2] and this narrative must confine itself mainly to the activities of the Royal Air Force.

It immediately became clear to Mountbatten and his staff that the modest British forces originally intended for Java would be totally inadequate. Lieutenant-General Sir Philip Christison, who had commanded XV Corps in Burma, was appointed C-in-C Allied Forces Netherlands East Indies (AFNEI) and despatched to Batavia with a nucleus of his Corps staff. He arrived there on 29 September, supported by 23 Division, with a Brigade Group from 26 Division going to Sumatra where the situation was at that time relatively quiet. It was fortunate that the influence of Dr Soekarno's government had had insufficient time to spread either to Sumatra or to the outer islands, with the result that the initial occupation of those areas met with no resistance and little hostility.

To provide the essential air support for General Christison, Air Headquarters, Netherlands East Indies (AHQNEI) was hastily formed from HQ 221 Group in Burma, and flew immediately to Batavia under the command of Air Commodore C A Stevens CBE MC. On arrival he joined General Christison, forming with him a joint headquarters. These moves were rapidly followed by the arrival of 904 Wing, under the command of Group Captain D J P Lee OBE.

904 Wing, it may be recalled, was one of the P47 Thunderbolt Wings originally intended to participate in Operation ZIPPER, but diverted to its new occupation task at short notice. It was decided that only two of the four squadrons in the Wing should go to Java and these, 60 and 81 Squadrons, left the Wing airfields in India to position themselves in Burma and subsequently at Kuala Lumpur, to await a call forward to Batavia. The Wing Headquarters embarked at Madras, as if for ZIPPER, in a small convoy of one Landing Ship Infantry (Large) (LSI (L)) and two MT and stores ships. In addition to the airmen for 60 and 81 Squadrons, a Wing and two squadrons of the RAF Regiment, a Servicing Commando and many supporting units made up the complement, a total of some 2,600 airmen in all.

The LSI(L) was one of the older Union Castle liners, the *Llanstephan Castle*, a very comfortable and pleasant ship for airmen on active service, and her conversion to a Landing Ship had necessitated little more than replacing the lifeboats by Landing Craft (Assault) (LCA) which hung from the davits around the boat deck. After sailing

---

[2]History of the Second World War—The War Against Japan, Vol V, HMSO 1969

from Madras this small 904 Wing convoy had to maintain wireless silence throughout the voyage: this was particularly important while transitting the Sunda Straits between Java and Sumatra owing to uncertainty about Japanese naval and air movements. The voyage itself was uneventful but the total lack of knowledge about the situation in Java gave cause for a great deal of anxiety as to whether the reception at Batavia would be hostile or friendly. The Commanding Officer took the precaution of parading his two Regiment squadrons on the boat deck in preparation for a ceremonial entry into Batavia on one day, while on another the airmen manned the LCAs in preparation for an assault landing. During this latter exercise the *Llanstephan Castle* hove-to for an hour while the loaded landing craft were all lowered into the water, engines started and several circuits of the ship completed.

Daylight was fading as the convoy approached Batavia on 17 October and it was decided to hove-to some twenty miles out to sea and make no attempt to approach or contact the shore until the following day. An all-night patrol of landing craft circled the ships as a guard against possible limpet mine attack. It was an unnecessary precaution, but a sensible one in the circumstances. As a brilliant tropical dawn broke, the three ships moved slowly towards the distant shoreline. Suddenly a signal lamp flashed from a position dead ahead and several miles offshore:— "Who are you and what are you carrying?" A reply was flashed from the bridge of *Llanstephan Castle*:— "*Llanstephan Castle* and two store ships carrying 904 Wing, RAF".

A long pause ensued during which it became evident that the signal came from a low grey ship which looked like a destroyer, at anchor some two miles ahead. Eventually a further signal was flashed to the convoy:— "I am guarding the starboard side of a swept channel through a minefield. The channel is 800 yards wide. Proceed at five knots between marker buoys into harbour. Beware sunken ship across harbour mouth".

Slowly the convoy moved in line astern down the swept channel which was clearly marked. The sunken merchant ship blocked half the narrow entrance to the inner harbour but this was safely negotiated. Whereupon a scene of utter chaos met the eyes of the astonished airmen. As was subsequently learned, a Japanese ammunition ship had blown up some months earlier and completely devastated the Tandjoeng Priok dock area. Every warehouse and building had been wrecked and, apart from some attempt to clear rubble from the dock sides, no effort had been made to repair the damage. A light signal from what turned out to be the office of the Naval Officer in Charge (NOIC) indicated where the three ships were to dock, a manoeuvre which was safely accomplished without any outside assistance. Indeed, the docks appeared to be lifeless and deserted. There was no reception committee, no greeting or welcome of any kind—just silence, dust and devastation with the temperature mounting rapidly into the 90s.

A pause ensued while the CO of 904 Wing and the Captain of *Llanstephan Castle* considered what to do in this extraordinary situation. Obviously they could not sit in the ships and do nothing. Equally obviously the 2,000 or more airmen could not go ashore with no knowledge of conditions in Batavia, five miles distant, and without even knowing which airfield was to be taken over by the Wing, and where it lay.

Finally it was decided to wait for two or three hours and at lunchtime, if nothing had transpired, to swing two jeeps ashore. The CO with a strong escort of Regiment riflemen would then drive cautiously towards the city in the hope of finding British forces in occupation. Three hours passed, during which the CO explained the position to his airmen and outlined his intentions. They were scattered round the decks in the sweltering heat, trying to find a breath of wind or square foot of shade, but all with their rifles loaded and ready for any eventuality. Such cheerful remarks as "Have we come to the right place, sir?" and "Can we go home now?" echoed the CO's own private thoughts as to whether he had become involved in some terrible administrative 'cock-up'.

However, as the two jeeps were being off-loaded onto the dockside, a lone Group Captain was seen hurrying up the gangway. Group Captain Sorel-Cameron announced himself as the Senior Officer i/c Administration (SOA) of the hastily formed AHQNEI. "Thank goodness you've arrived; the AOC knew you were coming but we had no idea when," were his first words. He went on to explain that General Christison had taken over in the city and set up his AFNEI headquarters, of which AHQ was a part. 904 Wing was to take over Kemajoran[3] airfield, which had originally been the civil airport of Batavia, and to bring in the Thunderbolts of 60 and 81 Squadrons as soon as possible from Kuala Lumpur. He described the political

---

[3]Pronounced "Kem-ire-on"

situation as extremely delicate, and although the Indonesians were not basically hostile to the British, the risk of being mistaken for Dutch troops was considerable and dangerous.

By the time these discussions were finished and a broad plan for the movement of the Wing from the docks drawn up, only a few hours of daylight remained. It was decided to start unloading vehicles and equipment but to delay movement to Kemajoran until the following morning. As 904 Wing and all its units were established on a mobile basis, sufficient vehicles were available in the three ships to move everybody and all the equipment without calling for outside assistance. This was one of the more fortunate aspects of the situation. Throughout the hot, sultry night the unloading of vehicles continued, using the floodlights and derricks of the ships, as all lighting and lifting gear normally associated with dockland seemed to have been destroyed. In the meantime Group Captain Sorel-Cameron returned to Batavia to organise accommodation to the best of his ability.

On the following morning the CO with two of his staff and a strong, well armed Regiment escort drove to Kemajoran ahead of the vanguard of the airmen. 904 Wing was becoming accustomed to shocks and the airfield was yet another. It was littered with damaged and unserviceable Japanese aircraft and its two short runways, each of about 1,600 yards, consisted of rough, uneven tarmacadam. There were two small corrugated iron hangars, three single storey buildings and a most inadequate domestic site of flimsy barrack blocks. Power, light and telephones were virtually non-existent and water would only come from standpipes within two feet of the ground, so low was the pressure. It was a little better than some of the airfields occupied by the Wing in Burma, but that was all that could be said for it. Had the Wing not been mobile and, therefore, virtually self-sufficient, it would have taken weeks to settle in. But within a few days, tents had been erected, power and light laid on, telephones organised by the Air Formation Signals Regiment which formed part of the Wing, and the water system improved.

However, the first task was to clear away the wreckage and make at least one runway suitable for the Thunderbolts to come in. This was not easy. 1,600 yards were barely adequate for a Thunderbolt and the surface would clearly play havoc with tyres. A ramshackle control tower of wood construction mounted on poles was quickly fitted up by some of the Mobile Signals Units (MSU) with VHF and a manual D/F installation. For good measure a wind sock was mounted above the tower and a signals square laid out in front of it. That was all that could be done in the 48 hours before the two squadrons were called forward. Fortunately the prevailing weather was good and Kemajoran, being close to the city and docks, easy to find.

On the morning of 21 October, a total of 26 Thunderbolts of 60 and 81 Squadrons arrived, being ordered to fly in formation around the city before landing. They were an impressive sight not only, one hoped, for the Indonesians, but also for the airmen who had not seen their aircraft for some weeks. No problems arose with the landings although the showers of stones and loose tarmac flying about indicated that some immediate work would be necessary on the runways.

The Thunderbolt

The Republic P47 (Thunderbolt II), to give it its full title, was one of a family of Lend/Lease aircraft from the United States and deserves special mention, partly because it bore the brunt of the RAF's active operations in the NEI. It also remained in 904 Wing long after the type had disappeared from all other RAF units.

Powered by a 2000 HP 18 cylinder air-cooled Wright engine, the Thunderbolt II was an extremely tough and rugged single-seater. Although originally designed as a high altitude interceptor fighter capable of a speed of 440 mph with a ceiling of 40,000 feet, it had to be used by the RAF mainly as a ground attack aircraft in the Far East. As such it was excellent, being armed with eight 0.5 calibre guns mounted in the wings and capable of carrying a variety of weapons or alternatively long range fuel tanks on universal mountings. Three long range tanks could rapidly be exchanged for $2 \times 1,000$ lb bombs and 1×500 lb bomb. It possessed the very useful radius of action of 637 miles.[4] In the context of Java, this meant that Soerabaya could be covered by Thunderbolts operating from Batavia, more than 400 miles distant. It had a high landing speed of more than 100 mph which, coupled with a long take off run when fully loaded and using water injection, restricted its use on short runways or rough surfaces. Even when the essential improvements to the Kemajoran runway had been carried out, it was never possible to operate the Thunderbolt at maximum load, but the restrictions which 60 and 81 Squadrons had to impose for safety reasons did not seriously limit the tasks for which it was needed. Its roomy cockpit, excellent field of vision and great

---

[4]Information from Jane's All the World's Aircraft 1945–46, Sampson Low, 1946

stability made it a popular and delightful aeroplane to fly: failure of the robust Wright engine was virtually unknown.

Sumatra and the Outer Islands

Had the situation which confronted the SEAC forces in the remainder of the Netherlands East Indies been as serious as that in Java, it would have been almost impossible for Mountbatten to accomplish his occupation tasks. Fortunately it was not so. The declaration of Indonesian independence, encouraged and made possible by the Japanese in Java, had insufficient time to spread its influence throughout the territory, and particularly in the outlying islands where hostility towards the Dutch was far less acute than in Java and Sumatra.

In Sumatra the reaction to the arrival of British forces, comprising a brigade of 26 Division, was on the whole peaceful and no difficulty was encountered in evacuating APWI personnel. As early as the end of September all of the 2,200 British, Indian and Australian prisoners-of-war had been released and moved to Singapore. The Japanese forces were co-operative and helpful and were responsible for concentrating some 13,000 internees, mostly Dutch and Asiatics, into areas for evacuation. As a precaution 28 (Spitfire) Squadron flew in to the Medan airfield, where it came under the control of AHQNEI in Batavia. Beyond 'showing the flag' and undertaking various reconnaissance tasks, it had little operational work to do, and could resume normal training. Inevitably, however, repercussions from Java began to affect Sumatra, and fears of a resumption of Dutch control gained in strength. In spite of a number of incidents, British forces did not become seriously involved and were able to withdraw during 1946, having accomplished their initial occupation tasks.

In Borneo, the other large island, which was part Dutch and part British, Australian forces carried out the initial re-occupation. They had in fact been fighting in British North Borneo when the war ended and so were well placed to accept the Japanese surrender and liberate the relatively few APWI in that area. By January 1946, Mountbatten was able to make British units, with a small RAF element, available to relieve the Australians who had taken on a somewhat larger commitment than their limited manpower really justified.

This left the problem of the many outer islands which, because of their isolation, had been unaffected by events in Java. The eastern islands, notably New Guinea and Timor, were occupied, and remained an Australian responsibility whereas the remainder were occupied at leisure by other SEAC forces. For example, Bali, which contained only about 300 Japanese, was not occupied until early in 1946 after a reconnaissance had revealed that no opposition or trouble was likely to arise. These islands were not actively hostile to the Dutch with the result that, in many instances, small parties of Dutch forces were able to take them over.

Reinforcements to Java

Even before 904 Wing arrived at Kemajoran, it was clear that its two Thunderbolt squadrons would be insufficient to provide all the air support that General Christison and his land forces would need to fulfil their essential tasks. Within a few days of its arrival, 904 Wing was therefore reinforced by the addition of three detachments of Mosquitos, from 84, 47 and 110 Squadrons stationed in Singapore. The 47 Squadron aircraft were capable of firing rocket projectiles (RP) while those of 84 and 110 Squadrons carried bombs only. Eventually the whole of 84 Squadron was deployed to Kemajoran and remained for the duration of the occupation.

To these reinforcements was added 31 (Dakota) Squadron. It was a large 'unit' with no less than 24 aircraft and was to become one of the hardest worked squadrons in the Royal Air Force for the next twelve months, most ably commanded by Wing Commander B R Macnamara who achieved the rare distinction of being awarded a 'peacetime' DSO for his leadership in the Netherlands East Indies. A small detachment of Photographic Reconnaissance Spitfires of 681 Squadron and one of Beaufighters from 27 Squadron for Air/Jungle Rescue were then added to the Wing, while 321 (Dutch) Squadron located some of its Liberators and Catalinas on the airfield, but was controlled directly by AHQNEI.

Within about a month Kemajoran had an aircraft strength of about 110, which placed an almost unmanageable burden upon the airfield, and upon 904 Wing. It was impossible to use both of the runways as the only parking area was a triangle of grass between them which was totally inadequate and which, in any case, was turned into a quagmire as soon as the rains came in November. The shorter and rougher of the two runways became a parking area, most of which was taken up by the exacting demands of 24 Dakotas and the RASC organisation needed to load and unload them. This left one 1,600 yard runway with an indifferent tarmacadam surface for all flying. Not surprisingly it began to disintegrate within a month with considerable risk to the Thunderbolts and Mosquitos in particular. There were no alternative airfields and the single runway had to be kept in use at all costs. An unusual and brilliantly conceived remedy was proposed by the Works authorities, namely to cover the whole of the runway surface with layer upon layer of bituminized hessian (Bithess). This, it was argued, would preserve the foundations and provide a soft, waterproof cover which should last for the duration of 904 Wing's stay.

A labour force of Japanese POWs was drafted in to a tented camp alongside the runway and the work was completed in what must have been record time. The result was most peculiar: it certainly produced a soft pliable surface, but so undulating was it that huge puddles formed all over it after rain which caused the Dakotas to disappear in clouds of spray on landing. In addition the strips of Bithess were liable to come unstuck and fly up in the slipstream, sometimes wrapping themselves round a tailplane after a landing. In order to rectify this problem, several Japanese with buckets of tar and large brushes were positioned along the runway sides during flying hours with instructions to run out and stick down the offending strips. The whole project was a desperate measure but it achieved the object of keeping Kemajoran fully serviceable for more than a year.

Initial Operations in Java

The reception accorded to the SEAC forces in Batavia made it crystal clear to the C-in-C and the AOC that the island, containing as it did some 50 million people, could not be fully occupied in order to repatriate APWI, disarm and send home the Japanese and hand back control to the Dutch. Such a task was estimated by General Christison to require at least five divisions with naval and air support to match. Even if forces of that magnitude were available—and they were not— the casualties to be expected from the Japanese-armed Indonesians would be quite unacceptable in the circumstances. In practice AFNEI had 23 Division, later reinforced with elements of 5 Indian Division, and the RAF force already described. Any occupation plan had to be broadly attainable with those forces.

The plan which was formulated restricted the SEAC forces to occupying three bridgeheads, one in West Java encompassing the three main cities of Batavia, Buitenzorg and Bandoeng, the second on the

north central coast around Semarang, and the third at Soerabaya in
East Java. Each of these bridgeheads (see Map 3) contained a port and
airfields, and it was hoped that from them it would be possible to reach
all the known prison camps and rescue the inmates. No attempt would
be made to occupy the mountainous backbone of the island or the
south coastal plain, and wherever prison camps were inaccessible to
the land forces, it was hoped to negotiate with the Indonesians for the
evacuation of the prisoners by air, eg from Soerakarta.

904 Wing was called upon to carry out its first operational task
within a few days of arrival. This consisted of a full-scale demonstration
flight by all serviceable Thunderbolts of 60 and 81 Squadrons over
Soerabaya on 25 October, to coincide with the landing of 49 Brigade
from 23 Division. It was a long and tiring round flight of more than
900 miles using long range tanks which permitted about half an hour's
formation flying over and around the port and town. No opposition
was encountered initially but the Proclamation leaflets which were
dropped resulted in a cool reception, and it soon became clear that
the occupation would not be well received. The town was full of
undisciplined young Indonesians, many of whom were well armed and
even possessed Japanese Armoured Fighting Vehicles (AFV).

In view of the distance from Batavia, it was appreciated at this early
stage that frequent close support of the ground forces in Soerabaya
would not be feasible and, if severe fighting were to break out, it would
be essential to position Thunderbolts much closer to the target area,
preferably on the airfield at Soerabaya itself.

On 28 October, similar demonstration flights by a large formation
from the two squadrons took place over Bandoeng and Buitenzorg, the
two principal towns in the Batavia bridgehead. The activity by aircraft
taking off, forming up and landing at Kemajoran was ample evidence
to the citizens of Batavia itself that the RAF meant business. No
particular demonstrations over Semarang, the third bridgehead, were
considered necessary but all aircraft flying between Batavia and
Soerabaya kept to the north coast of the island and thus overflew
Semarang where the airfield provided a useful emergency landing
ground.

Developments in Soerabaya

After the comparatively peaceful landing of 49 Brigade, covered by
the Thunderbolt demonstration already described, the situation in
Soerabaya deteriorated rapidly. This was largely due to increasing

suspicion that the British were hand in glove with the Dutch, and the difficulty which the Indonesians found in distinguishing between British and Dutch military personnel. This deterioration was greatly exacerbated two days after the landing when Brigadier Mallaby, the Brigade Commander, was brutally murdered while engaged in negotiations with Indonesian leaders. At the same time a small party of RAF officers, led by Wing Commander Kerr, which had been flown down from Batavia to make arrangements for the proposed detachment of Thunderbolts and Mosquitos, was ambushed and captured on the road from Soerabaya airfield to the town. The party was flung into jail in appalling conditions for two days before being released. They were extremely fortunate to escape with their lives. It was another example of confusion with Dutch forces, but Wing Commander Kerr eventually managed to convince his Indonesian captors that he was an Australian and the rest of his party British airmen.

The situation was too dangerous for a single brigade to attempt to occupy the town and 49 Brigade confined itself temporarily to consolidating in the dock area and the area where many of the internees were being held. Reinforcements in the shape of two brigades of 5 Division arrived on 9 November, followed immediately by the RAF detachment from 904 Wing of eight Thunderbolts of 60 Squadron and two Mosquitos of 110 Squadron, all under the command of Wing Commander M C Maxwell DSO DFC. Although he was, in fact, the Commanding Officer of 84 Squadron, he was detached to take command of the Soerabaya airfield as an emergency measure.

Greatly strengthened by these land and air reinforcements, General Mansergh, the GOC 5 (Indian) Division, was able to issue an ultimatum to the extremist factions to lay down their arms. This was rejected and resulted in three weeks of severe fighting in and around the town which cost the Indonesians some 10,000 casualties. Throughout these operations the Dakotas of 31 Squadron maintained a steady flow of supplies and ammunition, flying many sorties daily from Kemajoran and returning with APWI who were taken out from the town to the airfield under heavy escort. Thunderbolts and Mosquitos were called upon to attack a number of buildings occupied by extremists, including the Post Office, the Courts of Justice and several fortified buildings within the town. Accuracy was excellent: in one operation on 10 November $18 \times 1,500$ lb bombs were dropped, 10 of them being direct hits and the remainder very near misses. All the buildings attacked were either destroyed or rendered unusable.

There was no pause in the evacuation of APWI during the fighting so that more than 10,000 of these unfortunate people had been taken to safety by air or sea by the end of November, and the town had been completely occupied. A considerable amount of AA fire was encountered, much of it accurate and intense from light Bofors type guns as well as from machine guns and small arms. Although no aircraft were destroyed during these three weeks many hits were received, not only by the Mosquitos and Thunderbolts, but also by the more vulnerable Dakotas while landing and taking off. With the occupation of the town area, fighting died down but only because the Indonesian forces moved inland to new defence positions. From the accuracy of the AA fire, it was often thought that the weapons must be manned by Japanese, but no direct evidence of this was ever established. Nevertheless, in handing over their weapons, they must undoubtedly have given a considerable amount of instruction to the Indonesians.

The Soerabaya incident, or more correctly 'battle', showed conclusively that Dr Soekarno and his government had little control over the densely populated island. In spite of his efforts to restrain the extremist elements, the repercussions from Soerabaya created intense anti-British hostility elsewhere as propaganda pouring out from radio stations lent conviction to the suspicion that British forces were there to facilitate a return to Dutch colonial control. The situation was not ameliorated by certain militant statements emanating from Holland, and by the behaviour of some of the released Dutch personnel in Java who, perhaps understandably, were bitter and frustrated on their release from prison camps.

Operations in Central Java

The landing of SEAC forces at Semarang on 19 October, some days before that at Soerabaya was, as in the latter case, initially quiet and unopposed. Patrols of Gurkhas were pushed south as quickly as possible towards Magelang and Ambarawa where it was known that there were several prison camps containing many internees. All went well until the repercussions from Soerabaya reached the area, whereupon an ugly situation arose. A company of the 3/10 Gurkhas was surrounded at Magelang when endeavouring to rescue 4,000 internees. There was a distinct possibility that the Gurkhas would be overwhelmed but Dakotas of 31 Squadron arrived in time to drop supplies and ammunition to the beleaguered garrison. This was immediately followed by a Thunderbolt attack on targets in the vicinity. The attack was highly successful but the Indonesian reaction was to cut the road from Semarang, thus isolating the Gurkhas from their base. However, they were kept supplied by the Dakotas which were repeatedly hit by automatic fire during the process, but without loss. Heavy and concentrated bombing attacks along the Semarang road resulted in the Indonesian positions being captured and the road re-opened on 20 November.

On the following day the Gurkha garrison was withdrawn from Magelang to Ambarawa, but only reached there after severe fighting with constant air support from Mosquitos and Thunderbolts. Nevertheless the operation had permitted nearly 10,000 internees to be concentrated in and around Ambarawa. Even so the Gurkhas had been unable to prevent one prison camp being broken into and nine women and children murdered with a further twenty seriously injured and mutilated. These operations also cost 81 Squadron Flying Officer Crawshay-Fry whose Thunderbolt received a direct hit when attacking an anti-aircraft gun beside the lake and this extremely promising young officer had, only the day before, been strongly recommended for a permanent commission. The intensity of the opposition in this area may be gauged by the fact that 95 mortar shells fell in one RAPWI camp on one day.

These operations lasted for about three weeks, resulting in many casualties on both sides, and it became clear that the SEAC forces could not penetrate inland much beyond Ambarawa without incurring great risks, not only to themselves but also to the thousands of internees who were still incarcerated in and around Jogjakarta, the capital city of Central Java which was thought to be the headquarters of the extremist movement. Patient negotiation through the official Indonesian Government in Batavia seemed to be the only way in which these unfortunates, who were now being regarded by the extremists as hostages, could be released. General Mansergh's forces therefore held their ground in the Semarang—Ambarawa area where the fighting died down at the end of November.

The Situation in Western Java

The city of Batavia, being strongly held by 23 Division and 2962 and 2943 RAF Regiment Squadrons, remained fairly quiet apart from frequent clashes between hot-headed Dutch Ambonese troops and extremists, clashes in which British troops and airmen occasionally became involved by accident. This was about the only area in which Dr Soekarno and his Government were able to exercise some control.

Outside the city, however, the situation was extremely unstable and dangerous. So much so that no attempt was made to occupy or even enter the western end of the island and it was declared a prohibited area for flying as well as movement on the ground. Since there were no prison camps there it could be virtually ignored. The main concern was with the two towns of Buitenzorg and Bandoeng, the latter being particularly important as the hill station and secondary commercial capital of Java in which large numbers of internees were held.

After the initial Thunderbolt demonstrations had taken place an attempt was made to send a train containing food and supplies through to Bandoeng. It was ambushed, many of the Gurkha guard being murdered, and only one wagon reached its destination. After that incident it was necessary to send supplies either by Dakota, which carried APWI to safety on the return flights, or by heavily escorted road convoys with Thunderbolt and Mosquito cover. Even so, one convoy was ambushed near Soekaboemi on 9 December. A pitched battle ensued with many casualties among the British escort. Two of these were the RAF officer and his wireless operator who were controlling the aircraft from their jeep—both were killed in the battle. As in Central Java, the extremists turned upon the prison camps where several cases of atrocities were reported, including an incident in which 14 internees including some women were locked in a house and burned to death. Road convoys had to be restricted to the minimum and responsibility for maintaining Bandoeng devolved upon the RAF with 31 Squadron taking over the commitment to deliver 425 tons each week.

As the distance was comparatively short, a single Dakota could complete three or even more sorties to Bandoeng in a day but the limiting factor became that of loading the aircraft at Kemajoran and unloading at the other end of each flight. The RASC Air Despatch unit attached to 904 Wing was hard pressed to maintain the flow of supplies even with large gangs of coolie and Japanese labour. At times during November, the rate of aircraft movement on the single runway amounted to one every three minutes from first light until mid afternoon.

As the news of Indonesian success in Soerabaya filtered through, extremist activity increased in Batavia itself. So dangerous did the city become after dark that the C-in-C was compelled to order a

5. Before the arrival of NAAFI at Kemajoran in Java, October 1945

6. Internees deplaning from a 31 Squadron Dakota at Kemajoran with Indian troops waiting to emplane

7. Thunderbolts of 81 Squadron at Kemajoran with Dutch Catalinas and a B25 in the rear

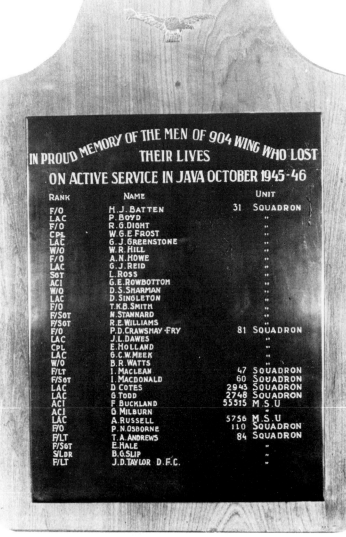

Rank	Name	Unit
F/O	H.J. BATTEN	31 SQUADRON
LAC	P. BOYD	"
F/O	R.G. DIGHT	"
CPL	W.G.E. FROST	"
LAC	G.J. GREENSTONE	"
W/O	W.R. HILL	"
F/O	A.N. HOWE	"
LAC	G.J. REID	"
SGT	L. ROSS	"
ACI	G.E. ROWBOTTOM	"
W/O	D.S. SHARMAN	"
LAC	D. SINGLETON	"
F/O	T.K.B. SMITH	"
F/SGT	N. STANNARD	"
F/SGT	R.E. WILLIAMS	"
F/O	P.D. CRAWSHAY·FRY	81 SQUADRON
LAC	J.L. DAWES	"
CPL	E. HOLLAND	"
LAC	G.C.W. MEEK	"
W/O	B.R. WATTS	"
F/LT	I. MACLEAN	47 SQUADRON
F/SGT	I. MACDONALD	60 SQUADRON
LAC	D COTES	2943 SQUADRON
LAC	G TODD	2748 SQUADRON
ACI	F. BUCKLAND	55515 M.S.U
ACI	G MILBURN	"
LAC	A. RUSSELL	5756 M.S.U
F/O	P.N. OSBORNE	110 SQUADRON
F/LT	T.A. ANDREWS	84 SQUADRON
F/SGT	E. HALE	"
S/LDR	B.G. SLIP	"
F/LT	J.D. TAYLOR D.F.C.	"

IN PROUD MEMORY OF THE MEN OF 904 WING WHO LOST THEIR LIVES ON ACTIVE SERVICE IN JAVA OCTOBER 1945-46

8. RAF Roll of Honour made by the airmen of 904 Wing in October 1946

curfew from dusk to dawn. One of the worst incidents which caused this tightening of regulations in the city occurred when a RAF funeral party was ambushed and attacked in the city cemetery. Fortunately an escort of 2962 RAF Regiment Squadron was present and the senior NCO in charge, Sergeant Haines, organised a defensive withdrawal and beat off the attackers. The coffin had to be left on the ground temporarily and neither the Padre nor the escort was injured. It was a most unpleasant incident and, but for the presence of mind of Sergeant Haines, who subsequently received the Military Medal, there would undoubtedly have been casualties. No 904 Wing was compelled to consecrate a piece of ground inside the perimeter of Kemajoran airfield and bury all subsequent casualties there.

By far the worst case of terrorist activity occurred on 23 November, resulting from the loss of a 31 Squadron Dakota. This aircraft was taking 19 Indian reinforcement troops to Semarang, but was compelled to return owing to engine trouble. It failed to reach Kemajoran and was forced to land about five miles south-east of the airfield. A wheels up landing in a paddy field caused no injuries and little damage. A Thunderbolt diverted to escort the Dakota saw it land and all the occupants get out, before returning to the airfield to report. When a crash party reached it, no signs of the crew or the passengers could be seen and a howling mob of Indonesians surrounded the Dakota. A whole battalion was then sent out to comb the area and locate the occupants who had apparently been taken to the village of Bekasi.

It was not until 1 December that information was obtained from a Christian Ambonese woman in Bekasi jail that she had seen the crew and passengers murdered and buried near the jail. Eventually the dismembered and mutilated remains of 22 bodies were unearthed, one short of the complement of the Dakota. Owing to the terrible mutilation and decomposition of the bodies, it was impossible to distinguish Indian from British, and all but three had their hands tied behind their backs. In his report on this tragedy the Deputy Air Commander-in-Chief, Air Marshal Sir George Pirie, wrote:—

"The Royal Air Force and Indian Army may well be proud of these men who gave their lives in carrying out their duties, not in defence of their own homes and country, but for the sake of humanity in a foreign land".

It was clear from this incident that Bekasi village had become the stronghold of a notorious gang of terrorists known as the 'Black Buffaloes'. An operation to clear the area was accordingly planned and carried out by the Army who razed the village to the ground. Feelings ran so high among 904 Wing personnel that the RAF was wisely excluded from the operation.

November and December proved to be the busiest months for the RAF of the whole twelve months for which the occupation of the Netherlands East Indies lasted. No 31 Squadron was hard pressed to maintain supplies to Bandoeng at a rate of 28 sorties a day as well as to fly essential supplies and troops to Semarang and Soerabaya. Moreover, its aircraft had to return with full loads of internees, as it became increasingly necessary to bring as many as possible to the comparative safety of Batavia for concentration, essential medical treatment and subsequent evacuation. Many of the loads of suffering humanity which filled the Dakotas were pitiful in the extreme. A typical load of, say, 25 would contain six or seven on stretchers, a dozen starved and emaciated children and the remainder so weak that they could not climb the ladder into the Dakota unaided. Often one or more would die on the flight to freedom in spite of every effort on the part of the 31 Squadron crews to fly them at low altitudes by the smoothest possible route. Every man in 904 Wing and its units was intensely moved by the daily flow of these desperately sick people through the airfield.

Mosquitos and Thunderbolts worked equally hard, daily escorting convoys to Bandoeng and strafing terrorist positions in and around Bandoeng itself where a great deal of looting and attacks on prison camps and military installations took place on an increasing scale after the news of Indonesian successes in Central and Eastern Java spread to the West.

The casualty rate among the SEAC forces was high. Between October and mid December the Army had no less than 1,063 casualties, of whom 350 were killed or missing. The RAF lost 21 officers and airmen killed or missing and had 5 injured. It was calculated that, in the first few months in Java, 23 Division lost more men than during a year's hard fighting in Burma. These were appalling losses during what should have been a peaceful period of occupation after the successful conclusion of a long and hard-fought war. The price of that success was high indeed in Java.

The Tide Begins to Turn

As the first Christmas for the forces in Java approached there was a noticeable decrease in terrorist activity in the main cities of Batavia, Semarang and Soerabaya. A large scale cleaning up operation by

British troops in Batavia brought a calmer atmosphere; shops began to open and the civilian population went about its business more freely. Outside the city, however, and notably in Bandoeng and Buitenzorg, the violence continued with many incidents of sniping, looting and arson. Every road convoy had to be constantly escorted by relays of Thunderbolts and Mosquitos while the Dakotas of 31 Squadron continued with their daily sorties to Bandoeng. In Central Java, only Semarang was held securely and the greatest anxiety was felt for the thousands of internees who were still being held inland in areas quite inaccessible to the available British and Indian forces.

However, a moderate Prime Minister, Sjahrir, had gained a certain measure of control throughout the island and he fully appreciated that negotiation and not military force was the only successful way to obtain the release of the internees. Had it not been for the continued intransigence of Dutch personnel and the bitter hatred of the Indonesians for the Dutch, Sjahrir's efforts to calm the situation would undoubtedly have achieved quicker results. Nevertheless, the tide gradually turned and the prospects for 1946 looked considerably brighter.

Living and Working Conditions

Little has so far been said about the conditions under which officers and airmen had to live and work. Initially they were indescribably bad, but initiative and improvisation, bred doubtless in the jungles of Burma, slowly produced conditions which were tolerable, but never good.

The inadequacies of the airfield at Kemajoran have been described. At peak times, as many as 110 aircraft were parked around the single runway. When the monsoon reached Java in November the whole station became a sea of mud in spite of the vast quantities of PSP which were laid to improve aircraft standings. Movement became extremely difficult. Fortunately it was found that the mud affected only the top few inches as a solid foundation lay beneath: this prevented aircraft bogging down, but it did nothing to relieve the surface misery. Hangar space precluded all but major servicing being carried out under cover and the Dakota was too large to go into either of the two small hangars. This meant that engine changes had to be effected in the mud, a fairly frequent occurrence with the intensive flying being carried out by 31 Squadron.

Many of the airmen had to be accommodated in tents, but the monsoon flooded them to an extent which made them uninhabitable so that, by December, all tentage was abandoned and whole streets of houses were requisitioned on the outskirts of the city. Recreation was almost non-existent until Batavia quietened down and it became possible to use sports facilities in the centre, such as the old European 'Box Club' which was rehabilitated. A 904 Wing team played in the first post-war game of cricket to celebrate the re-opening of this famous old club. Liberty runs for sea bathing were organised and eventually it became possible to send small parties of airmen to one of the many uninhabited off-shore islands for a few days lazing in the sun, fishing and swimming. In spite of heavy monsoon rain temperatures and humidity remained extremely high: 95° was not unusual in the middle of the day but work had to continue throughout the day to satisfy the operational commitment.

Strangely enough, money provided one of the few bright spots in an otherwise austere way of life. The Indonesian shopkeepers would not accept the Dutch guilder—the pre-war currency of the Netherlands East Indies. Sterling and Indian rupees were unobtainable for the troops and the only acceptable currency to the Indonesians was the Japanese guilder which had been in use throughout the war. Large stocks of this paper money had been taken over from the Japanese and it was decided to issue a small weekly allowance to all personnel until the NAAFI was able to set up an organisation in Java. Sterling was used for the payment of mess and canteen bills but, for essential toilet requisites, etc, the Japanese guilder was used. Thus for several months airmen were able to save most of their pay. This unique situation was too good to last, but it continued into 1946, by which time NAAFI had become firmly established and was able to provide all the necessities of life. The only people who were delighted at the cessation of this free issue of cash were the Accounts staff who had been dealing in as many as a dozen different currencies, a nightmare situation for them.

Initially, all messes remained on wartime 'Compo rations' which were adequate but unappetising to men who had lived on them for years. Tins of M and V (meat and vegetables) were little more than a variation of the bully beef of World War I. Java, however, is one large vegetable garden and it was not long before contracts were placed locally for excellent fresh vegetables. Nobody enquired too closely as to how they were grown and fertilised!

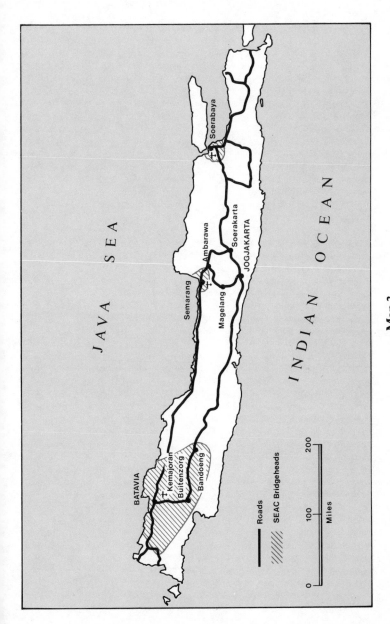

Map 3
Java

The New Year Brings Improvement

For the first time since the occupation, the month of January, 1946, saw no offensive air operations in either Java or Sumatra. Except for 31 Squadron which continued to be fully employed on supply missions, troop movements and APWI evacuation, flying was confined to tactical and photographic reconnaissance, and the escorting of road convoys from Batavia to Bandoeng.

This was an immense relief, partly owing to a serious manpower shortage resulting from the programme of release and repatriation, and partly due to the onset of bad weather making flying conditions difficult. So bad were they on several days that 31 Squadron suffered its second serious accident when a Dakota crashed on a mountain top during its return flight from Bandoeng to Kemajoran. The wreckage was not sighted for several days despite an intensive search. Photographs then showed that it had crashed in an inaccessible area of jungle, and had been burned out with no sign of life. Fortuitously it had been carrying no passengers, being loaded with APWI luggage, but it meant the loss of another crew for the squadron.

January also saw some reorganisation of both Army and RAF units. Soerabaya was established as a Royal Air Force station under the command of Wing Commander J D Warne DSO DFC, with 60 (Thunderbolt) Squadron, 321 Dutch (Catalina) Squadron and detachments of 47 (Mosquito) and 656 (AOP) Squadrons based there. Warne's primary task was to give air support to 5 (Indian) Division in Soerabaya and Semarang.

No 904 Wing remained with its squadrons as before at Kemajoran but 84 (Mosquito) Squadron was brought up to full strength with the arrival of its remaining airmen from Singapore. At the same time 155 (Spitfire) Squadron moved into Medan in Sumatra where the airfield had been resurfaced. The arrangements for Air/Jungle rescue were changed as 27 (Beaufighter) Squadron became due for disbandment, the essential task being assumed by 81 Squadron at Kemajoran where a section of Thunderbolts was maintained on permanent standby to fly to any reported crash. With minor alterations this remained the battle order in the Netherlands East Indies for the final stages of occupation.

As February came in the rains of the north west monsoon became even heavier, Batavia frequently registering more than one and a half inches in a day, making life at Kemajoran exceedingly difficult and unpleasant. Several aircraft came to grief in these conditions by skidding off the all too short runway. Excellent though the Bithess was in preserving the runway, it could and frequently did become extremely slippery, causing poor braking and sometimes aquaplaning.

The situation in the Bandoeng/Buitenzorg region began to deteriorate again in March with several road convoys ambushed, necessitating a resumption of offensive action by the escorting Thunderbolts. This deterioration was thought to be largely due to the introduction of more Dutch troops into Java and the reappearance of a certain amount of Dutch currency, giving the Indonesians the impression that British forces were co-operating closely with the Dutch authorities. More atrocities were perpetrated against internees and several camps were shelled and mortared. The convoy protection duty was a heavy commitment for 81 Squadron, calling for 16 sorties on each day that a convoy was on the road. The Thunderbolts flew in pairs, fully armed and at instant readiness to be called in to attack a target by the Air Contact Team which accompanied every convoy. Nevertheless, the intensity of operations remained well below that of the last two months of 1945.

Failure of the Mosquito

After several months of heavy rain and high humidity serious technical troubles began to affect the Mosquitos of 47 and 84 Squadrons. It must be remembered that these splendid aircraft were of all wood construction, having been designed and built during World War II when certain metals were in short supply. Their performance in the temperate conditions of Europe was exemplary, and it was for that theatre they were specifically designed. When deployed to the Middle and Far East theatres after the war, however, their particular form of construction proved unsuitable. The intense dry heat of the Middle East caused shrinkage in various vital components with the result that the aircraft had eventually to be grounded and the squadrons re-equipped with metal aircraft.[5] In the Far East the high humidity revealed other weaknesses, in main spars, glued joints and warping skin. There was no question of keeping the Mosquitos of 47 and 84 Squadrons in the two small hangars available at Kemajoran, and so they were constantly exposed to the worst possible conditions for their type of construction. Repairs were highly specialised and almost

---

[5]See Flight from the Middle East, page 6, Sir David Lee, HMSO, 1980

impossible under such conditions. The best that could be done was to patch them up temporarily and keep them airworthy for as long as possible. Eventually, in March 1946, 47 Squadron was disbanded and its remaining serviceable Mosquitos handed over to 84 Squadron to keep the latter going until the end of the occupation. It needs to be emphasized that this was no reflection on a very fine design, produced to meet an urgent need at a particular time. Whether it was wise policy to deploy it to the overseas theatres after the war is another matter, but here again it is important to realise that many squadrons, previously equipped with American aircraft under the Lend/Lease programme, had to disgorge their aircraft, and the Mosquito was one of the few British aircraft available to fill the gap. One of the saddest duties which befell 904 Wing before it left Java was to burn the remains of more than 20 Mosquitos on the perimeter of Kemajoran airfield.

Problems with the Mosquito were instrumental in a redeployment of 904 Wing's squadrons. By April the situation in Soerabaya was sufficiently under control to permit the return of certain Dutch forces. So it was decided to move 60 (Thunderbolt) Squadron back to Batavia to take the place of 84 Squadron which was to be transferred to Kuala Lumpur where it would exchange its Mosquitos for new equipment. Although not known at this time, this fine old Middle East squadron, whose airmen still sang *Those Shaibah Blues*, on every suitable occasion, was destined to return to Iraq after the briefest of stays at Kuala Lumpur. Almost since its formation 84 Squadron had been identified with Iraq, and it was appropriate that it should return to the desert.

Release of Internees from Central Java

The concentration of APWI in Soerabaya, Semarang and Batavia and their subsequent evacuation from those ports had been going well during the first quarter of 1946, but great concern was felt for several thousand of these unfortunates who were still incarcerated in various camps in Central Java. It was known that they were in a pitiable condition and virtually held as hostages eight months after the war was over. Even if sufficient forces had been available to rescue them by military operations, it was almost certain that they would have been murdered by their captors before help could reach them. Consequently negotiation and diplomacy were the only methods likely to effect their release, and these were desperately slow in the circumstances of Java.

But they did eventually succeed. At the end of April an agreement
was reached with the Indonesians to send in British aircraft to Solo,
the airfield for Soerakarta, in limited numbers to ferry out the
internees who would be brought to the airfield by road from their
various camps. This was the looked for break-through, and on 20
May, two Dakotas of 31 Squadron flew into Solo for the first time,
somewhat fearful of their reception. The organisation on the ground
was haphazard and the scores of heavily armed Indonesians surround-
ing the airfield did little to ease the tension. Nevertheless, the two
Dakotas made six sorties from Solo to Semarang and returned to
Kemajoran with their last load of the day.

Two Dakotas each day were allowed and the operation continued
without serious interruption. It was too dangerous to allow aircraft
and crews to remain overnight at Solo and, should an aircraft become
unserviceable while there, it was planned to leave it until the following
day while its crew returned to Kemajoran in the other Dakota. In
fact this situation never arose. An example of the sensitivity of this
arrangement occurred one day at the end of May when the CO of
904 Wing, Group Captain Lee, participated in the Solo operation,
and happened by chance to be flying the first Dakota received in
Java with red, white and blue RAF roundels on it. Throughout the
campaign in Burma, the red circle had been omitted from the roundel
owing to possible confusion with Japanese aircraft whose Rising Sun
emblem was painted on transport aircraft which bore a striking
resemblence to the Dakota. Consequently all the 31 Squadron Dakotas
which went initially to Java had blue and white markings only.

As the Group Captain stepped from his aircraft, he was greeted by
an Indonesian General who, pointing to the newly painted roundels,
asked tersely why he was flying a 'Dutch' aeroplane. The explanation
in halting Malay and pidgin English that those were the normal
peacetime markings of the RAF carried little conviction and the crew,
surrounded by heavily armed natives, were in some danger of being
arrested. Fortunately an English speaking internee was able to elucid-
ate but, with the comment that the Group Captain was exceedingly
lucky not to have been shot down while approaching to land, the
matter was closed except for the instruction from the General that
the Dakota was not to be used in the evacuation, but was to return
empty to Batavia. Needless to say, this incident resulted in the red
circle being omitted from all roundels for the remainder of the
occupation of the Netherlands East Indies.

Prickly incidents continued to occur from time to time, but the operation continued for many weeks and resulted in all the APWI being eventually rescued from Central Java, some 10,000 of them being flown to safety by 31 Squadron.

Handing Over to the Dutch

During May the political negotiations reached a stage at which the handing over of British control to Dutch forces could make gradual progress. The main tasks of the British forces, namely the evacuation of APWI and the rounding-up of Japanese forces, were within sight of completion, and it was imperative that they should leave the Netherlands East Indies as soon as those tasks were finished.

Soerabaya was the first of the three bridgeheads in Java to be handed over, the responsibilities of 60 Squadron being assumed by a Dutch Kittyhawk squadron whereupon the RAF squadron and all personnel returned to Kemajoran. Shortly after its return, 81 Squadron was disbanded and 60 Squadron assumed its tasks, notably the protection of the Bandoeng road convoys which continued to meet with occasional opposition.

Semarang was next in line to be handed over, releasing the British brigade which returned to Singapore. The Dutch continued to handle reception arrangements for APWI being daily flown out of Solo by 31 Squadron, a commitment which was not completed until August. A few weeks later control of Bandoeng was also relinquished to Dutch forces, a move which was met with considerable hostility from extremists, resulting in some resurgence of sniping and other terrorist activity. The road convoys to Bandoeng were also handed over gradually to Dutch control with the air escort duty being shared between 60 Squadron and a detachment of B25 Mitchells of 120 (Dutch) Squadron which was located for convenience at Kemajoran. The two squadrons provided the escort aircraft on alternate days.

It was perhaps understandable that July should see a general flare up in anti-British activity everywhere—in Sumatra as well as in Java. It was undoubtedly the rapidity of the handover of control which convinced the extremists that the British were now firmly in the pockets of the Dutch. Not only the main islands but also the outer islands were, in Indonesian eyes, returning to the hated prewar colonial rule. For a while the flow of APWI out of Solo was stopped and, once again, delicate political negotiations were necessary before the situation calmed down and the daily Dakota run to Solo was resumed.

Very little credit has so far been given in this narrative to the RAF Regiment. No 2962 Squadron at Kemajoran and 2739 Squadron at Medan were kept intensely busy in preventing the constant looting, thieving and sniping which continued unabated around the airfields in particular. Hardly a night passed without some incident involving petrol stealing or the theft of cloth which was desperately needed by the Indonesians. The windsock was removed from its pole at Kemajoran on at least three occasions, the outside canvas was removed from tents and there were frequent attempts to break into storehouses. The vigilance and courage of the Regiment gunners throughout this difficult period was beyond praise and they suffered a number of casualties.

Rundown and Departure from the Netherlands East Indies

From August the rundown of RAF units gathered momentum in anticipation of an early departure from both Java and Sumatra. No 155 (Spitfire) Squadron at Medan had already been reduced to one Flight of eight aircraft and during August it was disbanded, having had a useful but somewhat frustrating stay in Sumatra. Unlike its companion fighter squadrons in Java, it had not been called upon to take any offensive action but, nevertheless, its tactical reconnaissance work had proved of inestimable value to the Army. One Flight of 60 Squadron was detached from Kemajoran to take its place at Medan for the few remaining weeks.

In September, it was the turn of 31 Squadron to be disbanded, but to be re-formed in India as part of the permanent postwar Royal Air Force. The operational record of this Dakota squadron is remarkable. During its one year and six days in Java, it flew 11,000 sorties, carried 127,800 passengers and 26,000 tons of freight. Praise for its work was unstinted from British and Dutch authorities alike, and the award of the DSO to Wing Commander Brian Macnamara, who had commanded the squadron throughout, was richly deserved.

The next two months saw the gradual assumption of control of all sections at Kemajoran by personnel of the Royal Netherlands Air Force who operated under RAF supervision until fully conversant with procedures and equipment. No 60 Squadron remained on the station until the final withdrawal on 28 November. Its Thunderbolts, which had proved so rugged and effective, were broken up before departure, and the squadron moved to Singapore to be re-equipped with Spitfires. No 904 Wing, the last of the ACSEA wings, was also disbanded, having retained its mobile role and equipment throughout its 14 months at Kemajoran. Similarly AHQNEI, formed for a specific purpose under Air Commodore Stevens, had completed its task and was disbanded.

In Retrospect

Withdrawal from the Netherlands East Indies brought to an end the many and difficult occupation tasks with which SEAC forces were faced in August 1945. It had taken 15 months to rescue and repatriate the many thousands of APWI from their terrible conditions, none worse than in the East Indies. All Japanese forces had been disarmed and, if not repatriated, at least concentrated for eventual repatriation. The Royal Air Force had played a notable part in all these activities, and it is appropriate to end this chapter by quoting from the final Report of the Air Commander-in-Chief on the work of the RAF in the Netherlands East Indies. He said:

"In retrospect, the British role in the Netherlands East Indies appears to be considerably enhanced by its spirit of tolerance. The part played by the Royal Air Force in this connexion, though spectacular, should be remembered as a striking contribution to the cause of world rehabilitation during an exacting and delicate period of transition".

The RAF suffered considerable casualties and losses during its time in the Netherlands East Indies. Some of these have been mentioned but a full record of the aircraft lost and casualties incurred will be found at Appendix A.

5

Reductions in India and Ceylon

From Indonesia, where the RAF's task was short and sharp, it is time to turn to India where the RAF had been committed since its earliest days.

The sub-continent had been built up from 1942 onwards as the main base for the support of the Allied forces engaged in the war against Japan. As soon as the war in Europe was over, reinforcements poured out to the Far East and the Indian base assumed an even greater size and importance. By the middle of 1945 India had become one vast depot, not only supporting the campaign in Burma and the air route to China over the 'Hump', but also absorbing the additional supplies and personnel which it was expected would be needed for ZIPPER and subsequent operations. A quick glance through the Location of Units publication[1] for mid 1945 reveals hundreds of miscellaneous units, depots and establishments, varying from small Anti-Malarial and Mobile Signals Units to large Repair and Salvage Units, Hospitals, etc. These were still in process of expansion when the war abruptly ceased on 14 August. An additional volume of this narrative would be required to describe in detail the huge task of sorting out the base units needed to tackle the immediate post-war commitments as well as to satisfy the release and repatriation programme. This chapter is, therefore, confined to outlining the principal organisational changes which took place in 1945 and 1946 as the base was reduced, and as India moved steadily towards independence in 1947.

Ceylon must also be regarded as a subsidiary base for the Royal Air Force at this time, in that its primary role had been to support the war at sea by housing and maintaining the flying boat and long range general reconnaissance squadrons operating over the Indian

---

[1] SD 161 Location of Units in the Royal Air Force, 1 June 1945.

Ocean. Its location, facing the Bay of Bengal to the east, the Indian Ocean to the south and the Arabian Sea to the west, made it ideal for covering these large sea areas which were the hunting grounds of Japanese submarines. Ceylon was also fortunate in possessing a number of secure anchorages and lakes which were suitable for Sunderland and Catalina bases. The strategic importance of this island, dominating the main sea route to the Far East, was immense.

When South-East Asia Command (SEAC) was established, Ceylon was a natural choice for the location of its headquarters. Although at first sight it seemed far removed from the centre of the fighting which was mainly in Burma, and for this reason was not a popular location, there was a considerable Japanese threat to the eastern seaboard of India. Siting HQ SEAC and its associated single service headquarters at Kandy, in the hills of Ceylon, not only provided a secure location against any further advance to the west by Japan, but also ensured that the Supreme Commander and his staffs were well placed to control the Allied forces when able to advance and re-occupy Malaya, Singapore and the remainder of South-East Asia. Events were to show that the selection of Kandy was a sound decision which eventually facilitated the return of the various Far East headquarters to Singapore.

Post-war Organisation and Role

At the end of the war there were four major RAF formations under HQ ACSEA in India and Ceylon. HQ Base Air Forces (BAFSEA) was a non-operational administrative headquarters of considerable size and complexity, located in New Delhi. As its name implied, it administered the Indian base of the RAF and provided the personnel and the technical and administrative support for all the squadrons and ancillary units located forward in the operational areas.

Secondly, there was Air Headquarters Burma which remained in India, at Calcutta, but only until the way was clear for it to move to Rangoon as the fighting in Burma died down. It represented, therefore, the first of the reductions which took place in India during the closing stages of the war.

Thirdly, Headquarters 222 Group, at Colombo, was the operational formation which controlled all the squadrons stationed in Ceylon, largely of a maritime nature. Its stations were spread widely across the Indian Ocean and included those on the Cocos Islands Diego

Garcia. The area of responsibility of 222 Group was, therefore, very large indeed.

Finally, Headquarters 229 Group, also at New Delhi, was one of several Transport Command Groups located round the world, the day to day operations of its squadrons being controlled locally in accordance with a policy dictated from the United Kingdom to ensure that the most efficient and economical use was made of transport aircraft world wide.

For the first few months of peace, the importance of India as a base for the Royal Air Force was undiminished. The serious shortage of merchant shipping due to wartime losses necessitated the use of every available ship for the immediate tasks of feeding the population of the re-occupied countries, repatriating Service personnel, prisoners-of-war and internees, providing for the essential needs of the widely dispersed SEAC forces and many other high priority tasks. It stood to reason, therefore, that until Singapore and Malaya could be rehabilitated, the RAF would have to continue to depend upon base units in India for the major servicing of aircraft and equipment and the bulk of those administrative services normally provided by a main base area.

Nevertheless, it was possible during those early months to disestablish and reduce in size many units no longer needed to support the front line. It could have been effected more rapidly had there been adequate shipping and aircraft available to repatriate the airmen. Every transport aircraft that could be spared was pressed into service together with Liberators, Halifaxes, Lancasters and even Sunderlands which were diverted to the transport role, but they were still unable to meet the full demands of the release and repatriation scheme. This was one of the primary causes of the wave of 'strikes' and disaffection which spread through RAF stations in India and Ceylon at the end of 1945, and which has been described in Chapter 1.

Changes in Ceylon

As units were reduced or moved forward to the newly occupied areas of SEAC, some reorganisation took place. The first formation to be disbanded was 222 Group at Colombo. On 15 October 1945, this formation became AHQ Ceylon,[2] a much smaller headquarters under

---

[2] SD 155/1945 (2530) Secret Organisation Memoranda

the command of Air Commodore C E Chilton CBE, incorporating the Base Headquarters, Colombo, which was also disbanded.

The order of battle of AHQ Ceylon during this last quarter of 1945 was considerable, comprising six Liberator squadrons (Nos 99, 356, 203, 8, 160 and 321), the last named being a Dutch squadron. There were also four Sunderland squadrons (Nos 205, 209, 240 and 230), and No 136 Spitfire Squadron. Of this force 99, 356 and 136 Squadrons had been based in the Cocos Islands for the latter part of the war, standing astride the main sea route from Europe to Australasia. This isolated group of islands, containing a single airstrip, had played an important part in harassing Japanese submarines and surface ships in their efforts to penetrate the Indian Ocean and disrupt Allied shipping. The Liberators, defended by the Spitfires of 136 Squadron, had ranged far and wide over the long sea crossing from the Cape of Good Hope to Australia with considerable success under control from Ceylon.

Now, however, with the threat to the Indian Ocean gone, the role of the Cocos Islands was reduced to that of a staging post in the UK to Australia route, a role which was destined to continue only until facilities for four-engined aircraft could be provided in Singapore (Changi), whereupon all long range transport aircraft would be routed to and from Australia via Singapore.

Nos 99 and 356 Squadrons were disbanded but their last task before flying their Liberators to Maintenance Units in India for disposal was to evacuate the majority of the Cocos Islands airmen to India and Ceylon. The versatility of these Lend/Lease aircraft had been used to the full—as bombers, maritime reconnaissance and anti-submarine aircraft, transports and, in the case of 8 Squadron which was also disbanded, for special operations. With Dakotas and Thunderbolts they had provided an extremely valuable asset to the RAF in the closing stages of the war against Japan. Two Liberator squadrons, 160 and 203, were to remain in Ceylon for a few more months.

During the latter part of November, the situation in Singapore had stabilized to a point at which Mountbatten was able to transfer his Supreme Headquarters from Kandy to Singapore, a move which had always been contemplated when circumstances allowed. At the same time Air Chief Marshal Sir Keith Park similarly transferred his flag, so that by the end of the month ACSEA was firmly established at the centre of gravity of the majority of its forces. With the departure of the multitude of supporting units needed by the complex of inter-Service headquarters, Ceylon returned to its relatively quiet peacetime role of guardian of the Indian Ocean air routes.

The Rundown in India

In India a further major reorganisation was shortly to take place. Early in 1946 the political situation was developing rapidly in the direction of eventual independence for the sub-continent. With the war over and the disappearance of the threat from Japan, the demand for the return of its fighting troops became increasingly vociferous, as did the desire to obtain freedom from British rule. Militant demonstrations were more frequent and it became firm British Government policy to reduce its dependence upon the Indian base as quickly as possible.

Thus, on 1 April 1946, HQ BAFSEA was disestablished as a separate formation, those of its sections and personnel still required being amalgamated with AHQ India, with the combination retaining the latter title at New Delhi.[3] The units under command of the new headquarters comprised a mixture of Royal Indian Air Force (RIAF) and Royal Air Force squadrons and establishments, all under the command of Air Marshal Sir Roderick Carr KBE CB DFC AFC.

These were difficult months for the new Air Headquarters. It faced both ways in discharging its responsibilities, in that it had a heavy residual task of supplying and building up the units which had moved forward to the re-occupied countries while at the same time reducing its own strength as rapidly as possible and keeping the repatriation programme moving. The debris left by the war was immense, as in every other theatre, and it had to be cleared and accounted for efficiently. When all these conflicting tasks were viewed against the background of mounting political strife throughout India as the desire for independence increased, it is no little credit to AHQ India that it succeeded so well.

After the amalgamation of the two headquarters, 12 RAF squadrons were left under AHQ India. These squadrons, which are listed in Appendix B, were on loan to the Indian Government, an arrangement which followed closely the system which had pertained before World War II. The RAF personnel were paid, housed and provided for by the Indian Government in return for supporting the relatively few

---

[3] SD 155/1946 (481)

RIAF squadrons in their 'watch and ward' peacekeeping duties. India was committed to providing all necessary training facilities for the RAF squadrons to enable them to maintain full operational efficiency.

It was logical at this point for AHQ India to be removed from the control of ACSEA and to be placed directly under the joint control of the Indian Government and Air Ministry—a further step towards the eventual independence of the sub-continent and the final departure of the RAF. The staffs of AHQ and its subordinate formations were by this time made up of both RAF and RIAF officers and airmen. The war had understandably given a great impetus to the expansion of the RIAF which had been in existence for only six or seven years when war broke out. The training of Indian officers by the RAF had continued without cessation and, by 1946, a large nucleus of competent and well-trained officers was working efficiently alongside their British counterparts. As an example, the Wing Commander in charge of Air Training at AHQ India was Wing Commander S Mukerjee. He had been one of the first six Indian officers to be trained at Cranwell in 1930, and he subsequently rose to become Chief of the Air Staff in later years.

An unusual and important commitment which fell to the staff of the Air Headquarters, having been acquired from the defunct BAF-SEA, was planning and mounting the RAF and RIAF contingents for the British Commonwealth Air Forces of Occupation in Japan (BC(AIR)). Although Japan lay outside the South-East Asia theatre of responsibility, it had always been regarded as politically important that the Commonwealth should be strongly represented in the occupation force to be despatched to Japan. Planning proceeded during late 1945 and early 1946 on the basis of two RAF Spitfire squadrons (11 and 17) and one RIAF Squadron (No 4). These were to be joined in Japan by three RAAF Mustang squadrons and a Corsair squadron of the RNZAF. The ground personnel for this contingent were despatched from Madras by sea in the Spring of 1946, to be followed by the aircraft which were conveyed by aircraft carrier. Once the departure of the force had been completed, control passed to ACSEA, and AHQ India had no further responsibility. Mention of the work of these squadrons in Japan will be made in a later chapter.

Throughout 1946 and the early part of 1947 the rundown of RAF units in India continued rapidly and the repatriation and release programme made good the initial backlog as more shipping and, in particular, BOAC civil aircraft became available. As in other theatres, repatriation of airmen and airwomen due and overdue for release created severe shortages in the Command and made the tasks of closing down units efficiently most difficult. The return or disposal of many hundreds of Lend/Lease aircraft—Thunderbolts, Dakotas, Liberators, Catalinas and Expeditors to name but a few—gave many a headache to the Engineering and Equipment staffs who also had to cope simultaneously with re-equipping squadrons with British Tempests, Halifaxes, Lancasters and the latest versions of the Spitfire. As units were disbanded the top hamper of Group headquarters was also drastically reduced, from seven Groups in March 1946, to four by November when only 229 (Transport) Group remained as an RAF formation, the remaining three being RIAF Groups.

The independence of India was proclaimed on 14 August 1947 when Pakistan became a separate and independent country. The bloodshed which arose over Partition did not directly involve the Royal Air Force and, therefore, is irrelevant to this narrative. All RAF operational squadrons had been withdrawn before these events took place and 10 and 31 Dakota Squadrons alone remained temporarily at Karachi (Mauripur) which had by then become part of Pakistan.

The sub-continent had provided a magnificent training ground for the RAF for twenty years prior to the outbreak of World War II, and a splendid base for operations against the Japanese during that war. Since independence many officers and airmen of India and Pakistan have continued to receive RAF training in Great Britain and this had been accompanied by a constant exchange of technical and other information. It is pleasing to be able to conclude this brief resume by reflecting on the closeness and harmony that have characterized relations between the RAF and the indigenous air forces.

6
Development of the Singapore Base

It was Lord Alanbrooke, the wartime Chief of the Imperial General Staff, who said in his memoirs:—"With the loss of India and Burma, the keystone of the arch of our Commonwealth defence was lost".

As India, closely followed by Burma, approached independence, a new arch had to be constructed over Malaya, Singapore, British Borneo and Hong Kong, and the keystone of this new arch clearly had to be Singapore Island. Japan had laid bare the appalling weaknesses in the prewar defences of Singapore; the lesson of air power had been learned at great cost and the myth of the invincibility of the Malayan jungle had been exploded. Singapore was still vulnerable from sea, land and air, but its vulnerability was, by 1945, well understood. However, it was also defensible and its natural harbour, well protected naval base, airfields and barrack accommodation provided the facilities required to develop it into a splendid base for Britain's post-war forces in the Far East. It is significant that the batteries of 15-inch naval guns which had been its main protection before the war were never again to be activated and were left as rusting memorials to the inadequacy of the earlier defence policy.

As Mountbatten's forces completed their widespread occupation tasks throughout South-East Asia, those which were not disbanded gradually converged upon Singapore and Malaya to be assimilated into the pattern of a peacetime garrison, designed to safeguard Britain's remaining interests in the theatre. By 1946 it was already clear from the political activity in the Netherlands East Indies, India, Burma, Indo-China and Malaya that the future promised only instability, with the passionate desire for independence precluding any possibility of a permanent return to colonisation. The maintenance of internal security and a controlled relaxation of colonial rule was the policy which had inevitably to be accepted by the British, Dutch and French Governments.

Headquarters ACSEA

Air Chief Marshal Sir Keith Park transferred his headquarters from Ceylon to Singapore in November 1945, and was compelled to house his staff temporarily in a number of civilian buildings requisitioned in the vicinity of Collyer Quay in the centre of the city. This was not entirely satisfactory, the headquarters being separated by many miles of congested and indifferent roads from the airfields on the island: but at least it was close to Mountbatten's Supreme Headquarters—an advantage in view of the constant policy discussions which were initially required. For the first six months the staff was excessively busy with the problems of repatriation and release of airmen, the need to support the continued fighting in the Netherlands East Indies and, at the same time, to disband as many units as possible and rehabilitate the neglected airfields.

The wave of disaffection which spread through all the stations has already been described in Chapter 1 but it brought home to the staff how vital it was to clear the grossly overcrowded island of unnecessary troops with maximum speed, even if efficiency suffered to some degree in consequence. The Organisation staff was, therefore, instructed to disband and run down units at a quite alarming rate: no less than 140 units were disbanded in the month of February 1946, alone, although admittedly one hundred of those were small Mobile Signals Units whose tasks were assumed by the static stations. Gradually this activity had the desired effect and as soon as the airmen could see the efforts being made to get them repatriated, disaffection died down and was soon little more than an unpleasant memory.

The airmen were not alone in airing their grievances, for a wave of civilian labour strikes spread through the island at this time. Inadequate housing, low wages and food scarcity were given as the main reasons but, in fact, Singapore was seeing the first effects of communist influence taking advantage of the long standing differences between the Malay and Chinese populations. Factions which had united in their opposition to the Japanese during the years of occupation began to formulate their separate political requirements and, as elsewhere in South-East Asia, the communist influence was strong and vociferous. It could not be seen at the time, but these strikes at the end of 1945 sowed the seeds of disaffection which led three years later to the start of the thirteen years of the Malayan Emergency. The immediate effect of the civilian strikes upon the RAF was to

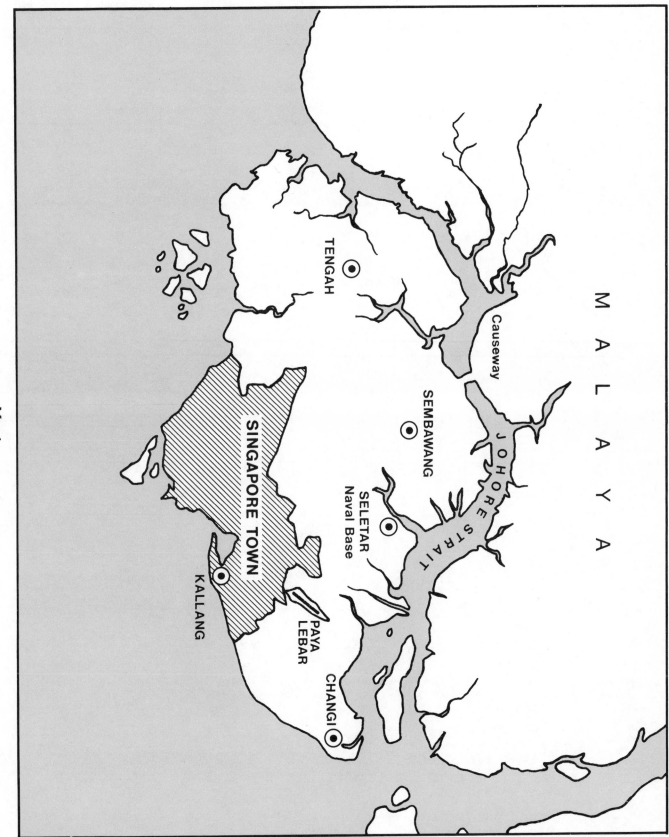

Map 4
Sketch map of Singapore Island
note: Paya Lebar was the site for the new international airport to replace Kallang.

slow down the whole programme of rehabilitation and development of the base.

To begin with, all stations and units on the island were directly controlled by HQ ACSEA as it was thought that AHQ Malaya was too remote in Kuala Lumpur to take them under its wing. It has, however, never been satisfactory for a Command headquarters to administer directly a mass of relatively small units, and this arrangement was regarded as no more than a temporary post-occupational measure. As the reduction of units on the mainland progressed, the responsibilities of AHQ Malaya declined until it was judged expedient to place the Singapore units under its control. This transfer took place on 15 February 1946 and, at the same time, plans were drawn up to transfer the AHQ to Singapore as soon as suitable accommodation could be found.

The Singapore Airfields

The island's four RAF airfields, Kallang, Changi, Tengah and Seletar (see Map 4)[1] had been hurriedly occupied in 1945 by those squadrons and types of aircraft most suited to the facilities found on arrival. The process of repairing and developing them for peacetime use became one of the priority tasks, and it was greatly facilitated by the presence of a number of Airfield Construction squadrons which had originally been included in the ZIPPER order of battle. Although the numbers of airmen in these squadrons were being rapidly reduced by release and repatriation, the expertise with heavy earth moving equipment of those who remained proved invaluable.

It was not a difficult task to decide the future role for each airfield: location, available facilities and potential for further development determined the future use almost automatically.

Kallang, which had originally been designed as Singapore's civil airport, was clearly destined to return to that role. Its location close to the city centre was ideal. It possessed a rudimentary terminal building with a control tower, and a good restaurant. The runway was, however, inadequate for the post-war generation of four-engined airliners and great care was necessary, particularly when landing over the harbour wall which bordered one end of the runway. Eventually the inevitable happened and a Constellation hit this wall during its

---

[1] Sembawang was initially allocated to the Royal Navy, and used by disembarked Fleet Air Arm aircraft.

approach in poor visibility, resulting in a terrible conflagration and much loss of life. This accident and many less serious incidents then decided the civil aviation authorities to abandon Kallang and to build a new international airport suitable for the jet age at Paya Lebar. However, the RAF decision in 1946 was to hand over Kallang to the Singapore Government as soon as Changi could be developed to four-engined standards.

The Japanese development of Changi has already been described. In spite of the marshy ground on which it had been built, the location near Fairy Point, well away from the city, gave excellent unobstructed all round approaches and was the obvious choice for the RAF transport base. It was to be some years before the expensive and difficult project of laying a concrete runway on the marshy subsoil could be undertaken, but improvement and extension of the PSP runway were pressed ahead, with the result that Changi was opened to four-engined traffic in April 1946. This enabled the Transport Command schedules from the UK to Australasia to be routed through Changi, and the Cocos Islands airfield to be closed. At the same time, 48 Dakota Squadron moved into Changi from its temporary base at Kallang.

In the north-west of the island, Tengah selected itself as the air defence centre and base for the operational squadrons of Spitfires and Mosquitos. The main runway, hard standings and dispersal areas met the demands of these combat aircraft better than those elsewhere and, furthermore, space was available for providing the technical and administrative buildings which were lacking. The decision over Tengah was a wise one. In later years it became a fine modern station fully capable of housing and operating the most advanced jet aircraft, and providing a pleasant home for airmen and families. It was far enough from Singapore City to be away from urban interference but close enough to satisfy the social needs of those who lived on the station.

Seletar, the oldest and best developed of the stations, did cause some head scratching among the planners. It had by far the best accommodation of all kinds, including the flying boat base with its complex of moorings, slipways and hangars which could not be provided elsewhere. Since it was close to the naval base on the Johore Strait, supplies could, under certain circumstances, be delivered to Seletar direct by sea, and it also enabled RAF marine craft to be serviced without difficulty. On the other hand, little could be done to extend or develop the airfield, that beautiful inverted saucer of grass which had been so highly praised before the war. The single PSP runway built at one end of the grass circle was short, sloping and quite unextendable. The Spitfires and Mosquitos of 1946 could use Seletar with care but it did not possess operational viability and it was apparent that future generations of combat aircraft would find it unusable.

The future plans of ACSEA, based upon British defence policy, were indicating that the peacetime strength of the RAF in the Far East would settle down at about 100 front-line aircraft. In view of the distance from the UK source of supply, a sizeable float of reserve aircraft and spares would also have to be held in the Command and, for the same reason, major servicing, salvage and repairs would have to be carried out in Singapore. In short ACSEA would need to be more self-sufficient than, say, the Middle East and certainly the home commands. This reasoning dictated the need for a comprehensive supply and maintenance base and one to which aircraft could be flown for overhaul and repair. Seletar was the obvious choice to fill this need and so it became the home of 389 and 390 Maintenance Units as well as the base for the Sunderland squadrons and any other flying units and detachments which could safely use the limited airfield facilities.

Move of ACSEA to Changi

As pressure increased for the Command headquarters to vacate the civilian accommodation which it had requisitioned on Collyer Quay, a suitable location away from the city was sought and the eyes of the planners lit upon Changi. Changi had been built prewar as an Army barracks, chiefly for the Royal Artillery, and the Army had returned to it in 1945. The construction of the airfield below and around the camp necessitated some accommodation being made available for the RAF in the vicinity, and Selarang Barracks were appropriated close to the main runway for this purpose. The subsequent decision to convert Changi into the main air transport base and to relinquish Kallang, however, demanded much more RAF accommodation than Selarang Barracks could provide, and the transfer of the whole of Changi to the RAF became desirable.

The camp had been splendidly built to peacetime standards with large, airy barrack blocks, messes and married quarters. Situated high above the Johore Strait as it wound its way up to the naval base, it caught all the breeze and fresh air that was available in the humid, damp island. Not unnaturally the Army was most reluctant to give up what was undoubtedly the most attractive site in Singapore. Prolonged negotiations eventually resulted in the RAF making an unassailable case and it was agreed that it should become the location for the Command headquarters in exchange for Selarang Barracks which were transferred to the Army, and which provided excellent housing for one battalion.

On 7 April 1946, HQ ACSEA moved out from the city to Changi and converted some of the barrack blocks into offices by means of internal partitioning. It was far from perfect but any disadvantages in the office accommodation were more than offset by the excellent social facilities and the layout of the camp. On the following day, 8 April, Sir Keith Park formally opened the airfield and welcomed 48 Squadron on its arrival from Kallang. This was one of the Commander-in-Chief's last official functions before he handed over the Command to his deputy, Air Marshal Sir George Pirie KBE CB MC DFC. Sir Keith had completed a long and difficult tour of duty in both Kandy and Singapore and guided ACSEA through the transition from war to peace. His final achievement had been to lay sound foundations for the RAF in the Far East in future years.

Reductions Continue

By the middle of 1946 most of the Lend/Lease aircraft were either on their way back to American custody or had been reduced to spare parts to maintain those remaining. Among the last to go, apart from some Dakotas and a few Thunderbolts in the Netherlands East Indies, were the Liberators of 160 and 203 Squadrons from Ceylon which were flown back to the UK where both squadrons were disbanded. Dakotas could not be spared as no equivalent British transport aircraft yet existed to take their place owing to the wartime policy whereby British industry concentrated upon combat aircraft production, leaving the building of transports almost entirely to the United States. Excellent though the Lend/Lease agreement had been, its cessation left the RAF with many difficulties in re-equipping its squadrons until a healthy postwar production flow commenced.

Meanwhile great efforts were made at Seletar to repair the dozens of Mosquitos which had failed to stand up to the climate, but it was a hopeless task. The man hours needed were excessive and, finally, 390 MU was instructed to concentrate all its efforts upon repairing the Mosquito 34, the Photographic Reconnaissance version used by 684 Squadron. Much aerial survey work in the occupied areas of SEAC remained to be completed and the specialized camera installation in the Mark 34 could not be rapidly duplicated in any other aircraft. All other Mosquitos were destroyed as they became unserviceable and were eventually replaced by the Beaufighter 10. Having had experience of the Beaufighter with 27 Squadron in the jungle rescue role, ACSEA was happy to have this rugged and relatively simple aircraft as a stopgap replacement for the temperamental Mosquito.

For versatility the Sunderland vied with the Liberator over the expanses of ocean which predominated in South-East Asia. Like its landplane counterpart the flying boat was used not only for maritime reconnaissance and anti-submarine operations, but for transport duties as well. A daily schedule was flown from Ceylon to Singapore for many months and a high proportion of newly posted and repatriated personnel was carried in safety and considerable comfort. But, by April 1946, the time had come to reduce the strength of the four Sunderland squadrons which still existed.

No 205 Squadron at Koggala was therefore reduced to a cadre of five boats while 209 Squadron lost two of its twelve Sunderlands and moved from Hong Kong to Seletar, leaving a detached flight behind to take care of the interests in Hong Kong and those of the occupation force in Japan. No 230 Squadron at Seletar returned to Pembroke Dock in the UK and 240 Squadron was disbanded. Some 25 Sunderlands were rendered surplus by these reductions and Seletar was instructed to prepare twelve of them for sale to the Royal New Zealand Air Force. Two flying boat alighting areas, namely at Penang and Rangoon, were transferred to BOAC, and the RAF was able to relinquish responsibility for handling the civilian Empire Class flying boats at these two staging points on BOAC's Far Eastern route.

These reductions marked the beginning of the end of the flying boat era. Admittedly the Sunderland remained in service for several more years, and continued to do splendid work in the Far East, operating from Ceylon, Singapore and Hong Kong. There was, however, to be no successor to this fine aircraft as the development of long range landplanes, such as the Shackleton and eventually the Nimrod, enabled the maritime reconnaissance and strike roles to be effected with greater speed and economy. Bearing in mind that the first aircraft ever to reach Singapore were floatplanes and flying boats (see Introduction), the departure of so many Sunderlands from the Command in 1946 was viewed with great regret and many a 'web footed' airman shed a quiet tear into his beer!

The second half of 1946 saw a steady continuation in the reduction of the Command. Occupation of the Netherlands East Indies came to an end, as we have seen, and relieved ACSEA of its largest and most unwelcome commitment. Similarly, RAF commitments in Siam, Indo-China, Burma and Borneo steadily reduced, leaving little more than staging posts in all except Burma where the Air Headquarters remained with residual tasks for transport and photographic reconnaissance aircraft.

Manpower problems

Rapid as was the reduction of units at this time, the rundown of manpower due to the demands of the release and repatriation programme was even faster. Not only was it faster but it was unbalanced as far as the various trade groups were concerned. Acute shortages in certain trades and an embarrassing surplus in others began to appear— an inevitable consequence of releasing airmen and airwomen strictly in accordance with their individual priorities. But this had to be done and, with the threat of war removed, it was not unreasonable to saddle the Service, in the Far East as elsewhere, with the temporary inconvenience of unbalanced manning.

Shortages in the Signals trades were among the most serious, necessitating the closing down of many communications links. Priority was always given to the safety of aircraft in the form of navigation aids, radar equipment and air traffic control systems. Armament trades were similarly affected: to such an extent that, at one time in 1946, their strength was down to only 35% of the establishment in the Command. The effect of this situation was to bring the overall strength of ACSEA down to 14,448, well below the official establishment.

As the experienced wartime airmen departed for home, a great dilution of skill took place, many of the replacements being hastily trained National Servicemen who had neither the technical skill of the departing tradesmen nor any knowledge of the climate and working conditions. ACSEA's method of tackling these problems was to allocate priority manning to those units which had the most urgent tasks to perform, and then to set appropriate levels of manning for every other unit in the Command. Thus a very high priority was given to photographic reconnaissance as a number of survey tasks, notably in Java and Sumatra, had to be completed before the SEAC forces were withdrawn. This meant that every effort had to be made to repair and maintain the Mosquito 34's of 81 Squadron[2] which now bore the burden of the PR work. The structural problems affecting all types of Mosquito could not have come at a less opportune moment but, nevertheless, the various surveys were completed as planned, leaving ACSEA with valuable and up-to-date coverage of the whole theatre.

One method of alleviating the shortages in RAF manpower was the enlistment of indigenous Malays and Chinese. Some progress with such a policy had been made before the war and the threads were picked up again in 1946. Local enlistment took many forms, but one of the most imaginative was the formation of the RAF Regiment (Malaya). This was accomplished by disbanding certain RAF Regiment squadrons and using those officers, NCOs and gunners who were not due for repatriation to form the nucleus of the new Regiment.

Slowly the manning situation began to improve and this was particularly noticeable when families were again allowed to accompany their husbands. Singapore had always been an excellent and highly popular family station but, in 1946, married quarters were extremely scarce. Very few junior officers and airmen had been married before the war, as marriage was officially discouraged for officers below the age of 30 and for airmen below 26. With the postwar relaxation of these out-of-date regulations and the high incidence of marriages among both officers and airmen, the 'accompanied tour' became a pressing requirement if recruiting was to be encouraged. Consequently a large married quarter building programme was initiated on all three stations, resulting in some delightfully sited houses at Changi and Seletar in particular.

Squadron Re-equipment

The manpower shortages had some effect on the operational squadrons but, as they naturally received a high priority for the available tradesmen, the effect was not catastrophic. The sudden and unexpected failure of the Mosquito, and particularly the fighter/bomber Mark VI version, alleviated the manning situation in one respect: shortage of aircraft necessitated reducing some squadrons to a cadre basis until replacement aircraft could arrive from the UK. As there were virtually

---

[2] 81 Squadron was the old 684 Squadron renumbered.

no active operations, other than in the Netherlands East Indies, this remedy was acceptable as a temporary measure and, furthermore, gave a welcome opportunity for Tengah to be rebuilt to modern standards without creating gross overcrowding elsewhere. For the greater part of 1946, therefore, Tengah was emptied of squadrons while the main runway was reconstructed and the domestic and technical sites completely rebuilt.

The two squadrons most affected by the Mosquito problem were Nos 45 and 84. It had been intended to keep the former on the Mosquito VI at Negombo until the new Bristol Brigand came into service in 1947. That was not possible and so 45 Squadron was re-equipped in Ceylon with the Beaufighter X. No 84 Squadron, temporarily located at Seletar, was similarly re-equipped after being reduced to a cadre of eight Mosquitos while awaiting its new aircraft. No 60 Squadron which, it will be recalled, played a notable part in the Netherlands East Indies operations, mounted on Thunderbolts, continued as a day fighter squadron on withdrawal from Java and was re-equipped with the Spitfire XVIII; with 28 Squadron it returned to Tengah when the reconstruction of the station was completed. So successful was the Sunderland in its unaccustomed role as a transport in the area of Hong Kong, Japan and Borneo that 1430 Flight at Hong Kong was given a specially modified transport version of the flying boat, with an all-up operating weight of 58,000 lbs. The Flight, which was renamed 88 Squadron in September 1946, flew a thrice weekly service from Hong Kong to Iwakuni in Japan and thus maintained the RAF element of the occupation force.

The End of SEAC

Lord Mountbatten returned to London to attend the Victory Parade held on 8 June 1946, and while he was at home the Chiefs of Staff decided upon the policy for the disestablishment of South-East Asia Command. With the Dutch gradually assuming control in the Netherlands East Indies, it was decided that all British and Indian forces would be withdrawn from that area by 30 November and, upon that date, SEAC would cease to exist. Furthermore, it was decided that Mountbatten need not return to Singapore and that his deputy, Lieutenant-General Stopford, should act in his place for the last few months of SEAC's existence, in addition to holding his Army command as C-in-C Allied Land Forces, South-East Asia (ALFSEA).

This reorganisation naturally affected the Air Command, ACSEA being no longer an appropriate title. On 30 November, the Headquarters at Changi adopted the new title of Air Command, Far East (ACFE) with Air Marshal Sir George Pirie continuing in command but in the new style of Air Commander-in-Chief. No longer was a Supreme Commander considered necessary with the result that both Naval and Army Commands changed their titles appropriately. This did not mean that the three Services went their own ways. The Commanders-in-Chief formed a Co-ordination Committee, answerable to the Chiefs of Staff in London on all policy matters concerning the Far East. More detail about the changes in the Command structure will be found in the next chapter.

SEAC had been formed as essentially a wartime command, following the pattern which had been so successful in Europe and also in the Pacific. Had it not been for the continuation of hostilities in Java and Sumatra, SEAC would probably have been disbanded much earlier, but so complex was the postwar situation in the Far East that it was deemed necessary to prolong its life for fifteen months after VJ Day. As in Europe, the principles of supreme command had been vindicated and the welding together of the total Allied effort under Lord Mountbatten had worked smoothly and efficiently. It is appropriate here to recall that, in the preface to his final report on post-surrender tasks to the Combined Chiefs of Staff, Mountbatten paid a sincere tribute to his forces by stating how difficult, urgent and complex were their tasks and how well they met the challenge.[3]

Final Steps in Consolidating the Base

For the purposes of this narrative, it is reasonable to take the end of 1947 as the time at which the RAF achieved its peacetime level. At no time was it entirely stable, but at least the Singapore base could be said to have settled down to the organisation and deployment of units which had earlier been planned for it. 1947 was a year of continued reduction in units and manpower as the last of the wartime commitments were completed. These reductions resulted in the strength reducing steadily by between 100 and 200 men per month, and this allowed manning levels in the remaining units to rise substantially towards the full establishment figures.

---

[3] Preface to Section D of Report to the CCS by SACSEA. AIR 23/2083

The last postwar operational task which remained to be completed was the photographic survey of various areas, which it was vital to finish while the RAF still had access to them. This task fell to the heavily committed 81 Squadron. The survey of Burma, where flying and photographic conditions were always badly affected by severe monsoon conditions, proved difficult and arduous, but the squadron, part of which was detached from Seletar to Mingaladon, managed to produce an excellent survey by the end of August 1947. This left North Borneo and Sarawak, of which only the most rudimentary maps existed. This survey too was finished by the end of the year, thanks to the Mosquito 34 which, despite all its vicissitudes, enabled the 81 Squadron crews to provide the material with which to bring all the Far East maps up-to-date. The importance of all this survey work may not have been fully appreciated at the time but, years later, when the Malayan Emergency, followed by the Indonesian Confrontation in Borneo, were at their height, the great value of this earlier work was realised.

In the engineering field 1947 saw the introduction in the Far East of a new technical organisation which had for some time been operating in the home commands. This was the third element of what now became known colloquially as 'the three prong' organisation. In effect it banded together all the technical arms—engineers, armourers, technical signals, etc—under one Senior Technical Staff Officer (STSO). In the Command Headquarters he held air rank and equivalent status to the SASO and AOA, resulting in three 'prongs' to the staff under the Commander-in-Chief. It was a most important reorganisation, bringing an unprecedented co-ordination to all the technical services as well as ensuring them a status equivalent to the air and administrative staffs at all levels from the Command down to stations. Not unnaturally it took some time for the change to percolate through to all levels but it was one of the important events of 1947 in consolidating the Singapore base. The operative date for the inauguration of the new scheme was 24 March 1947 .

Another milestone during this year was the arrival in Singapore of the first RAF jet aircraft for tropical trials. First, two Meteors were shipped to Seletar and, after erection, carried out their trials at Tengah, flown by Wing Commanders Bird-Wilson and Wilson. They were followed at the end of the year by two Vampire IIIs which were tested for twelve months, one in intensive flying trials and the other by ground exposure to Singapore's varied climatic conditions. Being the first jet aircraft seen in the Far East, these high performance fighters created immense interest and were much in demand for displays. Their presence was also immensely valuable in assessing the suitability of the stations and facilities on the island for the future operation of jet aircraft.

It is fitting to end this year of 1947, and also to end this chapter on the development of Singapore base, with the departure of the Commander-in-Chief, Air Marshal Sir George Pirie, who was succeeded on 18 November by Air Marshal Sir Hugh P Lloyd KBE CB MC DFC. Ten days earlier AHQ Malaya had been taken over by Air Vice-Marshal J Whitworth Jones CB CBE, succeeding Air Vice-Marshal Breakey who had seen AHQ Malaya through so many moves and changes since the end of the war.

It can truly be said that Singapore had now assumed India's previous role of forming the keystone of the arch of Commonwealth defence in the Far East.

7

Command Organisation

This narrative covers a period of 27 years, from 1945 to 1972. During that time so many significant changes took place in the RAF command organisation in the Far East that it is appropriate to devote a complete chapter to the subject so that the evolution can be clearly followed and further frequent references to organisation changes avoided. These changes were necessitated partly by political developments as a succession of Far Eastern countries achieved their independence and, perhaps more importantly, by the post-war evolution of British defence policy which was greatly influenced by lessons learned during the war.

The rapid growth of air power between the two wars, followed during the years of World War II by experience in the Battle of Britain, the Battle of the Atlantic and other campaigns, showed conclusively that both the Navy and the Army would, in future, depend heavily upon adequate air support in the majority of their operations. Had this been fully understood earlier, the catastrophe of Singapore might have been avoided.

This 'interdependence', a term by which the closer association of the Services became known, tended to dominate Whitehall defence thinking and, naturally enough, was reflected in the structure of command, not only in the Far East, but in all overseas theatres. Furthermore, as economic and financial stringency began to cause severe reductions in Britain's armed forces during the 1950s, it became increasingly apparent that Britain would have to combine with Allies in any future operations on a major scale. The outcome was the establishment of a number of international defence pacts, of which NATO, the Baghdad Pact and SEATO were the most important. 'Interdependence' thus assumed a wider connotation than just closer liaison between Britain's Services; it also came to mean close links in the fields of operations, administration and logistics between the participants in the various international treaty organisations. The principle of unified command had already been most successfully demonstrated in war and what was more natural than that it should be extended into peace wherever appropriate. It was therefore not surprising that its strongest protagonist was Lord Mountbatten, who prior to his appointment as Supreme Commander, South-East Asia, had been Britain's first Chief of Combined Operations, in which capacity he had initiated the first operations in which the three Services were closely integrated.

To begin with, however, it seemed in the Far East as though the lessons had been forgotten; as we have seen in Chapter 6, SEAC, Mountbatten's wartime command, was disestablished on 30 November 1946. This left the emergent RAF Command Headquarters (ACFE) once again answerable directly to Air Ministry although Sir George Pirie combined with his Navy and Army colleagues in the formation of the British Defence Co-ordination Committee, Far East (BDCCFE) to consider Chiefs of Staff directives and other policy matters affecting the theatre. In effect the responsibilities of the wartime Supreme Commander were now assumed by the Chiefs of Staff in the UK acting through a committee in Singapore, while each Commander-in-Chief was responsible to his particular Service Ministry for his own forces and their administration and logistics.

The traditional RAF chain of responsibility from a command headquarters through a number of subordinate formations to stations and thence to squadrons had proved highly successful and adaptable in war, and it had the great merit that it could be expanded or contracted to meet changing circumstances by adding or subtracting squadrons, stations and groups without affecting the basis of the organisation. The Far East was admirably suited to this system of delegated authority. It comprised a number of regions, geographically compact and homogeneous, but differing widely in other respects. The problems of Hong Kong, for example, were as different from those of Burma as were those of Ceylon from Malaya. The establishment of a subordinate headquarters to conform to each region was clearly a sound method whereby the C-in-C could delegate his authority, and it also ensured that each subordinate commander controlled a relatively compact area. This regional system differed from the functional system, which had been appropriate overseas during the war when there were very large numbers of similar types of aircraft and which was continued after the war in the UK alone.

Only in the case of transport aircraft was this type of organisation continued overseas in peacetime, and then for no more than a brief period until the number of transport squadrons had been reduced to a point at which a group headquarters to control them was no longer economical.

Thus by the end of 1946, ACFE had been slimmed down to its basic peacetime size, with five subordinate regional headquarters as shown in Fig II.

Figure II

FAR EAST COMMAND ORGANISATION
31 December 1946

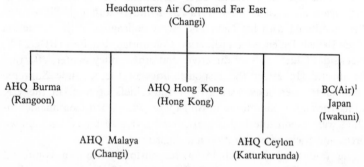

Headquarters Air Command Far East
(Changi)

AHQ Burma
(Rangoon)

AHQ Hong Kong
(Hong Kong)

BC(Air)[1]
Japan
(Iwakuni)

AHQ Malaya
(Changi)

AHQ Ceylon
(Katurkurunda)

Note: BC(Air) in Japan is shown under ACFE for convenience, but this is not entirely accurate as ACFE retained only limited administrative and logistic responsibilities for the RAF squadrons and units in Japan.

For the next two and a half years there were only two changes of significance in the command structure. First, as the date for Burma's independence approached, AHQ Burma moved out from the centre of Rangoon to the airfield at Mingaladon on 1 January 1947 prior to being disbanded on 31 December of the same year. Independence for the country came three months later when Burma opted not to remain in the Commonwealth. Secondly, during 1948 the occupation forces in Japan began to withdraw, most of the RAF component leaving by 31 March: 1315 Communications Flight alone remained as the only RAF flying unit until 15 November when BC(Air) was disbanded and the involvement of the RAF in Japan ceased officially. Air Vice-Marshal C A Bouchier CB CBE had been in command since the

---

[1] British Commonwealth Air Forces

inception of BC(Air) and thus completed a particularly long tour in operational command in the Far East which had started during the Burma campaign.

The independence of Ceylon was also proclaimed in 1948—on 4 February—but as Ceylon elected to remain in the Commonwealth, the Air Headquarters continued, moving from Katurkurunda to the RAF station at Negombo on 23 February.

While these changes were taking place, Whitehall had been giving much thought to rationalising the styles and titles of the overseas commands. Many changes had taken place in the Middle East[2] but, by the end of 1948, all the overseas commands of the RAF had achieved some degree of stability after the difficult years which were inevitable in the aftermath of the war. It was decided to give the two commands in the Middle and Far East comparable titles, not only more appropriate to their peacetime roles, but also in conformity with their sister Services in those theatres.

On 1 June 1949, therefore, the command in the Middle East, hitherto known as 'Mediterranean and Middle East' (MEDME) became 'Middle East Air Force' (MEAF). Simultaneously ACFE changed its title to 'Headquarters Far East Air Force' (FEAF) and the Air Commander-in-Chief was then designated 'Commander-in-Chief Far East Air Force'[3] an appointment which was held by Air Marshal Sir Hugh P Lloyd KBE CB MC DFC. No alterations were made in the titles of the subordinate formations but, as we have seen, by now they were only three in number, as shown in Figure III.

Figure III

FAR EAST COMMAND ORGANISATION
1 June 1949

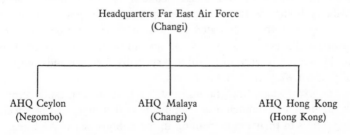

Headquarters Far East Air Force
(Changi)

AHQ Ceylon
(Negombo)

AHQ Malaya
(Changi)

AHQ Hong Kong
(Hong Kong)

---

[2] See Flight from the Middle East Chapter 2, Sir David Lee, HMSO, 1980
[3] Air Ministry Secret Organisation Memorandum 303/49

Throughout the next decade there were no major changes in the overall RAF organisation. Contraction and expansion took place periodically to meet the needs of the Malayan Emergency, the war in Korea and the Borneo Confrontation but these alterations largely took the form of adding or subtracting stations and squadrons to or from the basic organisation, thus demonstrating its inherent flexibility. It became necessary, for example, for AHQ Malaya to push forward an advanced headquarters to Kuala Lumpur at one period to handle operations in Malaya. One significant change only took place before the RAF eventually withdrew from the Far East, and that did not come until the 1960s.

The Principle of Unified Command

The tactics and weapons which had resulted from lessons learned during and after World War II had, as mentioned earlier, shewn the interdependence of navies, armies and air forces. Almost every form of operation required the participation of two, and usually all three, of the Services, and the designation 'combined operation' had grown from a small scale rarity to a universal description which accurately fitted most military actions. It stood to reason that this interdependence in the field should be reflected in the organisation of high command. Supreme Commanders, selected for their experience and ability from any Service, or indeed from any Allied nation, had proved their effectiveness in war, and the defence authorities in Whitehall were greatly attracted towards introducing a similar organisation in peace.

For several years during the 1950s the merits of various forms of integration and unification were debated. Such schemes were attractive to politicians and senior officials as they conjured up visions of immense economies and greater control of the military machine. Military leaders were not opposed to these developments in defence thinking, but they advocated caution in their adoption, and could visualise distinct limits to which the unification of Armed Forces could proceed in view of the highly specialised nature and complexity of modern weapons and equipment.

The expressions 'integration' and 'unification' constantly crop up in discussion of command developments at this time, and it is well to be clear as to their exact meaning in the military sense. An integrated command, if such an organisation were to be created, would comprise a single commander-in-chief with a staff in which an officer belonging to one Service, say the Army, would be required to carry out his particular operational or administrative duties for the Navy and the RAF as well as for his own Service. Although this is feasible in certain fields of activity common to all the Services and is, indeed practised to a limited extent, successive governments have been quick to allay justifiable Service fears by declaring in, for example, the 1962 White Paper on Defence, that they had no intention of fully integrating the Armed Forces.

A unified command is a less far-reaching and certainly less controversial type of organisation, although not without its critics. A single commander-in-chief, who has his own small secretariat and joint planning and intelligence staffs, relies upon three subordinate commanders, each in direct command of his own Service, and each with his own single Service staff. A feature of this type of organisation is that it permits many administrative functions, which may be undertaken by a single Service on an agency basis for the others, to be controlled by a single commander-in-chief. Storage, housing, rationing and the control of movement are typical of facilities which can be provided in this way. Although unification could be described as a step along the road towards integration, full integration has never been regarded as a desirable or attainable goal for Britain's Armed Forces.

The first major step towards unification took place in 1958, when a centralised policy staff was created in the Ministry of Defence designed to serve in particular the newly established Chief of the Defence Staff. The next step was to establish a unified command in the field. The Middle East was selected for this experiment at a time when the deterioration of relations with Egypt following the Suez Canal crisis and the worsening Arab/Israel situation had caused Britain to strengthen her forces based on Aden. Aden had for many years been a single inter-Service headquarters, controlled by the Royal Air Force which provided most of the facilities for the other Services. Furthermore, it had been placed directly under the Chiefs of Staff, and no intermediate headquarters stood in the way of the experiment. A unified command, subsequently to become Middle East Command, was therefore inaugurated in Aden on 1 October 1959.

This experiment proved so successful that the Chiefs of Staff decided to extend the system to the Mediterranean, which became the Near East Command, and later to the Far East. Thus, on 1 January 1963, Headquarters Far East Command was formed at

Phoenix Park in Singapore, the first Commander-in-Chief being Admiral Sir Varyl Begg. The intention was that the appointment should rotate between the three Services, always provided that an officer of suitable experience and seniority could be made available by the appropriate Service. The same rotational principle applied also to the other two Commands ensuring that an equitable allocation of senior appointments was maintained.

Below the four star Commander-in-Chief each Service was headed by a subordinate commander usually of three star rank who had direct access to his own Service Ministry on all administrative, logistic and technical matters which remained single Service responsibilities. It is important to make this point because it was the firm intention to place as many supporting services and facilities as possible in the hands of one Service which would make provision on an 'agency' basis for the other two.

It was in this field that the Middle East Command started with a big advantage. As Aden had always been commanded by the Royal Air Force which had provided the majority of supporting services and facilities, it was easy enough for it to continue to be the universal provider even though the forces under command expanded greatly during the 1950s and 1960s. No such universal provider had ever existed in the Far East where the three Services had always been fully independent, each with its own chain of supply depots and establishments of every kind. It was understandable, therefore, that each Service was reluctant to place its requirements in the hands of another, having built up over the years an efficient administrative and logistic chain running back to its own Ministry in London which provided its specialised needs. In this respect, but in this respect alone, unified command in the Far East was not an immediate success although, in the brief period of its existence before Britain's withdrawal from the Far East, some progress was made. The Army, which had by far the largest force in the theatre, eventually became the universal provider of a small number of categories of common supply.

Where the unified principle certainly did succeed was in the conduct of policy and operations. In contrast to other overseas Commands, the Commander-in-Chief had forces of several different nations under his control. Furthermore his command encompassed a large number of countries, not all of which were members of the Commonwealth, and he was deeply involved with the South-East Asia Treaty Organisation (SEATO) and with the pacts which linked Australia, New Zealand, the United States and the United Kingdom (ANZAM/ ANZUK).

These complex relationships, containing a high political content, necessitated much negotiation and a great deal of travelling. It was obviously unsatisfactory for three commanders to share these duties, but the establishment of a single commander-in-chief of a very senior rank ensured that Britain's Far Eastern policies were interpreted by one voice, whether it was in negotiation with the Australian Chiefs of Staff, the Tungku in Malaysia or the Government of Ceylon. This arrangement had the additional and extremely important advantage of leaving the single Service commanders relatively free to command and operate their own forces.

With the inception of the new headquarters, the British Defence Co-ordination Committee, Far East (BDCCFE), which had previously co-ordinated all policy matters, was superseded by the C-in-C's own committee comprising the three single Service commanders, a political adviser and several other specialists and staff officers. The layout of the Command was then as shown in Figure IV.

Figure IV

**FAR EAST COMMAND ORGANISATION
1 January 1963**

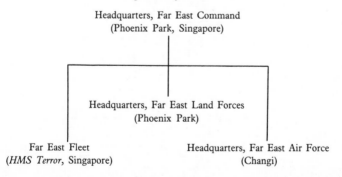

Headquarters, Far East Command
(Phoenix Park, Singapore)

Headquarters, Far East Land Forces
(Phoenix Park)

Far East Fleet
(*HMS Terror*, Singapore)

Headquarters, Far East Air Force
(Changi)

After Admiral Sir Varyl Begg had initiated the unified Command, he was succeeded in 1965 by the first RAF officer to hold the appointment, Air Chief Marshal Sir John Grandy KCB KBE DSO. He in turn gave way to an Army officer and rotation of the appointment was continued until final withdrawal from Singapore.

The withdrawal of British forces from the Middle and Far East and reductions in the Near East spelled the end of three unified Commands before any of them had existed for a sufficient time to reveal the full benefits of this type of organisation. Even so, there can be little doubt that they were developing along efficient and economical lines, matching the evolution of the Ministry of Defence. Sufficient experience was gained to indicate that 'unification', stopping well short of 'integration', was sound and acceptable and, should the need arise, could form the basis of any future command structure. Little more will be said on this subject in the following chapters, but a list of the RAF officers who held the posts of Commander-in-Chief or RAF Commander in the Far East will be found at Appendix C.

8

The Malayan Emergency—I

By the beginning of 1948 British forces in the Far East had virtually discharged their immediate postwar responsibilities, demobilised the 'hostilities only' Servicemen and women and repatriated all but a few of the Japanese forces. Fighting units and supporting establishments had been run down to what the policy makers decided was to be the peacetime level and Singapore had been set up and furbished as a comfortable and efficient main base.

In the RAF the reductions were striking. From a total of 124,718 men and women in ACSEA in mid 1945, manpower had sunk to 8,676 in ACFE by 1 June 1948. Similarly the front line strength had been reduced from 1,324 operational aircraft in more than 70 squadrons to $11\frac{1}{2}$ squadrons containing little more than 100 aircraft. This latter force comprised:

2 Squadrons of Beaufighters
2 Squadrons of Spitfires
3 Squadrons of Dakotas
1 Squadron of PR Mosquitos
3 Squadrons of Sunderland flying boats
1 Flight of AOP Austers.

This force, with its Navy and Army counterparts, was expected to be adequate to garrison the Far East territories during what was hoped to be a period of stability after the traumatic experiences of World War II. This hope was not to be fulfilled and 1948 marked the beginning of a long and exhausting campaign against communist guerillas in Malaya, a campaign which was not finally concluded until 1960.

The Importance of Malaya

With India now independent and thus lost to Britain as a military base, Malaya and Singapore had become not only the main military base but also the centre of Commonwealth influence in the Far East.

Economically Malaya was the world's largest rubber producing area and a major producer of tin. She was therefore an important dollar earner with an invaluable contribution to make to Britain's balance of payments. The Service commanders in Singapore wrote prophetically early in 1948: "Malaya ..... is likely to constitute the main long term target in South-East Asia for communists and other disruptive elements." The loss of Malaya, in the official view, would soon lead to communist domination of the whole of southern Asia between India and China, and thus sever the chain of Commonwealth communications.

No less valid reason for resisting communism was the belief that the people of Malaya as a whole were opposed to it and wished Britain to fight it on their behalf. The Federation of Malaya contained at this time some 4,900,000 people, of whom two and a half million were Malays, something less than two million Chinese and the remainder mainly of Indian origin. Singapore, which was ruled separately from the Federation, had a population of 941,000 but, in contrast to Malaya, the Chinese outnumbered Malays by six to one. Taking the two areas together there was a slight preponderance of Chinese. The nature and course of the Emergency were strongly influenced by these racial divisions. The Malays were the indigenous, mainly agricultural population whereas the Chinese were traders and businessmen, most of whom still owed loyalty to China.

Geography of Malaya[1]

In 1952 the Federation of Malaya covered an area of 53,240 square miles, a little larger than England. It stretched some 400 miles from north to south with a maximum width of 200 miles. Malaya was ideally suited to the techniques of guerilla warfare, with a central backbone of mountains rising to over 7,000 feet and four-fifths of its area covered by jungle, whose topmost storey provided an almost unbroken canopy at an average height of 150 feet from the ground. The lower layers were so dense that visibility was limited to 25 yards or less in most places. The remaining one-fifth of the country comprised rubber and coconut palm plantations, tin mines, rice fields, native villages and towns.

There are few seasonal changes in the climate which is hot and extremely humid all the year round. Monsoon conditions, moving down

---

[1] Throughout this narrative, mention of 'Malaya' refers only to the Federation of Malaya (ie the Malay Peninsula), and does not include the Colony of Singapore (ie Singapore Island).

from Burma and the Kra Isthmus, lose something of their intensity by the time Malaya is reached but, even so, frequent and prolonged tropical storms accompanied by a rapid build-up of dense cumulus clouds are a constant feature which accounts for the luxuriant foliage throughout the country. Fortunately for the airmen storms and cloud formations tend to be localised and fast moving with clear, often brilliant, weather around them making it possible for aircraft to avoid the worst conditions or to await the passing of a storm. Nevertheless great care is essential as the more formidable cumulus clouds are extremely turbulent and dangerous to the less robust aircraft.

Origins of the Emergency

Communist infiltration into South-East Asia can be traced back to the early 1920s with the establishment at Shanghai of a Far Eastern Bureau of the Comintern, Russia's organisation for the dissemination of communism abroad. Six years later the Malayan Communist Party (MCP) was formed with the firm intention of establishing a communist controlled democratic republic in Malaya. It met with little response despite some infiltration of schools and craft guilds of the Chinese community. However, by 1937 it had gained some hold on the labour force and had to be declared illegal. Apart from a few MCP inspired strikes, little of serious consequence happened before the outbreak of World War II.

When the Japanese invasion of the Malay Peninsula appeared imminent in 1941, it was considered necessary to establish a network of subversive agents who would work for the Allied cause should the country be overrun. It is ironical that the only organisation capable of carrying out this task was the MCP. Expediency prevailed, despite misgivings and, after the fall of Singapore, 200 of its members retired into the jungle under British instructors to serve as the mainspring of the resistance movement. This band formed the nucleus of the Malayan People's Anti-Japanese Army (MPAJA) and the situation then became complicated; suffice it to say that, by the end of the war, most of the resistance was being directed by a highly organised and well armed MPAJA force of 4,000 guerillas and 6,000 ancillary personnel.

When British forces re-occupied the Peninsula the MPAJA was kept in being to effect some control over the disorderly elements scattered throughout the country, and was not officially disbanded until December 1945. This was the signal for the pre-war MCP to re-emerge and revive its original aim of overthrowing the administration and establishing a communist state. Although all members of resistance movements were ordered to come forward and hand over their arms in exchange for a gratuity and civilian employment, an order with which 6,000 complied, several hundred remained in the jungle as a clandestine military force under the control of the MCP. Prompt British action forestalled any attempt at a coup d'etat, but subversion continued through the fomenting of labour strikes and infiltration of public organisations.

By the beginning of 1948 it was evident to the MCP that their efforts were little more than an irritant and they embarked upon a programme of intimidation and violent demonstrations, followed by a carefully planned series of murders and sabotage as the Government stepped up its measures against them. The scale of insurrection throughout the newly created Federation reached such a level that Emergency Powers were invoked by the Federal Government on 16 June, and the military authorities were called in to assist the civil administration in restoring law and order. This then must be regarded as the start of what has come to be called the 'Malayan Emergency'.

Having openly committed itself to armed resistance the MCP adopted a three stage programme: first, to cause terror and economic chaos in rural areas by assassination and sabotage; second, to 'liberate' selected rural areas and establish local communist administration and, third, to 'liberate' urban areas and declare a communist republic. The MCP estimated that six months would be needed to accomplish each of these stages and that two years would see Malaya transformed into a communist state. In the event, as will be seen, the MCP failed to complete even the first stage but it took the Government and Security Forces no less than twelve years to bring the Emergency to a successful conclusion.

Roles of the Air Force in the Emergency

AHQ Malaya bore the prime responsibility for RAF operations during the Emergency. The principal role of the RAF continued to be the air defence of Malaya, Singapore, North Borneo and Sarawak against possible enemy attack. Its secondary role was co-operation in defence with the Navy and the Army. These roles took precedence over the campaign against the terrorists which was therefore conducted by only a small proportion of the total air forces available in the theatre.

9. An early type of basket stretcher for casualty evacuation by Dragonfly helicopter at Grik in Northern Malaya, March 1952

10. A Dragonfly with external stretcher attached

11. Hornets of 33 Squadron over Malaya

12. Supply dropping into the Malayan jungle in July 1951. The dotted line is the DZ

For the Emergency the task of the RAF was stated to be "to operate in conjunction with and in support of the ground forces".[2]

It was clear that, in an internal security campaign of this nature conducted mainly in dense jungle by police and ground forces, the capability of air forces would be strictly limited but, nevertheless, as the campaign progressed it was found that the participation of the RAF was invaluable. Broadly its main tasks were 'to hit, to carry and to reconnoitre'. It was, perhaps, in discharging the first of these tasks that the nature of the terrain imposed the greatest restrictions upon the aircraft. Targets were so fleeting and their identification so difficult that bombing attacks were often unproductive. Attacks by rocket and cannon tended to be more effective particularly if ground forces were able to mark a target accurately with smoke or to give a pilot good radio directions. As in the Burma campaign several years earlier, it was air transportation, the positioning of airborne and parachute forces and air supply which formed the RAF's greatest contribution. When, during the early 1950s, helicopters began to be deployed in Malaya and were able to position troops and supplies in the smallest jungle clearings as well as to evacuate casualties with great speed, the air contribution was immensely strengthened.

Reconnaissance, the third of the RAF's main tasks, played an important part. Thanks to the survey work previously undertaken mainly by 81 Squadron, knowledge of the interior of Malaya was accurate and up-to-date, and this was constantly improved by additional surveys of specific areas of terrorist activity. When to this was added visual and tactical photographic evidence of potential targets and damage assessment, the ground forces were able to rely upon a wealth of intelligence material which facilitated what became a long and arduous campaign.

Early Operations

Prior to the declaration of a State of Emergency the RAF was called upon only to carry out photographic and visual reconnaissance of an area in North Perak where the MCP had stepped up extortion and intimidation of the local inhabitants (see Map 5). In order to produce intelligence at short notice for the force of British and Gurkha troops sent to deal with this situation, one Spitfire of 81 Squadron and a mobile photographic and interpretation unit were sent on detachment to Taiping, a civil airfield close to the affected area, which had often

---

[2] Emergency Directive No 2, para 23. Quoted in AP3410 'The Malayan Emergency'.

been used by Service aircraft in the past. This small task force remained at Taiping for about a month, by which time the known terrorist camps and hideouts had all been occupied but, as was to happen so frequently in the future, the occupation only caused the terrorists to disappear into even deeper jungle with few losses. If nothing else it showed that air reconnaissance could greatly facilitate the extremely tedious and exhausting operations which the ground forces were compelled to undertake if there was to be any hope of eliminating the pockets of activity.

It soon became apparent that the AOC Malaya, Air Vice-Marshal A C Sanderson CB CBE DFC, could not adequately control the increasing scale of air operations in Northern Malaya from his headquarters in Singapore some 300 miles away. He therefore established an Advanced Headquarters at Kuala Lumpur to control all squadrons taking part in the operations. A month later, in July, Kuala Lumpur was re-opened as an RAF station, whereupon the AOC moved up to his Advanced Headquarters there and formed an operational task force consisting of detachments of Spitfires from 28 and 60 Squadrons, Dakotas from 110 and Beaufighters from 45 Squadron in Ceylon. The variety of this task force not only reflected the marked increase in insurgent activity but also the realisation that the RAF could play a major part in supporting the ground forces.

Operations, under the overall code name of FIREDOG, continued to be largely confined to the upper Perak region but there was little sign of either side gaining a decisive advantage. The impenetrable jungle and fleet-footed terrorists clearly indicated that a long and arduous struggle lay ahead for the Security Forces. All RAF personnel engaged in FIREDOG were placed on an 'Active Service' status, Kuala Lumpur was made an official RAF station once again and a Joint Operations Centre was set up there to control and co-ordinate all aspects of the operations.

By early 1949 the terrorists had begun to realise the dangers of air attack on their jungle camps. Initially they tended to concentrate in collections of 'Basha' huts which, although set in deep jungle, often presented targets as large as 1,000 square yards in area and as much as 6,000 yards in length. By a combination of good intelligence from informers, confirmed by photographs provided by 81 Squadron Mosquitos and Spitfires, these were flushed out by bomb, rocket and cannon attack by Beaufighters and Spitfires with the object of driving the terrorists into prepared ambushes set up by the ground forces. In

Map 5
Malay Peninsula

one such attack on 28 February 1949, on a large camp in south-east Pahang, 84 and 60 Squadrons mounted a closely co-ordinated strike with 500 lb and 20 lb anti-personnel bombs, rockets and 20 mm and 0.5″ cannon fire. Eight huts were destroyed and a further 12 huts damaged causing considerable casualties. Unfortunately the effect of this and similar attacks was to discourage the enemy from concentrating his resources in large camps providing reasonable targets for air attack, and to disperse in small bands into even denser jungle where their identification and subsequent elimination became excessively difficult.

So fleeting were these targets that, although Spitfires and Beaufighters were maintained at as little as one hour's readiness on the airfields at Kuala Lumpur and in Singapore, it was often impossible to mount an attack before the target had disappeared. Even if aircraft could have been kept in the air on immediate call, along the lines of the 'cab rank' readiness developed during World War II, the necessity of ascertaining the position of security forces or civilians in the area would have precluded air support being provided in time to be effective. In addition, ground to air communications were reduced to 25 per cent of their normal efficiency in jungle conditions, and the current Army 62 wireless set weighed no less than 150 lbs (a ten-man load for jungle patrols) and also needed a tree aerial which took time to erect. The alternative use of a control vehicle was quite impracticable, as one could rarely penetrate into the area of contact. Furthermore, with large numbers of small patrols operating throughout the Federation at the same time, the number of contacts at any one moment could run into hundreds. For example, in one period of three weeks, more than 2,000 potential contacts were made by ground forces: some 145 of these developed into actual contacts but only one of these was suitable for direct air support.

It can thus be seen that, during the early months of FIREDOG, the number of occasions upon which direct air support was practical and effective was strictly limited. Nevertheless, the constant threat of air attack and the frequent presence of aircraft overhead undoubtedly kept the terrorists on the move and deterred them from setting up any permanent bases or concentrating in significant strength. The form of operation in which the Beaufighters and Spitfires were perhaps most effective at this time was in the defensive role of convoy protection. All road convoys had to traverse roads ideally suited to ambush and many were undoubtedly forestalled by the presence overhead of patrolling aircraft.

The largest element of the RAF to be deployed during the Emergency was undoubtedly the air transport support force. During the early phase of operations this comprised four Dakota squadrons namely 48, 52, 110 and the Far East Communications Squadron, all based at Changi but detached in rotation to Kuala Lumpur. In addition a light transport force, mainly of Austers, initially operated as far forward as rough jungle airstrips and clearings would allow. The helicopter, which was eventually to transform the operations of the ground forces, had not yet come into service in the Far East and was still in its infancy in the home commands and the Fleet Air Arm.

The Dakota squadrons virtually resumed the roles which had made them so invaluable during the Burma campaign five years earlier, namely supply dropping by parachute and free fall techniques, troop carrying to the forward airfields, and the general maintenance of ground forces in the field. Without their constant support, all supplies and ammunition would have had to be carried by road convoys under constant threat of ambush and then into the jungle by the ground forces themselves, thus severely limiting their depth of penetration. Beyond a range of five or ten miles from the jungle fringes the terrorists would, under these circumstances, have been virtually free from molestation, and the Security Forces would have been reduced to holding a series of more or less isolated defended areas. As it was the Dakotas and light aircraft enabled patrols to penetrate as deeply as they wished into the jungle, and to remain there for periods of up to three months instead of about four days without air supply.

Only one Dakota squadron was needed to fulfil the transport support commitment at Kuala Lumpur and 110 Squadron was the first to be detached there from Changi, being relieved in turn by 52 and 48 Squadrons at six monthly intervals. Requests for air supply were radioed from jungle patrols to Army or Police District Headquarters who passed them on to the Joint Operations Centre at Kuala Lumpur for confirmation and the allocation of tasks. At the same time details of the requirements were passed to the depot of 55 Air Despatch Company RASC who packed the supplies, attached the parachutes and provided the personnel to act as despatchers in the Dakotas.

The supplies, which usually consisted of rations, clothing, ammunition and medical necessities, were packed in 200 lb packs—the maximum size which air despatchers could reasonably be expected to handle in the air. The parachutes which were attached to the packs were expensive items of equipment since less than half of them were recovered and, of these, less than half were fit for repair and renovation. Irvin 'R' type parachutes cost some £32 each and the consumption rose to about 18,000 per year which added significantly to the cost of FIREDOG. Nevertheless, air supply proved infinitely more economical in men and materials than the alternative, had it even been feasible.

It fell to 110 Squadron to perfect the technique of locating and supplying the patrols. The selection of dropping zones was the responsibility of the patrol commander and, although every attempt was made to find some clearing or a patch of secondary jungle which could be cleared, the DZs seldom met the minimum desirable qualifications of size and visibility from the air. Most were no more than holes in the jungle canopy a mere ten yards in radius. Often drops had to be made with no visual contact between the Dakota and the ground. Pilots were briefed with the estimated map reference of the dropping zone but instructions were frequently inaccurate as, with a limited field of vision, ground patrols often had only a hazy idea of their own positions. As soon as the approaching aircraft was heard, therefore, a smoke grenade would be fired to indicate the dropping zone and coloured smoke and cloth panels used to indicate the aiming point during the run up. After discharging his load the pilot would await confirmation by radio that the packs were recoverable. This was vitally important bearing in mind that dropping zones were mostly located among trees 200 feet in height and any significant error would usually result in the supplies being out of reach, and the drop having to be repeated.

More than 60,000 lbs were dropped in this way during the first six months of operations, mainly by 110 Squadron from Kuala Lumpur, but, as the ground forces realised the value of air supply and penetrated deeper and deeper into the jungle, the tonnage increased rapidly so that in later years over half a million pounds of supplies were being regularly dropped each month. The Police were quicker than the Army to take advantage of this facility and as early as the first months of the Emergency two police posts as Batu Melintang and Gua Musang in North Kelantan were kept supplied entirely by air.

Significant as were offensive and transport support, the part played by air reconnaissance was no less important. Indeed, the strike and transport aircraft largely depended upon it for their own operations. Almost the entire photographic reconnaissance commitment during the whole twelve years of the campaign was undertaken by aircraft of

81 Squadron. It was the only squadron of its kind in the Far East, equipped initially, as we have seen, with six Mosquito PR 34s and two Spitfires. Owing to the structural problems already mentioned of maintaining the Mosquitos, they operated principally from the squadron's base at Tengah, but the two Spitfires were frequently sent forward on detachment to handle the short range tactical sorties.

The first and most important strategic photographic task was to up-date the large scale, one inch to one mile, maps of the Federation. 81 Squadron had completed a survey of the country by 1949 but no new maps had yet been printed. When the Emergency was proclaimed the only available large scale maps were prewar editions, and these covered little more than the populated areas of Western Malaya. Mosquitos of the squadron, in conjunction with 2 Air Survey Liaison Section of the Army, therefore completed a detailed survey of the whole country on a scale from which tactical maps of both 1 inch and $2\frac{1}{2}$ inches to the mile could be produced. These were essential for the accurate planning and routeing of jungle patrols, and for the navigation to dropping zones and target areas. It was a formidable task and was not completed until the end of 1952 when the Emergency had been in existence for more than four years.

Tactical reconnaissance was usually undertaken by the Spitfires as occasion demanded, from Kuala Lumpur or Taiping. These sorties had to be strictly limited as it was soon appreciated that aircraft flying below about 15,000 feet could be seen and heard by the terrorists, many of whom had been indoctrinated into the value of air reconnaissance while serving with the MPAJA during World War II. On the other hand tactical reconnaissance above 15,000 feet could not produce photographs to a larger scale than 1:10,000, and these showed insufficient detail to satisfy most of the requirement. During the early years, therefore, it was a case of assessing for each sortie whether it was wise to risk compromising the security of a possible ground or air attack in order to have the advantages of a large scale photograph, or to remain undetected and accept the limitations of a small scale picture.

As 1949 progressed towards the monsoon period the intensity of terrorist activity tended to increase in spite of the vigilance of patrols and the support from the air. On July 7 the largest air strike to date was mounted by 26 Beaufighters and a number of Sunderlands, Spitfires and Harvards. It took place in Johore as the result of intelligence from informers and was designed to drive a concentration of terrorists into the arms of the waiting Security Forces. It was partially successful but many escaped the high concentration of troops and faded into deep jungle. To quote from the Air Ministry Secret Intelligence Summary of August 1949, "there were no grounds for complacency at the rate of progress in the campaign." Although this large scale operation took place in the south of the Federation, this month saw a general shifting of the centre of operation to the north—from South Pahang into Perak—accompanied by sustained terrorist attacks on urban police stations and public utilities, such as water pipelines.

Communist successes in China at this time undoubtedly encouraged the MCP, and it was noticeable how closely they followed communist tactics in China, concentrating on gaining control of the remote areas and hoping later to use the villages to encircle and eventually control the towns. They adopted Mao's Four Golden Rules: when the enemy advances, we retreat; when the enemy halts, we harrass; when the enemy avoids battle, we attack; when the enemy retreats; we follow. As one writer put it; "Catching communists in Malaya is about as easy as looking for fleas in a sheepdog's coat".

Policy Developments

By the beginning of 1950 it was abundantly clear that the Security Forces, although harrassing the terrorists and keeping them constantly on the move, were not winning the battle decisively. The terrain was against them and the population at large lived in constant fear of intimidation. A new strategy was clearly essential, and it was the plan now prepared by Lieutenant-General Sir Harold Briggs, the first Director of Operations, that enabled the long campaign to be effectively fought and eventually won.

The Briggs Plan sought not merely to destroy terrorists but to prevent a recurrence of their activities. The prime task of the police and the military forces, working in close partnership, was to win the confidence and support of the people by dominating all the populated areas. It was a political aim and the control was civilian. The plan therefore aimed to cut off the MCP from the people, especially from the Chinese squatters on whom the terrorists depended for food and information. Accordingly troops and police began to move nearly half a million Chinese from isolated communities to new villages where they could be protected within barbed wire perimeters by police and locally recruited Chinese Home Guards. To minimize the discomforts of this wholesale movement, land, schools and social amenities were to be liberally provided in the new protected areas. Many other measures were incorporated in the Briggs Plan such as the issue of identity cards to all adults and the exportation to China of suspected terrorists. More than 100 million leaflets were to be dropped by the RAF to promote confidence and countless other steps taken to separate the population from the machinations of the MCP.

This then was the plan—clearly a long term plan—which was initiated in 1950. Eventually it was to succeed but not until a further ten years of hardship and casualties had been suffered by terrorists, villagers and Security Forces alike.

The Pressure Increases

For the first time since the Emergency arose the Briggs Plan brought a real sense of purpose and direction to the authorities who had undoubtedly been caught unprepared, and whose initial efforts to contain terrorism had lacked co-ordination. The RAF was now strengthened by the arrival of 33 Squadron equipped with the Tempest, a rugged single seater fighter which had already proved its reliability and hitting power in both European and Middle East theatres. The Royal Australian Air Force (RAAF) sent a squadron of eight Lincoln medium bombers to Tengah and the Dakota force was augmented by 41 Squadron of the Royal New Zealand Air Force (RNZAF) based at Changi. An additional RAAF Dakota squadron joined the medium range transport force at Changi in June 1950. These valuable reinforcements reflected the growing concern within the Commonwealth of the insidious spread of communism in South-East Asia, and the determination to join the British forces in combating it.

Nevertheless the terrorist offensive, based upon more effective planning, developed with increasing intensity to reach a peak of violence during the latter part of 1951. Attacks and incidents rose from about 100 a month in 1949 to over 500 a month in 1951 and in that year more than 500 members of the Security Forces and 500 civilians, including the British High Commissioner, Sir Henry Gurney, were killed. The reply to this increase of violence took a number of forms in implementing the Briggs Plan. Many troops were replaced in static duties by police, thus releasing many front line fighting units to penetrate even deeper into the jungle in pursuit of identifiable gangs. Where suitable targets could be located with certainty, the RAF was given priority to attack and destroy them. Air supply was stepped up to permit patrols to spend longer and longer periods in the jungle without relief and, finally, greater attention was paid to obtaining intelligence from villagers and informers.

Comprehensive records of the overall air effort exist but are too detailed to be reproduced here. However, it will be of interest to include a summary of the effort expended up to 1951 in order to show the significant increase in the tempo of air operations during the early years of the Emergency.

Operation FIREDOG Air Effort

	July 1948 to March 1949	April 1949 to December 1950	January 1951 to August 1951
No of Offensive Air Strike Sorties	403	6,011	3,278
Tonnage of Bombs	78	6,900	4,956
Rocket Projectiles	1,256	27,169	13,850
Air Transport Sorties	5,784	13,735	6,487
Passengers	9,639	18,324	10,273
Tonnage of Freight	423	3,518	1,716
No of Reconnaissance Sorties	1,339	3,606	2,199

The co-operation between ground and air forces became ever closer, controlled by the efficient Joint Operations Centre (JOC) at Kuala Lumpur. After one operation named JACKPOT in December 1950, the AOC Malaya reported as follows:

"This affords a typical illustration of major pre-planned ground operations supported by closely co-ordinated air action. This operation had as its object the destruction of the 2nd Regt of the MRLA, then located in South-Eastern Selangor and Northern Negri Sembilan and believed to total some 260 terrorists. The air forces were asked to help by attacking a concentration of 70 to 100 terrorists who had taken refuge in an inaccessible area. On three successive days heavy air strikes were made involving 98 sorties—19 by Lincolns, 32 by Brigands, 26 by Spitfires, 17 by Tempests, one by a Sunderland and

3 by Dakotas acting as an airborne Tactical Headquarters. These attacks had the desired effect of dispersing the gang and driving it out of the jungle into a rubber estate where it was engaged by the 1st Suffolks who killed five of the enemy and captured another five. During the seven weeks of the operation, the terrorists are known to have lost 44 of their number, 29 being killed, 10 captured and five surrendering. The final score sheet was not unsatisfactory although, as is so often the case, no direct casualties could be credited with certainty to air action".

For the effort expended, these casualties must seem very few but, nevertheless, they were typical and serve to illustrate the intense difficulties which ground and air forces alike encountered in locating, attacking and destroying the fleeting targets offered by the terrorists. The circumstances were such that the casualties inflicted were not an accurate guide to the effectiveness of the air operations. It was essential to maintain pressure on the guerillas to keep them constantly on the move, and there is no doubt that harrassment from the air achieved this with great economy of effort. Repeatedly the offensive support aircraft were used to strike at camps which might have remained undamaged because they were located in remote and often inaccessible areas. Attacks on pin-point targets were widely recognised for their usefulness and they became increasingly effective as target marking techniques were developed and refined. It is impossible to assess accurately the indirect effect that these air operations had on the elimination of terrorists, but it was by no means inconsiderable. It is known that by the end of 1950 police interrogation had revealed that 32 terrorists had surrendered and 12 had been captured as a direct result of air strike action.

The narrative in this chapter has covered the first three years of the Emergency. 1951 is a natural point at which to leave events in Malaya temporarily and to focus on developments elsewhere. After an initial period during which the gravity of the situation in the Federation was undoubtedly underestimated by the authorities, unrelenting pressure was applied to the terrorist incursions by an adequate force of police and Army units strongly supported by the RAF in accordance with the Briggs Plan, and it was already clear that, although victory would be slow in coming, it must inevitably arrive.

By this time the spread of communism was beginning to have serious repercussions elsewhere in the Far East, notably in Korea, and it is there that we must now turn our attention.

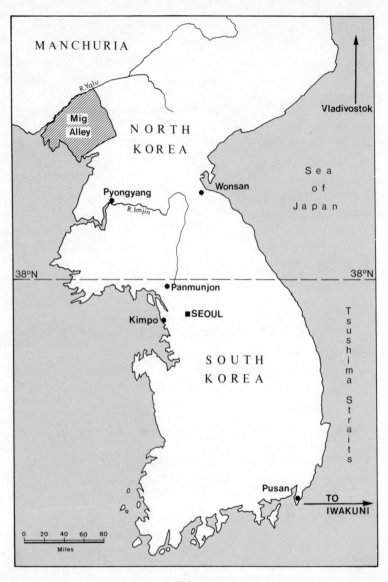

Map 6
Korea

9

Korean Interlude

The Far East Air Force seemed destined to become involved in one emergency after another. Barely three years after the start of the Malayan Emergency, and at a time when the mounting intensity of operations in the Federation was reaching its peak, attention was sharply diverted to the situation arising in Korea which, although not within the boundaries of the Far East Command, was nevertheless a serious threat to the stability of South-East Asia.

Background

The little known Asian peninsula of Korea had been annexed by Japan in 1910 and the Allies in World War II made a pledge that, when Japan was defeated, Korea should once again become a free and independent state. However, after Japan's defeat in 1945 the Soviet Union, exploiting her belated entry into the war in the Pacific, occupied northern Korea. United States forces then occupied the southern half, and, in order to facilitate the surrender of Japanese troops in Korea, came to a purely military arrangement with Russia to regard the 38th Parallel of latitude as the dividing line between their respective zones of occupation (see Map 6).

This demarcation was intended to be no more than a temporary arrangement until the promise of an independent Korea could be realised. Nevertheless, all attempts by the United States and the Soviet Union to reach agreement and to withdraw their forces failed and, after two years of haggling, the United States laid the whole matter before the General Assembly of the United Nations. In spite of agreement by the majority of members, Russia exercised her right of veto and refused to withdraw.

By this time the 38th Parallel had become much more than an arbitrary line of demarcation—it had developed into a strongly fortified frontier. Nevertheless the United Nations persisted with the holding of elections in South Korea which led to the establishment of the Republic of Korea under the presidency of Dr Syngman Rhee in August 1948, to be followed one month later by the setting up of the communist Democratic People's Republic of Korea at Pyongyang in the north. The stage was thus set for confrontation between the United States and Russia in yet another sensitive area. The situation bore a marked similarity to that existing in Germany.

As already mentioned Korea lay outside the boundaries of South-East Asia and the Americans also considered it to be beyond their own area of responsibility in the Pacific. Consequently they gradually withdrew their forces from South Korea after the Republic had been established in spite of the fact that skirmishes were almost daily occurrences along the line of the 38th Parallel. Russia, however, was well aware that possession of South Korea would greatly strengthen her Pacific defences and also give encouragement to anti-American factions in Japan as well as to those communist inspired elements in Malaya, Indo-China and elsewhere in the Far East. On 25 June 1950, with Soviet encouragement, eight North Korean divisions launched their invasion of South Korea from the 38th Parallel. What the Soviet Union miscalculated and did not expect was that armed aggression would be resisted by force from outside. They were wrong, but it took three years of extremely bloody conflict to restore the situation.

On the afternoon of 25 June, the United Nations called in vain upon North Korea to return to the 38th Parallel and two days later President Truman of the United States authorised the use of American naval and air forces to support South Korea. This was followed the next day by the Prime Minister of the United Kingdom, Mr Clement Attlee, placing elements of the Royal Navy in the Far East at the disposal of General MacArthur, who had assumed command of the US forces in the area. So serious was the position that on 30 June MacArthur was instructed to use American ground forces from Japan and to bomb targets in North Korea. Thus, within a matter of days, the United States and Britain were fully committed on behalf of the United Nations to a large scale conflict against Russian backed Chinese communist and North Korean forces.

The Land Campaign

Although this is primarily a Royal Air Force narrative, it would not be complete without at least a summary of the bloody land campaigns which ebbed and flowed beneath the Korean skies. 'Ebb and flow' is the correct expression because the United Nations forces crossed and recrossed the 38th Parallel, the border between North and South Korea, no less than three times during the three years of hard fighting.

The initial threat of the communist forces carried them almost completely through South Korea, leaving little more than a bridgehead for the United Nations forces around the port of Pusan. Under General MacArthur's astute leadership, his forces pushed the North Koreans back almost to the Manchurian border within the first five months. At that point the government of communist China despatched its 'volunteers' in great numbers to assist the shattered North Korean army, with the result that the United Nations forces were driven back beyond the 38th Parallel once again. They fought back to hold a line which straddled the 'waist' of the country and which crossed the 38th Parallel from south-west to north-east. This position was reached in July 1951, and the last two years of the war were characterised by bitter fighting in this narrow 'waist' while seemingly endless truce talks proceeded at Panmunjon. (See Map 6).

When a truce was eventually signed in July 1953, the United Nations forces had suffered heavily but the communist casualties were much greater. Approximately 350,000 United Nations men had been killed or wounded and the enemy casualties have been assessed at not less than 1,500,000, a terrible toll when it is realised that the truce was far from satisfactory and failed to unite the country in the manner that had been agreed at the end of World War II.

British Participation

This sudden, and to some extent unexpected, involvement in 'limited war' in a distant corner of the globe created many difficulties for Great Britain. Her forces world wide had been steadily and rapidly run down since the end of World War II and a fresh mobilisation was most unwelcome, both politically and economically. Nevertheless, a limited mobilisation was inescapable if the United Nations declaration was to be supported and a worthwhile contribution made to the Korean operations.

The Army which was heavily committed in Malaya and elsewhere found great difficulty in raising a force to support this new emergency. Nevertheless, a number of British brigades were formed, largely from Commonwealth regiments, during the first few months, and these were subsequently combined into the 1st Commonwealth Division on 28 July 1951.

The Far East Air Force, which was endeavouring to cope with the Malayan Emergency as well as maintaining the air defence of South-East Asia, had undoubtedly been allowed to run down too far and could spare little from its slender resources. Indeed, the personnel strength of AHQ Malaya at this time was less than 4,000.

There were, however, certain factors which worked to the advantage of Britain's small Far Eastern forces. The Royal Navy could play only a limited role in the Malayan Emergency in view of its mainly landlocked nature, and was thus able to provide a number of ships, including aircraft carriers, for General MacArthur's force. They were most welcome as Korea is a peninsula which can be effectively blockaded from the sea. Similarly the Far East Flying Boat Wing, comprising three squadrons of Sunderlands at Seletar and Hong Kong, could carry out only a strictly limited number of tasks in Malaya, and had sufficient resources to provide valuable reconnaissance and transport facilities for Korean operations. As far as other operational aircraft were concerned, the United States Air Force had retained a powerful array of fighters, fighter bombers and light bombers in Japan and the Philippines with bases for strategic bombers located well within range of North Korea. Fortuitously, therefore, Britain was able to make a contribution in those categories which were most welcome to the United States without diverting squadrons of operational landplanes from their heavy commitments elsewhere.

The Importance of Hong Kong

Being the nearest British base to Korea, Hong Kong had an important role to play in supporting the British forces of all three Services committed to the Korean campaign. Pressurised as it was on all sides by the advance of communism, the British Chiefs of Staff placed the defence of Hong Kong high on their list of priorities. It was defended always by one, and on occasion by two fighter squadrons and, as already mentioned, by the Sunderlands of 88 Squadron or by detachments from Seletar. Throughout the campaign it provided intermediate base facilities for the flying boats at Iwakuni, avoiding the necessity to undertake the 3,000 mile flight back to Singapore for major servicing or repair. It provided a staging post for many aircraft flying between the Korean zone and Singapore, and it also serviced and despatched Dakotas ferrying supplies up to Iwakuni.

Hong Kong has always been acutely vulnerable to a Chinese take over but much as they might wish to acquire it, they have always realised that it is worth more to them as a trading entrepot. Nevertheless the Korean war period exposed it to great danger as the Chinese realised how important a role it played in supporting the UN forces. Because this is essentially a Royal Air Force history, no mention has been made of the naval facilities at Hong Kong but it would be wrong to ignore their significance in supporting the not inconsiderable Commonwealth fleet which fought throughout the three year campaign. Hong Kong was of vital importance to the ships, aircraft carriers and naval aircraft of that force. In addition to the refuelling, victualling, servicing and repair services, the colony provided admirable amenities for shore leave, rest and recuperation for the many naval and air force personnel involved.

The Limitations of Air Power

The great weight of American air power was used to considerable effect throughout the campaign but it was subject to certain overriding limitations. Political restraints which inhibited air attacks on Chinese bases in Manchuria also prevented the use of nuclear weapons. Restricted thus to essentially tactical roles, the air forces gave intensive support to the UN ground forces, thereby reducing the effect of the communists' numerical superiority: but domination of the skies over the battlefield was not enough to enable the air forces to paralyse their opponents. Although bridges, power stations, factories and airfields in North Korea were relentlessly attacked and destroyed or damaged time and time again, vast reserves of labour and an expertise in camouflage enabled the communists to effect repairs in an astonishingly short time and to conceal their movements most effectively.

The North Korean air force, equipped with mainly obsolescent Russian aircraft, was quickly eliminated but the limitations in the use of the air became serious as soon as the Russian backed Chinese forces came into action, flying their MIG-15s from airfields in Manchuria which were politically secure from attack. Combats thus took place close to the Manchurian border when the American and Australian fighters were at the limit of their range and severely handicapped by the knowledge that their enemies were fresh and operating within a few miles of airfield bases which were immune from attack. There can be no doubt that these impossible restrictions prolonged the war considerably. But it is equally clear that any extension of the American air offensive to the Manchurian airfields would have widened the area of hostilities to a degree which can only be imagined.

Tactical Air Operations

The assistance which the USAF most desired during the early stages of the war was advice and guidance from the RAF on tactical operations, and particularly in night intruder tactics. Two highly decorated and experienced RAF officers, Wing Commander P G Wykeham-Barnes (later Air Marshal Sir Peter Wykeham) and Wing Commander J E Johnson (later Air Vice-Marshal Johnson) were therefore attached to the 5th United States Tactical Air Force.

Wykeham-Barnes used his night intruder experience to good effect. He flew on many sorties and at once saw that a lack of co-ordination between the three different types of aircraft which the Americans were using in this role was failing to produce the best results. He urged the establishment of a single intruder control working to a plan designed to eliminate communist troop columns, rather than harassing them in a somewhat haphazard way as had been the tendency before his arrival. He produced a 'charter' for night intruder operations in which squadrons were to be allocated specific target areas to avoid interference with one another; a technique using flares for identification of targets was to be introduced, and better air to ground communication established. To the great credit of Wykeham-Barnes, his 'charter' was accepted and implemented by General Partridge, Commander of the 5th TAF, and resulted in a general improvement in their night intruder operations. On his return to the United Kingdom, the Wing Commander was able not only to brief the Air Ministry fully on the Korean air situation from first hand knowledge, but also to give a comprehensive lecture to the Royal United Services Institution.[1]

Having paid the RAF the compliment of seeking its operational advice, the USAF then invited Wing Commander Johnson to fly with them in operations in Korea. He flew many unarmed missions in the B-26 light bomber, taking both day and night photographs of enemy concentrations. Like Wykeham-Barnes, he found a lack of co-ordination in the control of these operations between air and ground formations, including the age old problem of who should control operations in close support of ground forces.

---

[1] RUSI Journal, May 1952, pp. 149–163

These two officers established a close rapport with the USAF and they opened the way for more RAF pilots to be accepted with American squadrons. For example, Flight Lieutenant S W Daniel flew with the 334th Fighter Interceptor Squadron on F86-A Sabres for more than six months and was awarded the Air Medal and the American DFC. His experience against the menacingly efficient MIG-15 in the Yalu river area (which was colloquially known as 'MIG Alley') was probably the first RAF combat involvement of the war. Leading a flight of four Sabres on one occasion he encountered six MIGs at 28,000 feet, a height at which the Sabre could out-turn the MIG in level flight and diving turns. Splitting the enemy formation, Daniel pressed home his attack and after placing himself in a firing position and following one MIG through violent evasive manoeuvres, chased the severely damaged machine to the Manchurian border, firing at every opportunity. This and similar examples of skill and airmanship impressed his American colleagues and persuaded the USAF Chief of Staff to accept more RAF pilots in his squadrons. Accordingly four more Sabre trained pilots joined units of the 4th and 51st Fighter Interceptor Wings at Kimpo airfield. They were quickly in action in the clear winter skies over North Korea and acquitted themselves well. For his leadership against a greatly superior force of MIG-15s during one eventful sortie, Wing Commander Johnnie Baldwin DSO DFC AFC was awarded the American DFC, but sadly was himself shot down and lost nine days later.

Not all the allied squadrons were American. The Royal Australian Air Force also contributed with 77 Squadron, initially equipped with Mustangs, but converted to Meteors with the help of three RAF officers and one NCO pilot who joined them in February 1951. One RAF member of 77 Squadron, Flying Officer M O Berg AFC, had the somewhat dubious distinction of becoming the only RAF prisoner-of-war. He was forced to eject from his Meteor on 28 August 1952, after his aircraft was crippled by AA fire. He was uninjured and spent the remainder of the war in communist hands, successfully withstanding their fearsome brainwashing techniques and a great deal of solitary confinement. Six more RAF pilots joined 77 Squadron and, by the middle of 1952, a sizeable contingent of Commonwealth airmen was fighting in Korea.

These combat attachments were of course mutually beneficial. On the one hand the host squadron, American or Australian, acquired the experience of the RAF pilots, all of whom were carefully selected for their proven skill and specialised knowledge in a particular operational role. On the other hand the pilots gained invaluable jet combat experience which could be advantageously passed on to their contemporaries. By 1953, seventeen RAF pilots were fighting in Korea, either in 77 Squadron or in one of the USAF fighter squadrons.

This was not the sum total of attachments. The USAF was deficient in a number of skilled trades, not least that of photographic interpreter. The 5th TAF was therefore reinforced with a small team of officers and airmen sent out from the United Kingdom and specially trained in interpreting photographs of carefully camouflaged installations.

A question which was frequently asked at this time was why the RAF did not send tactical squadrons instead of individual aircraft and ground tradesmen to Korea. The answer is quite simple. The RAF in 1951–52 was fully occupied in maintaining 'cold war' vigilance in Germany, in monitoring a rapidly deteriorating situation in the Middle East and supporting the Malayan campaign. To have detached one or more squadrons from those theatres to Korea, when the USA had adequate tactical air forces available, would have necessitated an expensive and lengthy diversion of effort from other major commitments. Although the USA would undoubtedly have appreciated and welcomed a RAF Meteor or Vampire squadron, they fully understood the need to combat Soviet threats in other theatres and found the attachment of selected RAF personnel to their units equally satisfactory. To quote from the reply to a question on this subject given by Wykeham-Barnes: "It is better that a lot of individuals should get a little experience of it (the Korean war) than that a few people should have a great deal".

The Sunderland Squadrons

It must not be thought that RAF involvement was entirely confined to the attachment of individual personnel. Far from it. Although for reasons already stated, no close support fighter or bomber squadrons went to Korea, the Sunderlands of 88, 205 and 209 Squadrons participated fully throughout the three years of war. Together these squadrons formed the Far East Flying Boat Wing, commanded by Wing Commander D H Burnside DSO DFC, based at Seletar. At the outbreak of hostilities, 88 Squadron was stationed at Hong Kong and was thus nearest to the war zone. Almost immediately it moved to Iwakuni on the southern tip of Honshu under the command of Squadron Leader M Helme AFC, and was placed under American naval command. This was the start of a monthly rotation by the three squadrons in turn from their main Singapore base, 3,000 miles distant.

The Sunderlands were integrated at Iwakuni with patrol squadrons of the US Navy and their role, together with the United Nations naval forces, was to maintain the blockade of Korean ports. From the beginning it was evident that the task was an exacting one. The patrols required were long, often of 12 hours duration, and arduous. The weather, to say the least, was unkind to unheated, draughty Sunderlands: −20°C was no uncommon temperature during the long winter months, and icing was a frequent hazard. The terrain around Korea and Southern Japan is grim and forbidding and very mountainous. For example, the safety height for the airfield at Iwakuni was 4,000 feet and frequently the only way in and out of the bay for the flying boats was either to fly over the top at 4,500 feet in dense cloud or to crawl through a narrow gap visually at 100 feet or less. Flying was no picnic under these conditions.

It was essential to maintain the blockade around the clock, necessitating much night flying as well as long daylight patrols often as far north as Vladivostok. Daily anti-submarine patrols in the Tsushima Strait, which is an important focal point for shipping between Honshu and South Korea, were frequently allocated to the Sunderlands, and these proved to be among the more interesting missions as every ship seen had to be identified and often photographed. Mine surveillance and weather reporting all added to the busy lives of the crews on these sorties.

During the time that the Sunderlands operated over and around Korea, more than 1,100 lengthy missions were carried out by the three squadrons, amounting to 12,500 flying hours. This meant that each crew flew between 60 and 70 sorties, ie about 7 sorties per month during the period of each crew's attachment, many individual aircrew members achieving 2,000 hours of difficult but interesting flying during their tour with the Wing. Enemy contacts were few as most of the time was spent over the open sea. No Sunderlands were lost from enemy action and, as far as is known, no enemy aircraft were shot down by them. Clearly they were unsuited to participate in the land campaign but their value in the reconnaissance role was inestimable. The United Nations fleets depended heavily on the information they passed back to base and most of the carrier borne strikes, both American and British, were planned on reports received from these maritime patrol aircraft.

Within a short time of the opening of hostilities, the blockade of
Korean ports was complete and thenceforth it was almost impossible
for enemy supply shipping to use the ports on either east or west
coasts without being heavily attacked by aircraft called forward by
the reconnaissance aircraft. This was an extremely important factor
in the final victory.

AOP Operations

When the Commonwealth Division was formed in 1951, it was
essential to provide it with battlefield reconnaissance and artillery
spotting facilities. This requirement gave rise to an interesting military
hybrid which was established on an airstrip close to Divisional
Headquarters. No 1903 Independent Air Observation Post Flight of
the RAF was plucked from the relatively relaxed atmosphere of Hong
Kong, and 1913 Light Liaison Flight RAF was transported out from
the UK. These two units were equipped with RAF Auster aircraft,
flown by Army pilots and serviced by RAF and Army ground
personnel in roughly equal numbers.

No 1903 Flight with its aircraft, equipment and personnel embarked
in *HMS Unicorn* at Hong Kong on 9 July 1951 and landed at Iwakuni
eight days later. The five Austers were assembled and flew to Pusan
in Korea on 27 July, escorted by a Sunderland for the open sea
crossing. By 1 August the Flight was operational on the Division's
airstrip some five miles south of the Imjin river. After digging slit
trenches and camouflaging its equipment the unit began operating
over the 1,000 yards of no-man's land which at that time separated
the enemy frontline from the Commonwealth Division. As most of
the American units had never seen an Auster before, one of the most
urgent tasks was to take photographs of Austers in the air from every
angle for distribution to front line troops and, in particular, to AA
gunners. Thereafter the Flight became immersed in the arduous and
highly dangerous business of AOP, engaging targets for the artillery,
reporting the incessant ground activity and taking photographs. No
1913 Light Liaison Flight was located nearby at Fort George on a
bend in the Imjin. Its airstrip was 600 yards long but only 20 yards
wide with a surface of packed earth which tended to be either a dust
bowl or a quagmire. In the winter the mud on this strip froze so
hard that the Austers were often frozen to the ground in the morning
and had to be thawed out of the ruts before they could be moved.

Fortunately, in spite of the vulnerability of these fragile little aircraft, casualties were relatively light. Nevertheless two aircraft were shot down with the loss of their pilots, and after the first incident the wearing of parachutes was made compulsory for the first time. Some respite was obtained when the Commonwealth Division took its turn in reserve and this was more than welcomed, not only by the soldiers and airmen of the two Flights, but also by RAF Iwakuni where the problems of maintaining and supporting the Austers in the front line had become formidable. No less than 2,935 AOP sorties were flown during the campaign and it must be remembered that there were never more, and usually less than ten aircraft available to the two Flights.

MIGs, Meteors and Sabres

The arrival of the Russian built MIG-15 in Korean skies came as a considerable shock to the British and United States Air Staffs. Its speed and manoeuvrability established it as a superior aircraft to the Meteor 8 then being flown by 77 Squadron RAAF and, in certain respects, but not all, superior to the F86 Sabre, flown by the majority of the American fighter squadrons. At the time the Meteor 8 was the standard equipment of RAF Fighter Command and furthermore the F86 was being bought in considerable numbers to re-equip the RAF fighter squadrons in Germany. Consequently the confrontation in Korea for the first time between MIG-15s and Meteors and Sabres aroused intense interest, not unmixed with apprehension.

On 29 August 1951, the first encounter took place between eight of 77 Squadron's Meteors and a strong force of MIGs in the Yalu river area. One of the Australian Meteors was shot down and another badly damaged. It soon became apparent that the Meteor's limiting Mach number of 0.82 compared with the 0.9 of the MIG made it inferior to the Russian aircraft in almost every respect. The role of 77 Squadron was therefore immediately changed from providing high altitude top cover to giving medium cover for bombers and ground attack aircraft in circumstances where the Meteors could be afforded top cover by American Sabres. Disappointing though this development was for the Australian and RAF crews of 77 Squadron, it in no way reduced the value of the squadron's contribution. There was much protective work to be done at lower altitudes to provide cover for F51 Mustangs and F84s as well as the various categories of bomber and reconnaissance aircraft.

With regard to the performance of the Sabre in relation to the
MIG-15, Squadron Leader W Harbison, who flew with one of the
Sabre squadrons, reported as follows:

"The MIG can sustain a high angle of climb which can leave the
F86 at the point of stalling whilst the MIG is still climbing away
.... The 'zoom' climb of the MIG is outstanding when attacked
and is one of the evasive measures. A slight dive to gain speed,
followed by a climb estimated to be between 50 and 60 degrees is
something which has to be seen to be appreciated".

However, some comfort could be derived from Harbison's report
that below 20,000 feet, the F86 could out-turn the MIG in level and
diving turns, and in a sustained dive, it had the edge on the MIG.
Below 20,000 feet the level top speed of both aircraft was about the
same.

RAF Casualties and Awards

When measured against the USAF commitment and casualties the
contribution of the RAF was modest, but it was a contribution made
in those spheres of aviation which were valuable in making good
certain deficiencies in the American order of battle.

Those RAF officers and airmen who served, both in the air and on
the ground, during the campaign distinguished themselves. 21 pilots
served with various USAF fighter squadrons and a further 29 with
77 Squadron RAAF. Five of them were officially credited with the
destruction of one MIG-15 each and Squadron Leader G S Hulse
was additionally given half credits for two more.[2] For this and
other meritorious service 7 DFCs, 6 Mentions in Despatches and a
considerable number of American decorations were awarded, repre-
senting a high proportion of honours and reflecting the excellent
account which these officers and airmen gave of themselves.

Inevitably there was a price to be paid. Eleven RAF aircrew lost
their lives in Korea: one was killed while flying as an observer in a
Fleet Air Arm Firefly from *HMS Theseus*, and the remainder lost
their lives flying with the USAF and RAAF. Additionally, one leading
aircraftman was drowned in the Imjin when an Auster in which he
was flying as an observer crashed into the river. A Sunderland of
205 Squadron crashed in transit between Iwakuni and Hong Kong,
killing fourteen crew members and passengers.

---

[2] USAF Historical Study No 81 (1963).

The men who fell in this long and costly campaign are commemorated on a memorial plaque which was placed in the lobby of the General Assembly building of the United Nations headquarters in New York and unveiled on 21 June 1956. One hopes that it will serve as a reminder that, on one of the earliest occasions upon which the newly formed United Nations was called upon to take action, it did so decisively and successfully.

In Retrospect

It is not easy to draw specific conclusions from the war in Korea. Some may say that the United Nations forces should have carried the attack to the Chinese bases in Manchuria, using nuclear weapons if necessary to conclude the war quickly. Others may argue that a small country like South Korea was not worth the heavy toll in lives that had to be paid for its eventual freedom. The situation in Korea in 1953 bore a marked similarity to that in Germany. In both cases a nation had been divided by the peace lines drawn at the end of World War II. In both cases communism proved to be intransigent as far as agreeing to any form of reunification and thus contravened the principles of the United Nations to which many communist countries belong. As we now know with hindsight Korea was one of the earliest post-war manifestations of the determined advance of communist ideology, to be followed by a continuation of the Emergency in Malaya, by Vietnam, to some extent by the Confrontation with Indonesia, by Cuba and by events in Europe and Africa. Whether South Korea was important to the West or not is immaterial. The only conclusion that seems appropriate is that the advance of communism was halted in Korea. The campaign showed that communism could be halted, and this experience strengthened the determination of Western nations to stand firm against its encroachment elsewhere. It is a fact that the Armed Forces of the West were experiencing a natural reaction after World War II and were running down faster than was prudent in face of the threat of communism. Korea did much to arrest that process and alert Western governments to the reality of the threat. But for Korea, therefore, the forces of the West might well have continued to run down even faster, and to be less prepared for further aggressions which were to follow.

Although the Royal Air Force had played a relatively small part in the Korean war, it had learned a great deal from the experience of the individual pilots and airmen who participated. Experiences of the capability of the MIG-15, for example, sharpened the determination to hasten a new generation of jet aircraft. The importance of all aspects of air power in limited war was emphasised, and more cogent weapons of persuasion were placed in the hands of the Air Staff when the future of the Service came under discussion. Finally, the co-operation between the USAF, the RAF and those Commonwealth air forces which contributed was again consolidated after an interval of nine years since the end of World War II, and this could only be of benefit for the future.

10

A New Generation of Aircraft

During the early years of the Malayan Emergency and while the Korean war was running its course, FEAF enjoyed a major re-equipment programme—and not before it was due! At the conclusion of World War II it had understandably taken the British aircraft industry some years to repair the ravages of war and to bring into production a new generation of military aircraft. Once production commenced, thorough evaluation and service experience in the home commands were essential before the new types could be sent to squadrons overseas and, in this respect, FEAF tended to be placed well down the list of priorities.

Until about 1951, therefore, the aircraft which replaced those in use at the end of the war, some of which were American Lend/Lease types, such as the Thunderbolt and Catalina flying boat, had to be in the nature of stop gaps until post-war production got into its stride. Spitfires, Mosquitos, Beaufighters and Sunderlands formed the bulk of the British aircraft in the Far East, together with Dakotas which were retained for a much longer period than other American types. The Dakota could well go down in history as the most valuable and long lasting aircraft ever produced, and in no theatre did it provide better proof of this than in South-East Asia.

Light Bombers

Nos 45 and 84 Squadrons continued to provide the light bomber element of FEAF's strike force until the early 1950s. The technical problems associated with the Mosquitos have already been described and it was hoped to replace them straight away with the Brigand. However, the impossibility of keeping the Mosquito VI serviceable until Brigand production was available necessitated an interim re-equipment of these two squadrons, and they were allocated Beaufighters. Rugged and reliable though they were, they had been designed primarily as night fighters and maritime strike aircraft and were not entirely suitable for the light bomber role; moreover, production had already ceased to make way for the Brigand.

After a brief period the Brigand arrived and both squadrons settled down at Tengah to take part in Malayan operations with their new aircraft. Unfortunately it did not prove to be the happiest of associations. Within a few months of re-equipping 45 Squadron suffered two fatal accidents in January 1951. Both were thought to be due to the premature firing of incendiary ammunition, but no member of either crew survived to identify the cause positively. The firing of cannons was stopped immediately and a year passed before modifications were considered sufficiently satisfactory for the ban to be lifted. In relation to Malayan operations this was a most severe and unwelcome restriction, since at the height of the Emergency the two squadrons were confined to bombing and rocket firing.

Worse, however, was to come. In June 1951, the two squadrons had three more fatal accidents within 19 days, losing two officers and three NCOs due to the technical failure of propeller hubs. In each case the hub fractured around the base of the propeller blades after only a few hundred hours. The severe unbalanced forces thus created wrenched the entire engine from its mounting and the aircraft became uncontrollable. All Brigands were grounded on 19 June and it was August before 45 and 84 Squadrons were airborne again. Even when the major faults which had caused these serious accidents were rectified the Brigands continued to be plagued by hydraulic problems, and serviceability remained low. However, by November 1951, 45 Squadron was back to full operational status and during that month flew 144 sorties including 41 air strikes against jungle targets.

It was unfortunate that the Brigand—so suitable for its role in many respects—should prove technically unreliable when the operational need for it was at its height, and in a theatre so far from the bulk of the spares and the expertise in the UK. It was an example, and there have been others, of a new aircraft being exposed to the rough and tumble of overseas conditions and climate before being rigorously tested in service conditions at home.

A rapid decision was made to re-equip 45 Squadron with the de Havilland Hornet, of which more anon, and this change took place in February 1952, after the squadron had flown the Brigand for exactly two years. As the Hornet, although a single seat aircraft, was not unlike the Mosquito, several dual controlled Mosquitos were given to 45 Squadron to effect the conversion at Tengah.

While this unpremeditated change was taking place, 84 Squadron continued with the Brigand and was then transferred back to Middle East Command where it had spent most of its early life and where it had always been associated with Iraq in general and Shaibah in particular. Throughout its few years in the Far East this famous old squadron had continued to sing *Those Shaibah Blues* on every appropriate, and sometimes inappropriate occasion. Thus ended FEAF's short and not very glorious acquaintance with the Brigand.

The Air Defence Force

After the Thunderbolts were returned to the custody of the United States or otherwise disposed of, the Spitfire VIII served 28 and 60 Squadrons efficiently for several years in Hong Kong and at Tengah. By the end of 1950, however, they were long out of production in the United Kingdom and had been relegated to subsidiary roles. The era of the jet had dawned and highly satisfactory trials of the Vampire had been carried out in Singapore. The 'Mini-Jet', as it was affectionately known, had already proved itself in UK service and been sent to re-equip squadrons in Germany and the Middle East. It had flown the North Atlantic and also completed a successful long range flight from Iraq to South Africa and return, in the hands of 6 Squadron. For the difficult conditions of the Far East it had the great advantages of rugged construction and simple maintenance. It was easy to fly and possessed adequate performance and firepower for the theatre.

The first Far East squadron to receive the Vampire, 28 Squadron, one of the two squadrons charged with the defence of Hong Kong, received its Vampire Vs in February 1951 and found them ideal for their task. Their small size and ease of handling on the ground made them particularly suitable for the confined and congested Kai Tak airfield. No 80 Squadron, which shared Kai Tak with 28 Squadron at the time, retained its Mosquitos until rearmed with the Hornet for a brief period in 1952 before being disbanded after the Korean war when the air defence of Hong Kong could be left entirely to the single Vampire squadron.

Tengah had been the home of 60 Squadron with a few minor interruptions since it came out of Java in 1946. The squadron had watched with great interest the earlier trials of the Vampire and was now delighted to become the first unit in Singapore to receive jet aircraft. The rebuilding of Tengah had been completed by 1951 and it now had storage and technical facilities designed for jet operations. Conversion of the pilots was simple and straightforward so that 60 Squadron was back in the thick of jungle operations within very few weeks.

The Vampire proved to be such a good design for world wide RAF use that the de Havilland Company continued to develop it, producing from it in due course the Venom. Many of the RAF Vampire squadrons were rearmed with the Venom, and this applied to both 28 and 60 Squadrons during 1955 and 1956. Although not fundamentally different from the Vampire, its improved performance with a useful radius of action of 240 miles and with power operated controls on later versions gave it the greater versatility which was a much needed asset to FEAF.

The Tempest, which 33 Squadron had brought to Butterworth when some reinforcement of FEAF was needed for operations, could be described as the last of the single piston-engined fighters. It had been produced during the last years of the war, providing a valuable interim fighter until the Meteor/Vampire family of jet fighters came along. It was a good aircraft, heavily armed, fast and reliable but, in the Far East, it had the disadvantage of being the equipment of one squadron only, necessitating the holding of a complete range of spares and ground equipment for a handful of aircraft. However, 33 Squadron played a valuable part, being stationed up country in the midst of the terrorist activity during its brief stay in Malaya.

As soon as sufficient Hornets became available, the Squadron converted to them, remaining at Butterworth for a further period on active operations. Unfortunately Hornet production was slow and, despite the rapidity with which both 33 and 80 Squadrons converted to the new type, many months elapsed before they received their full complement of aircraft. The life of the Hornet in RAF service was relatively short, not because it was in any way unsatisfactory but because it was quickly outmoded by the new family of jet fighters. In 1956 33 Squadron, which was amalgamated with 45 and took the latter's number plate, was given the Venom and remained at Butterworth. This produced a homogeneous fighter force of three Venom squadrons in the Command, to the great relief of the Engineering and Equipment staffs who had been suffering for years from a plethora of aircraft types.

Transport Aircraft

By 1951 the Dakotas of 48, 52 and 110 Squadrons, all based at Changi, had completed many years of exceptionally arduous service. Many of them were veterans of the Burma campaign almost ten years earlier and all were shaken and battered by the relentless monsoon conditions. The exploits of these splendid load carriers in, for example, Java have been described in Chapter 4 and that was but one of the many areas in South-East Asia which had cause to be grateful to them. It has been said that, on more than one occasion in Burma, a Dakota was inadvertently double loaded with boxes of ammunition (a full load of these heavy boxes barely covered the floor of the fuselage). Yet, in each case it was able to stagger into the air and land safely without any disastrous results.

As the result of international wartime agreements, the RAF had depended upon the United States for medium range transport aircraft while British manufacturers concentrated on producing combat types. It therefore took some years after the war for transports to reappear from British industry and one of the first was the Valetta. Similar in most respects to the Dakota it was used to re-equip those medium range squadrons which remained in service, and that included the three FEAF squadrons which were fully occupied in Malayan operations, the Korean campaign and maintaining the scheduled services within the Command.

No 48 Squadron was the first to receive the Valetta early in 1951, followed by 52 and 110 Squadrons within a year to eighteen months. They remained based at Changi which had by this time been developed and extended into a first class transport airfield capable of accepting the largest aircraft. Arrival of the Valetta did not, however, signal the total disappearance of the Dakota from FEAF. No 41 RNZAF and 38 RAAF Squadrons continued to fly them from Changi with the usual up-country detachments for a few more years in their support of anti-terrorist operations.

Photographic Reconnaissance

No 81 Squadron, which moved around the three Singapore stations during the 1950s, continued to fly the Mosquito PR34. Priority was given to the maintenance of this single mark of Mosquito mainly because of its excellent camera and survey installation for which no comparable aircraft could be found until the advent of the Meteor

PR10. It was not easy to keep the PR34 serviceable but, with the priority given to it, 81 Squadron was kept flying with 8 Mosquitos until the middle of 1953 when it was rearmed with Meteors. It was regrettable that one squadron only of Meteors had to be introduced when some semblance of standardisation was at last beginning to appear, but it was inevitable if the highly specialised and important role of the squadron was to be fulfilled satisfactorily.

Introduction of Helicopters

Helicopters were to play a significant part in the second half of the Malayan operations and this will be fully described in later chapters. The Dragonfly (S51) was first introduced into FEAF when helicopters were still in an experimental stage of development, and the conditions of high temperature and humidity, uncertain weather, high altitude terrain and the steep angle of entry and exit into jungle clearings meant that they were constantly flown close to their operational limits, which were considerably less than those in the United Kingdom.

The Dragonfly formed the initial equipment of a Far East Casualty Air Evacuation Flight (CAEF) formed on 1 April 1950 at Changi, close to the RAF Hospital, with three of these small helicopters. The Dragonfly had a cruising speed of 70 knots at a temperature of 80°F in still air and a range of about 225 miles. It could carry two seated passengers or one stretcher case. Downward visibility for the pilot was poor which made it a tiring aircraft to fly in jungle conditions but, nevertheless, its introduction was a morale booster to the patrols whose hope of speedy evacuation if wounded was considerably increased. 26 casualties were successfully brought out of the jungle during the first few months of the Flight's existence, and several of these undoubtedly owed their lives to the helicopter rescue. Three more Dragonflies were added to the Flight in 1952, followed by re-equipment with the slightly larger Sycamore which could lift two stretcher cases, had a better performance and, what was particularly important, much better visibility for the pilot when entering and leaving small clearings. Eventually, in 1954, the CAEF was absorbed into 194 Squadron, a full size operational unit with a complement of 14 Sycamores, based at Kuala Lumpur and operating from many up-country strips.

13. The last sortie by a Beaufighter of 84 Squadron over Singapore harbour, 10 May 1960

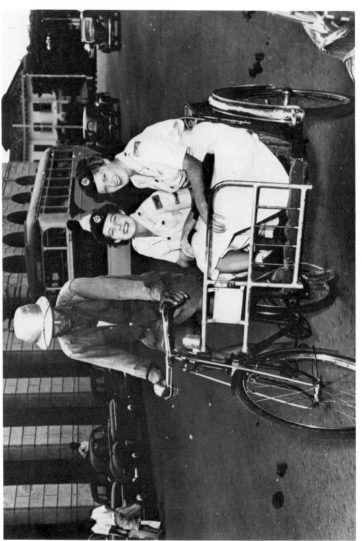

14. Members of the WRAF shopping in Singapore

15. The last operational Mosquito in the RAF. A PR Mark 34A of 81 Squadron over Seletar, 15 December 1955

16. The end of an era. The last Sunderland flying boat in the RAF leaving Singapore on 13 November 1959

Flying Boat Squadrons

Of all the squadrons in FEAF, only those equipped with Sunderlands saw no change in their aircraft until the end of the 1950s. This was largely because no flying boat replacement was available; with airfields in many parts of the world becoming increasingly suitable for large and powerful aircraft, the RAF had chosen to develop a four-engined landplane, the Shackleton, which could undertake maritime reconnaissance and strike operations more economically than the flying boat. The Far East, however, was still a difficult theatre for large landplanes, with open sea areas, many islands and other places which lacked modern airfields, eg Borneo, the Maldives, the Andamans and Penang, and here the Sunderland remained immensely valuable, as its contribution to the Korean war had already shown (Chapter 9). With excellent flying boat facilities available at Seletar, Hong Kong and Borneo in particular, it was clearly sound policy to leave the Sunderlands in FEAF for as long as they could be maintained. Natural wastage eventually dictated their demise but this was a gradual process. After the Korean war, 88 Squadron was disbanded in Hong Kong and its Sunderlands shared between 205 and 209 Squadrons at Seletar on 1 October 1954, At the end of that year 205 Squadron was amalgamated with 209, retaining the former number plate until it was re-equipped with Shackletons in 1958. And so the Sunderland soldiered on with the last flying boat squadron in service until almost the end of the Malayan Emergency.

Arguments for and against the retention of flying boats will doubtless continue as long as flying boat crews exist. They did a wonderful job, particularly in the less developed parts of the Commonwealth, but they were expensive to maintain and operate and as soon as long range landplanes reached a certain stage of development, the value of flying boats began to decline and eventually they had to be superseded for economic reasons.

Locally Recruited Air Force Units

Prior to the Japanese occupation of Singapore some effort had gone into creating a locally enlisted Auxiliary Air Force along the lines of the Royal Auxiliary Air Force in the UK. It was inevitably cut off in its infancy by the invasion and nothing more was heard of the project until March 1949. During that month the Air Council decided to augment the regular RAF fighter force by the formation of three auxiliary fighter squadrons, one each in Malaya, Singapore and Hong Kong. It was hoped that these would eventually relieve the regular squadrons of at least part of the internal security commitment in time of war and ensure that some fighter defence remained available in the Far East if the need should arise to withdraw RAF units. Looking well ahead, these squadrons should provide an outlet for volunteer enthusiasm and form the basis of the air forces which the Far Eastern possessions would need when they achieved independence.

By June 1950, the necessary negotiations had been completed with the local governments, who were required to foot part of the bill, but FEAF was instrumental in having the policy changed somewhat to allow the formation of four operational fighter squadrons in the Malayan theatre, supported by three fighter control units within four years, a period which was subsequently reduced to two years.

To cut a long story short, it was not a successful scheme. Recruiting for the Penang and Singapore squadrons got under way in May and June 1950, and for their complementary fighter control units six months later. A third squadron was formed at Kuala Lumpur in December 1951 and plans were advanced for a second Singapore squadron. These units were initially equipped with Tiger Moths and Harvards for training, the intention being to give them the Spitfires thrown up by the rearming of 28 and 60 Squadrons with Vampires.

Progress was disappointingly slow, as was recruiting, and it soon appeared that these squadrons were unlikely to be able to cope either with the maintenance or the operation of Spitfires unless excessive demands were to be made upon RAF personnel who could be ill afforded. By 1954 the whole project as envisaged had to be abandoned. Agreement was, however, reached that a regular Malayan Air Force should eventually be formed and, in the meantime, the AOC Malaya was to use MAAF units in the short range transport and visual reconnaissance roles on anti-terrorist operations. This change of plan resulted in three MAAF squadrons, each equipped with four Tiger Moths and four Harvards. They continued to do useful work, the ageing Harvards being replaced by Chipmunks, until some time in 1958 when the Royal Malayan Air Force (RMAF) came into being and assimilated the pilots and ground personnel of the MAAF, about 16 pilots and 170 airmen in all.

Apart from the introduction of the short range transport aircraft, the Single-Engine Pioneer, into 267 Squadron, the re-equipment of the majority of FEAF squadrons was complete by the end of 1955.

The SE Pioneer, built by Scottish Aviation Ltd at Prestwick, was a short take off/landing high-wing monoplane, reminiscent of but larger than the Auster. It was particularly suitable for operating in Malaya and, with the later variant, the Twin Pioneer, complemented the helicopter force in making full use of the many short airstrips which sprang up all over the Federation to bring the closest possible support to the patrols in the jungle.

FEAF Order of Battle—1956

Role	Aircraft Type	Squadron	Location
DF/GA	Venom FBI	28	Kai Tak
		45	Butterworth
		60	Tengah
P.R.	Meteor PR10	81	Seletar
MR/TPT	Valetta C1	48	
		52	Changi
		110	
F B	Sunderland GR5	205/209	Seletar
SR/TPT	Sycamore	194	Kuala Lumpur
	Whirlwind	155	Kuala Lumpur
	SE Pioneer CC1	267	Kuala Lumpur
AOP	Auster 5/6/7/9	656	Kuala Lumpur

Attached Units

Role	Aircraft Type	Squadron	Location
MB	Lincoln B 30A	1 (RAAF)	Tengah
DF/GA	Venom FBI	14 (RNZAF)	Tengah
MR/TPT	Bristol Freighter	41 (RNZAF)	Changi
SR/TPT	S55 Helicopter	848 (RNAS)	Sembawang
MB	Lincoln	Periodic dets from Bomber Command	Tengah

Thus, in the short space of about four years, FEAF was transformed into a modern force which is summarised in the table above. It will be seen that light bombers had disappeared from the order of battle, and that on the relatively few occasions when a heavy scale of bombing was required, it could be provided either by the Australian Lincoln squadron or by one of the periodic detachments of home based Lincolns from Bomber Command. The attachment of RAAF and RNZAF squadrons greatly strengthened the air support which FEAF could give to the up country operations. Without these reinforcements which are also listed above, FEAF would undoubtedly have required considerable strengthening from elsewhere in the RAF. Throughout these post-war years it was heartening to see the extent to which the Commonwealth appreciated the dangers to South-East Asia of the spread of communism, and provided generous support to combat it.

11

The Malayan Emergency—II

Early in 1950, after the Emergency in Malaya had been in existence for almost two years, there was some reason to think that Government and Security Forces had the measure of the terrorists. After having suffered several severe reverses they had now withdrawn into deep jungle and set about reorganising their army and supply forces for a protracted guerilla campaign, leaving behind small 'killer' squads in the populated areas to continue their policy of terrorism, intimidation and extortion and to occupy the attention of the Security Forces.

It was the marked decline in the rate of incidents resulting from the withdrawal which encouraged the belief that the campaign could be speedily brought to an end. No idea could have been more misleading as events were to prove. At about this time the Malayan Communist Party (MCP) changed its title to that of the Malayan Races Liberation Army (MRLA) in order to disguise their insurrection as a nationalist movement and to foster the impression that it included all races. Communist successes in China, Korea and Indo-China, followed by the official recognition of Mao Tse-Tung by Britain and Ho Chi Minh by Russia greatly heartened the MRLA. These events also gave serious food for thought to the Chinese community in Malaya who began to show a marked reluctance to co-operate with the authorities in case they jeopardised their safety under a future communist government.

The reconstituted MRLA launched an all-out offensive of violence and intimidation in June 1951 and the incident rate rose sharply to 606 in that month, the highest in the whole Emergency, and only fell below .500 a month on one occasion during the year. Although the majority of attacks were against 'soft' undefended targets with the object of terrifying the civilian population, a number of well planned attacks on the Security Forces were launched towards the end of the year, the most serious being one in which 11 members of

The Queen's Own Royal West Kent Regiment were killed. 1951 saw the highest casualties on both sides. The Security Forces suffered 505 killed and 668 wounded but they killed 1,025 terrorists, wounded 650 and captured 121.

Throughout this year the RAF squadrons flew unceasingly in support of the operations, achieving the highest monthly average of sorties, weapons expended, photographs taken and leaflets dropped, as well as passengers carried of any period during the campaign.

The Value of Air Support

After some three years of the Emergency it was now becoming possible to assess the value of air action in this unusual form of guerilla warfare and the many reports collected from Army and Police formations and units in the field made interesting reading. In particular one from HQ 26 Brigade in Johore, received in September 1951, summarised the general conclusions very well:

'Offensive air sorties in support of ground forces were considered to be very effective and should be carried out whenever possible. Strafing with cannon fire and rockets was undoubtedly the most fruitful method of attack on known or suspected terrorist locations, but bombing was generally less effective. There were seldom any pinpoint targets suitable for direct bombing attack and any form of pattern or blanket bombing, particularly in swampy areas, tended to be a waste of effort, producing few casualties. However it was interesting to note that heavy bombing caused a number of casualties from wood splinters due to the destruction of trees. This side effect could obviously not be regarded as a justifiable reason for ordering bombing raids and, although bombing continued against suitable targets until the end of the campaign, the scale tended to reduce considerably after 1951 in favour of widespread strafing attacks. Whenever bombing attacks continued to be ordered, however, a great advantage lay with those aircraft which could remain over a target area for three hours or more, dropping bombs at irregular intervals and using a mixture of instantaneous and delayed action fuzes. These tactics created uncertainty among the terrorists and undoubtedly had a significant effect on morale. A further valuable effect was to deny certain areas to the scattered enemy and to drive terrorists towards ambush positions prepared by the Security Forces. Many confused and disorientated MRLA men were captured in this way. Immediate air strikes on receipt of a call for support from a patrol tended to be much more effective than pre-planned attacks. In many cases an air strike within an hour of a call could be arranged, often with excellent results.'

But it must be said that transport support in all its forms provided the most valuable contribution to the ground forces in the field. The medium range transport squadrons, Nos 48, 52 and 110 ably assisted by 38 RAAF and 41 RNZAF Squadrons, also reached a peak in their effort during 1951. Undoubtedly supply dropping was the most important of their roles and, by enabling the offensive to be carried to the enemy, helped to ensure his ultimate defeat. Without this support the enemy would have gone almost unmolested in areas deeper than five to ten miles from the jungle fringe. During this year the squadrons were dropping, either by parachute or by free fall techniques, up to half a million pounds of food, ammunition and other supplies each month, enabling patrols to remain in the jungle for periods up to three months and isolated police posts to survive without overland supplies almost indefinitely.

It was impossible to transport some of the heavier items by overland means but assault boats, marine engines, water pumps and even tractors and earth moving vehicles were broken down and dropped by the Dakotas and Valettas for assembly in the jungle camps and forts which were built to extend the activities of the Security Forces. Even armchairs, furniture and livestock were successfully parachuted in and one rat infested camp site had a consignment of cats delivered safely on the end of a parachute.

The Dakota/Valetta force was limited by the fact that there were only seventeen airfields in the Federation suitable for their use and this placed an increasing burden upon the Short Range Transport Force which, up to the end of 1951, mainly comprised the Austers of 656 AOP Squadron and the first few Dragonfly helicopters of the CAEF. Even these light and undemanding aircraft were greatly handicapped by the paucity of airstrips before helicopters began to arrive in significant numbers. In August 1951, for example, there were only 50 airstrips suitable for light aircraft in the whole of Malaya. As will be seen later, their numbers were to increase considerably as the Emergency dragged on and, with the advent of the helicopter, it was eventually possible to cover the whole of the Federation with short range transport aircraft.

So few, and at times hazardous, were the road links in the Federation that much of the movement of bodies of troops, mainly from Singapore to suitable up-country airfields, was accomplished by air. Until the end of 1951 there were not sufficient Army and Police forces to patrol all areas and the transport force played a vital role in moving troops rapidly to reinforce those under threat. Lateral communications were particularly poor and airlifts from Ipoh or Taiping to Kota Bharu or from Kuala Lumpur to Kuantan (see Map 6) were of the greatest value in reinforcing the remoter parts of Kelantan, Trengganu and Pahang. Quite apart from the speed with which troops could be moved by air, significant manpower was saved in providing heavily armed escorts for road convoys.

Except for the dropping of leaflets, psychological warfare did not make much progress in these early years. Leaflets had, however, been distributed from the air since the beginning and these operations also reached a peak in 1951 when more than 50 million leaflets were dropped, sometimes on terrorist locations but often to bolster the morale of the civilian population as some sort of antidote to intimidation. Almost every type of aircraft could be used for leaflet dropping: Dakotas and Austers were particularly suitable but bundles were frequently hurled from Spitfires and Vampires and could, with some ingenuity, be dropped from bomb racks. It was always worthwhile to spread a little propaganda and make full use of a sortie over areas likely to be influenced.

In the photographic reconnaissance field the work of 81 Squadron has already been mentioned. By 1951 its Mosquitos and Spitfires were beginning to show their age; indeed, the Spitfires were then restricted to within 150 miles of their Singapore base and the Mosquitos were becoming increasingly difficult to keep serviceable. Nevertheless, 1951 saw the squadron averaging more than 100 sorties per month, keeping up-to-date the large scale maps, so essential for the jungle patrols, photographing suspected enemy locations and passing a wealth of intelligence information to the Joint Operations Centre at Kuala Lumpur. No single squadron worked harder than 81 during this intensive period, or made a more valuable contribution to the operations.

The Situation Improves

By the beginning of 1952 the Briggs Plan had begun to pay dividends and a distant light could be dimly seen at the end of the tunnel which had seemed so black during the previous year. Nearly half a million Chinese squatters had been rehoused in newly constructed villages and the operations of the Security Forces were being effectively co-ordinated with food denial. A policy of deporting Chinese communists from Malaya was being implemented and elsewhere—notably in Korea and Indo-China—the communists were being held. All these events had a marked effect on public confidence which in turn led to a greatly increased flow of information. The rate of contact with terrorists rose to its peak for the whole Emergency.

At this point, in February 1952, General (later Field Marshal) Sir Gerald Templer became High Commissioner and also Director of Operations, and for the first time there was supreme and unified control, not only of the Emergency but of all Government activities. His dynamic leadership was immediately felt. The complacency which was still evident in some Government departments was swept away, priority was given to training and reorganising the Police Force which was suffering from an over-rapid expansion, and the intelligence and information services were improved.

MRLA policy became less aggressive as all these measures began to bite and their efforts were turned increasingly to subversion. Many of their units were withdrawn to build up deep jungle bases with their own cultivation. Aggressive incidents likely to alienate the public, such as attacks on the railways and damage to the people's means of livelihood, were avoided: the number of murders decreased and tended to be confined to those who were unpopular and could be represented as 'oppressors of the poor'. The average monthly Security Forces and civilian casualty rate fell away from nearly 200 in mid 1951 to under 30 a month by the end of 1952.

During 1953 the improvement in the situation enabled troops for the first time to be concentrated for offensive action in chosen areas without weakening security dangerously elsewhere. It was decided first to attack the MRLA where they were weakest, namely in Malacca, Pahang, Selangor and Negri Sembilan, so that Police and Home Guard could subsequently take over in those States, freeing the bulk of the Army to concentrate on the toughest terrorist targets in Perak and Johore (see Map 6). In consequence it was possible for Emergency regulations to be lifted later in the year from a large part of Malacca, which then became the first 'White' area (as the liberated territories were known). Progress was so good that, by the middle of 1954, 7,500 terrorists had been eliminated, and only some 3,500 remained in the jungle.

The Build-up of Air Striking Power

After the intensive operational activity of 1951, the steady improvement in the measures taken by the Security Forces and the perfection of new techniques permitted some reassessment of air support policy. The Air Staff in London had for some time been concerned at the air strike effort being expended in Malaya, and the AOC was exhorted to consider every means of achieving reductions. For a short period the attachment of Lincolns from Bomber Command was discontinued, partly because it was thought that heavy bombing was not gaining results commensurate with the effort expended, partly because the aircraft had many important commitments elsewhere, and partly because the wartime stocks of 1,000 lb bombs were fast running out.

During 1953, however, full scale combined operations were planned in the Federation in the hope of terminating the campaign quickly. This coincided with the comprehensive rearming of the FEAF fighter and light bomber squadrons which created considerable serviceability problems as explained in Chapter 10. In order to increase the available offensive air support, Air Ministry therefore agreed to resume the Lincoln detachments, and 83 Squadron was sent out at full strength to Tengah to supplement 1(RAAF) Lincoln squadron. Thereafter these detachments were maintained until the back of the Emergency was broken.

Although the strike force was thus greatly strengthened, a much more selective and economical policy for its use was now evolved based upon earlier experience. Potential targets submitted by the ground forces were more carefully categorized and full support was provided only if there was thought to be a reasonable chance of furthering the aims of the Security Forces with a high probability of terrorists being present in the target area. These more selective policies applied equally to the fighter, light bomber and Lincoln attacks, and in the event they were just as successful as before with greater economy of effort.

Much credit must be given to the Australian and RAF Lincolns during this intensive phase of operations. The serviceability rate of the Bomber Command Lincolns only twice fell below 75 per cent in spite of the difficult climatic conditions for working on aircraft in the open air. They were somewhat inhibited by the fact that, allowing for the long flights between their home bases and Singapore, they had little more than 75 to 100 hours of flying available to them during each detachment. Their range, endurance and bomb capacity gave them immense advantages. With full tanks (2,850 gallons), an endurance of eleven hours and a load of up to 14×1,000 lb bombs, they were able to mount formidable attacks on any target in the Federation by day or night. On rare occasions, and only with the personal authority of the High Commissioner, 4,000 lb bombs were dropped by Lincolns. Their blast effect was not, however, proportional to their size and they also tended to have an unfortunate political connotation. The 1,000 lb HE bomb, nose fuzed, with a 'mean area of effectiveness' of 75,000 square feet proved to be the best weapon for both medium and light bombers.

When not occupied with the Korean Campaign, the Sunderlands proved their value as a limited addition to the strike aircraft, having extremely concentrated fire power and the ability to carry no less than 360×20 lb anti-personnel bombs. When sustained harassing attacks were more important than extreme accuracy, the elderly flying boat came into its own.

Apart from these conventional explosive weapons, various other devices were used experimentally at the instance of the Operational Research Section of AHQ Malaya. Napalm or jellified petroleum in 200 lb canisters was tried out but proved relatively ineffective in the green jungle. Depth charges were used with the same results but smoke bombs had some success when limited force only was required, for example to persuade reluctant aborigines to move to a new resettlement area. One successful device was a toxic spray used against cultivation, upon which the terrorists depended in their deep jungle camps. Finally, when the cost of weapon expenditure soared alarmingly in 1954, 'screamers', often made from empty beer bottles, were occasionally used during continuous harassing operations and, when interspersed with lethal bombardments, their alarming noise proved quite effective in inducing surrenders.

Control and Technique of Air Strikes

The first prerequisite of all successful air strike action was reliable intelligence information, without which neither ground nor aerial reconnaissance was likely to locate possible targets without detection. Reports from all branches of the Security Forces about terrorist locations were carefully graded but actual knowledge of enemy camps and concentrations came invariably from informers—usually captured or surrendered terrorists. Unfortunately, owing to the low mentality of these informers, and their inability to read maps or assess distances accurately, much of the target information was unreliable resulting in aircraft often being despatched on abortive missions. This problem was exacerbated by a natural inclination of the planning staffs to overgrade information in their enthusiasm to prosecute the campaign. Any attempt to verify information by investigation usually resulted in the terrorists being forewarned of an impending air attack and rapidly dispersing.

As the campaign developed it was recognised that opportunities for immediate air attack were extremely rare and increasingly such attacks were confined to carefully co-ordinated large scale combined operations. Whereas strikes had originally been arranged on an ad hoc basis by personal agreement between Army and RAF commanders, all were now ordered through the combined Land/Air Operations Room at GHQ Malaya District, Kuala Lumpur, which became the nucleus of the Joint Operations Centre (JOC), which expanded into its final form by 1954. This may seem an obvious development but it must be remembered that, in the early years, incidents were so numerous, so widespread and so fleeting that the temptation to deal with every one immediately it occurred was understandable, and some time elapsed before it was realised that this rapid reaction was proving wasteful of the valuable strike resources.

The second prerequisite of a successful air strike, after reliable intelligence information, was an accurate method of pinpointing the target in country where map reading by the ground forces was difficult and where an error of 100 yards in the aiming point could nullify the effect of an air strike. Aerial photographs played an important role here as, even with all the survey work by 81 Squadron, maps were rarely up-to-date in the detail needed. As pilots became experienced in flying over the jungle they acquired a remarkable knowledge of the terrain and could navigate by the light patches in the ground cover associated with areas of dead vegetation often caused by previous bomb explosions. However, it was rarely possible to make a single first time approach to a target and the need to circle for positive identification usually provided sufficient warning for terrorists to take cover, and thus avoid the worst effects of the attack.

Many developments in marking techniques were tried, namely, flying on a fixed bearing for a specific time from a known datum point, and using low flying Austers to mark a target with phosphorus grenades, smoke or flares. The latter technique was successful provided that the strike aircraft could follow the Auster so closely that terrorists had no time to take cover. A gap of a mere $1\frac{1}{2}$ minutes was often long enough for this to occur. Perhaps the most successful method devised was the positioning of ground markers at a known distance and bearing from the target, allowing the strike aircraft to make timed runs from the datum. Delayed action flares, allowing the ground party which positioned them to escape a possible ambush, were used in daylight, and searchlights trained vertically were effective for night raids. Small radio transmitters tuned to give a continuous signal on a specific frequency for 24 hours were also satisfactory as markers in some circumstances, but the variety of techniques adopted shows how difficult it was to locate and attack the type of target offered with any degree of accuracy.

Except in the rare instances where a pinpoint target was clearly visible, these difficulties in target identification and marking resulted in the general but obviously wasteful practice of laying down the largest possible bomb pattern in order to cover expected errors in target location. Not only was a broad bomb pattern necessary, but strikes by more than one aircraft needed to be highly concentrated to prevent terrorists dispersing before the later aircraft arrived. In this latter respect, intensive training by 1(RAAF) Squadron enabled it to operate up to five Lincolns in Vic formation on moonlit nights, and three aircraft on dark nights, and to lay down an exceptionally heavy, widespread and simultaneous pattern of 1,000 lb bombs.

1954 saw some of the heaviest bombing of the whole campaign, an average of about 25 attacks per month being undertaken. During this year a new technique was devised using Hornets to support a main attack by Lincolns. During operation ECLIPSE in July of that year, Lincolns attacked the main targets while Austers marked pinpoint targets nearby which were simultaneously attacked by Hornets with bombs, rockets and cannon. This operation took place in Kedah (see Map 6) and, after a continuous assault over a period of three days, it was subsequently found that thirteen terrorists had been killed, one had surrendered and 181 camps destroyed. But, once again, the relatively small enemy casualty rate in relation to the effort expended revealed the immense problems facing the Security Forces in eliminating the elusive enemy. Nevertheless persistent harrassment on this scale was the only solution and by the end of 1954, a year in which

426 air strikes had been mounted, definite signs that the MRLA were losing the battle began to be evident.

As air strike operations mounted to a peak in 1953–54 with the increasing number of well planned and co-ordinated combined operations, the ground forces penetrated ever more deeply into the jungle to comb out the terrorists disturbed by the heavy air attacks. This in turn put a steadily increasing load upon the transport squadrons to move the troops and keep them supplied in their outposts.

Air Supply

The dropping of supplies by parachute or by free fall continued to be the most effective method of supporting the troops and, as with the air striking force, the main problem faced by the crews of the medium range transport squadrons was that of locating and identifying dropping zones in featureless primary jungle. Responsibility for selecting the zones lay with the ground patrol commanders and, although an attempt was always made to find some clearing or a patch of clearable secondary jungle, these seldom met the minimum desirable qualifications of size and visibility from the air. Most of the DZs were mere holes in the jungle canopy, perhaps ten yards in radius, often necessitating a supply drop with no visual contact between the aircraft and the patrol on the ground.

As soon as the approaching aircraft was heard a smoke grenade was fired to identify the DZ, and coloured smoke signals and panels were used to provide an aiming point during the run up. Fortunately radio communication between air and ground was normally good and the pilot would await confirmation that the packs were recoverable before leaving the area. Once over the DZ, however, there was little margin for error as most were located amidst trees 200 feet high, often on the lee side of a hill or surrounded by swamp. It was generally extremely difficult to recover supplies that missed the aiming point by anything more than 50 yards.

Four or five separate drops were usually carried out during the course of one two and a half hour Dakota or Valetta sortie and the strain on the aircrews was considerable. Flying at less than 300 feet in intense heat, turbulent conditions and often in bad weather, it is not surprising that the aircrew frequently lost as much as three pounds in body weight during a single mission. What is truly remarkable is that less than one and a half per cent of all supplies dropped during the entire campaign were lost—surely a great tribute to the accuracy and airmanship of the squadrons. The casualty rate among supply dropping aircrew from all causes was, however, high and has been placed at four times the casualty rate of the infantry they were supporting.

By 1955 the number of troops deployed in the jungle had reached its maximum, placing a heavy burden on the squadrons. But welcome reinforcements arrived at that time in the form of Bristol Freighters for 41 (RNZAF) Squadron and the addition of extra RASC Air Despatch personnel to load the aircraft and despatch the supplies in the air. Mere figures are not of great interest, but it should be mentioned that the greatest weight of supplies dropped was reached in March 1955, when 808,035 lbs were dropped in 218 sorties during that one month, more than had been dropped during the entire first year of the campaign.

Paratrooping

The dropping of parachutists was a hazardous operation in Malaya but was nevertheless used on occasions when it was necessary to position small bodies of troops in terrorist-held areas without giving warning of their approach. The greatest danger to the paratroops was, of course, that of landing in the tops of the trees up to 200 feet above ground and initial experiments were tried with a knotted rope carried in each man's pack of sufficient length to enable him to reach the ground. These were a failure owing to the fatigue which resulted and a special abseil gear was evolved by the RAF Parachute Training School at Changi. It consisted of 200 feet of webbing carried in a bag attached to a special harness. This, with subsequent refinement, was reasonably satisfactory and, although there were casualties, they were little more than those normally suffered when dropping in open country.

Most of the dropping fell to the highly experienced men of 22 Special Air Service Regiment (SAS) and some of their operations in Northern Malaya, close to the borders of Thailand, were most successful. They did, however, place an immense responsibility upon the transport aircrews as the slightest error over a DZ could put the parachutist straight into the treetops. On one occasion, in Northern Perak, with a strong wind funnelling down a valley and exceptionally difficult flying conditions, 44 out of 48 paratroops fell into 150 foot trees, fortunately with few casualties, and they were able to concentrate for their attack on a terrorist target without undue delay.

Few opportunities occurred for major operations of this kind after 1954 as the expanding helicopter force in Malaya proved capable of introducing a greater number of less specialised troops into the jungle more quickly and with less risk of personal injury.

The Work of the Short Range Transport Force

As there were never more than 17 airfields in the Federation usable by the Dakotas, Valettas and Bristol Freighters, most of these being located in the populous coastal regions, the light aircraft and helicopters of the short range squadrons had to provide all the services between the main airfields and the many airstrips which were developed wherever sufficient space could be found or cleared. Some 68 of these airstrips were constructed, covering between them the whole of Malaya; while a few were suitable only for the Single Pioneer the remainder were safe for Austers and Beavers and, of course, all could be used by helicopters.

It is to 656 AOP Squadron that credit must go for being the only light aircraft unit to operate throughout the Emergency. This squadron rarely if ever operated as an entity and spent most of its life split into four Flights scattered throughout the country wherever their presence was most needed. For most of the campaign the squadron contained no less than 26 Austers which made it numerically by far the largest squadron in FEAF. In view of the varied tasks, its designation was changed to that of 656 (Light Aircraft) Squadron, Army Air Corps, but it continued to rely upon the RAF for technical assistance. Mention has already been made of the AOP tasks carried out by these small aircraft in marking targets for the strike and transport forces and in making low level visual reconnaissance to update photographs and generally to ensure that air attacks were not laid on fruitlessly. They were also constantly in use for communications flights, leaflet dropping, and casualty evacuation before the helicopters arrived to assume that role. During 1953 and 1954, 656 Squadron flew nearly 1,000 sorties per month, and it has been truly said that the Austers of 656 Squadron were the most versatile of all the aircraft that were deployed in the Malayan campaign.

Valuable though the Auster was it suffered from the severe limitation of being unable to carry more than one person in addition to the pilot with reasonable safety over the type of terrain encountered in

Malaya. If military commanders wished to be accompanied by one or more of their staff on visits to operational areas, a separate Auster had to be provided for each member of the party. Such demands were uneconomical and placed a great strain on the resources of 656 Squadron since its constituent Flights were located in widely separated areas, making rapid reinforcement impracticable.

The choice of an additional aircraft with characteristics similar to those of the Auster but with a greater carrying capacity fell upon the Prestwick Pioneer. This could carry up to four passengers and 600 to 800 lbs of freight in addition to the pilot, and yet was capable of operating from nearly all the improvised airstrips in the Federation. In fact the take off and landing performance of the Pioneer was somewhat better than that of the Auster and its introduction in 1953 effected considerable economies not only in maintaining communications between airstrips but also as an alternative to Dakotas or Valettas if the latter were required to operate well below their normal carrying capacity between the main airfields.

The first three Pioneers were placed in 1311 Transport Flight of 303 Helicopter Wing at Seletar. Two more arrived at the end of 1954 but production and build up of these Scottish Aviation aircraft were slow and it was a further year or two before a full squadron, designated 267 Squadron, was available. Their most important task was the routine supply and maintenance of the garrisons of a number of police forts which were established in the deep jungle and swamp of Central Malaya, mainly in South Pahang and North Johore from 1953 onwards. These forts served as strategic centres from which the indigenous aboriginal population of the areas, on whom the terrorists relied for support and security, could be controlled and protected, and from where offensive patrols could be mounted. Nine of these forts were originally constructed and, as few were accessible by ground communications, the advent of the Pioneer removed the need to maintain them by supply drop with its attendant hazards, or by helicopters which had to be reserved for situations in which fixed wing aircraft could not operate.

Although the serviceability record of 267 Squadron's Pioneers was generally good, it was not long before they began to show signs of wear as it had never been envisaged, when calculating their life, that the intensity of their operations would demand over 1,000 landings in arduous conditions by each aircraft every year.

Only occasional mention has so far been made of the work of the helicopter element of the Short Range Transport Force because, during the years 1952 to 1954, it was in process of introduction and expansion. During the middle and later years of the Emergency, helicopters were to play a most significant part in jungle operations of all kinds and the techniques of their operations will be dealt with fully in the next chapter.

Psychological Warfare

The main aims of the 'war of words' that was inaugurated during the campaign were to induce surrenders among the terrorists, by breaking their morale and causing disaffection within their ranks, and to win the battle for the minds and loyalties of the uncommitted populace in the face of the propaganda offensive that was launched by the communists. The local populace was indoctrinated largely through the media of the press, radio, films and itinerant information teams. Some of this material undoubtedly filtered through to the terrorists, but more direct methods were needed to reach those in the deepest jungle hideouts.

The air forces provided one of the main agencies for the delivery of both tactical and strategic messages devised by the Psychological Warfare Department. Often the dropping of leaflets and the broadcast of messages in the deepest jungle could be carried out only by aircraft. Broadcasting recorded messages from aircraft, often called 'sky shouting', was introduced by General Templer in October 1952, when he borrowed a US Army Dakota for experimental purposes. These experiments were sufficiently successful for two FEAF Valettas to be fitted with broadcasting equipment and begin a programme of 'sky shouting' early in 1953. However, the engine noise of the Valetta proved too intrusive and they were replaced by the now obsolete Dakota the following year. With quieter engines the quality of the broadcasting improved considerably, and the slower cruising speed of the Dakota also proved beneficial. In addition, two Austers were fitted up for use as more economical 'sky shouters' over small targets, on the fringes of the jungle and over roads, so that eventually the Voice Flight of 267 Squadron possessed three Dakotas and two Austers. It was calculated that, in good conditions and flying at 2,500 to 3,000 feet over a target area, a broadcast message could be heard up to 2,500 yards below and to the port side of the aircraft. These figures refer to a Dakota: the range from an Auster was somewhat less—of the order of 1,500 yards.

'Sky shouting' was closely co-ordinated with leaflet dropping, both being essential parts of the psychological warfare campaign which reached its peak during 1954 and 1955 when it was felt that the operational successes of the Security Forces were having a marked effect on MRLA morale. As mentioned earlier, every type of aircraft was used for dropping leaflets, usually combined with a main task such as a supply drop, and occasionally with an air strike. The highest monthly total of leaflets dropped during 1954 occurred in November when 7,220,000 were released during 30 supply drops.

In any battle for the minds and loyalties of men, it is not to be expected that quick or spectacular results will be forthcoming, and it was not until the number of terrorist surrenders reached the proportion of a major defeat from 1955 onwards that the full effects of the long and patient psychological offensive could be appreciated. The statement of one surrendered terrorist serves to summarise the effectiveness of this campaign.

"After the attack on our cultivation area we fled to another area where we saw many Government propaganda leaflets and safe conduct passes. I picked up some of the leaflets intending to use them when coming out to surrender. A few days later we heard voices coming from an aeroplane calling on us all to surrender and offering good treatment. We all agreed to this suggestion".

Reconnaissance

Much has already been said about the strategic photographic reconnaissance and survey work of the Mosquitos and Spitfires of 81 Squadron and the tactical, largely visual reconnaissance by the Austers of 656 Squadron. This did not, however, complete the reconnaissance effort, and mention must be made of the work of the Sunderlands flying from Seletar. Patrolling of the coastal waters of Malaya by these flying boats constituted a routine but important commitment.

The islands off the east coast had always been one of the routes by which seaborne illegal entrants had come and from the start of the Emergency it was felt that the dangers of such immigration and the smuggling of arms and equipment by sea had greatly increased. Illegal immigrants started from anywhere on the China coast and crossed the Gulf of Siam in small craft. Reaching the islands off the east coast of Malaya in daylight, they waited until they could slip across to the mainland under the cover of darkness. It was quite impossible for the Royal Navy alone to keep watch on all these islands from Kota Bharu in the north to the southern tip of Johore. On the other hand, aircraft were of little use by themselves as there was nothing they could do even if they did sight a suspicous vessel.

Consequently combined patrols, using one sloop or destroyer and one aircraft, were carried out in selected areas according to a pre-arranged plan based on available intelligence. There were two types of patrol—the 'Blue Water' patrol up to 80 miles out to sea and covering 100 miles of coastline in order to intercept craft attempting to run direct for the shore, and the 'Coastal and Island' patrol to investigate inlets and anchorages among the islands. Sunderlands, with their long endurance, slow speed and good radio facilities were particularly valuable and successful in this work and undertook the major part of it. By 1953 these patrols had become so efficient that few attempts were subsequently made to smuggle shipments of arms to the MRLA and it became possible to reduce their frequency to no more than one or two per week.

It has been said that aerial reconnaissance certainly made a signifi-cant contribution to the successful outcome of the campaign. No accurate figures are available of the number of terrorists who were killed or captured, or who surrendered during the operations in which reconnaissance was an important element, but there is no doubt that a major proportion of the total number of terrorist eliminations achieved by the Security Forces was attributable to it in some way. By 1954 it was becoming extremely difficult for MRLA camps to avoid detection by one form of reconnaissance or another and terrorist movements very rarely went unobserved.

In Sight of Success

This chapter has taken the narrative of the Malayan Emergency to the middle of 1954, an appropriate point at which to pause because 1954 was the year in which the dim light originally perceived at the end of a long tunnel brightened to a degree which showed that the journey though the tunnel was coming to an end. The Director of Operations said in his report in July 1954, "the threat of armed revolution is now broken".

In that month it was no longer considered necessary to continue to combine the functions of the Head of State and Director of Operations. A new High Commissioner, Sir Donald MacGillivray, was appointed and the post of Director of Operations was combined with that of the General Officer Commanding, Malaya Command. The task of eliminating the remaining terrorist gangs and disrupting their organisation continued, but an increasing measure of control passed to Malayan political leaders in preparation for independence.

Although several more years of jungle operations lay ahead, the Security Forces were clearly on top. The diminishing number of terrorists were being driven ever deeper into the jungle by the carefully co-ordinated ground and air attacks, and more and more terrorists were giving themselves up in response to the widely publicised amnesty terms. Their support from the local populace was dwindling as more and more resettled in safe areas with police protection. It was possible to declare more 'White Areas', notably in the south of the Federation as the remaining terrorists tended to seek refuge in northern areas close to, and even across, the frontier of Thailand.

12

Final Phase of the Malayan Emergency

During 1955 the first Federal elections were held throughout Malaya as an early stage in the transition from Colonial rule to independence. This step effectively deprived the terrorists of their strongest propaganda line and led the MCP leaders to attempt to negotiate a peace settlement. The Alliance Party in the Federation refused to negotiate but, appreciating that the MRLA were rapidly losing the military battle, declared an amnesty on 9 November 1955, and invited the Secretary-General of the MCP, one Chin Peng, to attend a meeting and hear the surrender terms.

After a short hiatus owing to the MRLA taking advantage of the temporary cease fire to commit further atrocities, the meeting took place at the end of December. It was totally abortive as Chin Peng made unacceptable demands for the return of all surrendered terrorists and formal recognition of the Malayan Communist Party. As these demands amounted to a licence for the MCP to continue to pursue their subversive aims unopposed, the Chief Minister of the Federation rejected them without further discussion, leaving Chin Peng to retire into the jungle declaring that the terrorists would continue to fight to the last man. It was evident from this episode that the Emergency was bound to drag on for a long time while the laborious task of mopping up the widespread pockets of resistance took place.

The only hope of the Communist Party now lay in leaving the jungle under some form of guarantee that it would be allowed to remain in existence, and to this end its members launched a 'peace offensive' early in 1956 in an attempt to lay the blame for the continuing Emergency on the Federal Government. There was some sympathy for this appeal amongst the Chinese element of the population and the Government was compelled to step up its counter-propaganda in order to persuade the civilian community of the need to maintain pressure on the terrorists. Civilian support was essential if the terrorists were to

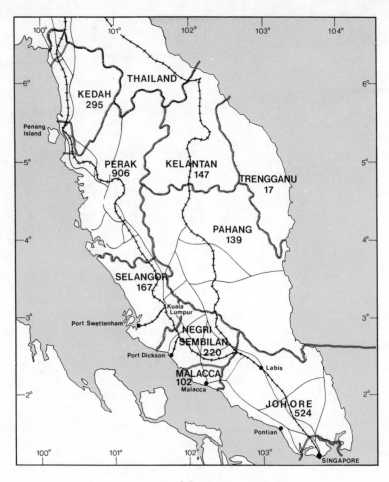

Map 7
Distribution of Communist Terrorists
throughout Malaya — 1956

be prevented from reorganising and rebuilding their strength and continuing as a malignant cancer in the body of the country.

By now most of the waverers amongst the terrorists had been eliminated and those that remained were well disciplined and virtually immune to propaganda appeals. Inspired by Mao-Tse-Tung's 20 years wait for power in China they were determined to avoid contact with the Security Forces and to sit it out in the jungle until external communist aid or some other opportunity presented itself. The number of active terrorists was estimated to be about 2,500 but, as will be seen from Map 7, they were widespread and present in every State in the Federation to some degree, although the concentration was greatest in Johore and Perak with an unknown number across the border of Thailand.

Command and Control

Concentration of operations against the weakened MRLA forces in Central Malaya necessitated some change in the command and control of the air forces involved. AHQ Malaya had, for some years, been split into a Rear HQ at Changi and an Advanced HQ at Kuala Lumpur. It was now decided to move the Rear HQ up to Kuala Lumpur and position it on the airfield. This did not, however, immediately join up with its Advanced HQ as the planning for joint operations required a Joint Operations Centre at the Army Headquarters in the town, and this necessitated the Air Staff of AHQ Malaya remaining with the Army HQ. As the offensive support tasks of the RAF in the campaign gradually decreased the Joint Operations Centre was moved to the airfield permitting the two parts of AHQ Malaya to amalgamate once more. The wheel had turned full circle and by April 1957 the AHQ was once again established in the location which it had left eleven years earlier.

This situation was, however, short lived. On 31 August 1957, Malaya gained its independence and the conduct of operations and the maintenance of law and order became the exclusive responsibility of the Governments of Malaya and Singapore. At their request, the Governments of the United Kingdom, Australia and New Zealand agreed to give such assistance as was practicable during the final phase of the Emergency. Thus the C-in-C FEAF and the AOC Malaya took their operational directions relating to anti-terrorist operations from the Federation's own Director of Emergency Operations.

With independence firmly established it became politically embarrassing for the AOC Malaya to retain that particular title and it was decided that his command should revert to an old designation—that of HQ 224 Group. This was highly appropriate since 224 Group had originally been formed in Singapore in 1941 and, on the capitulation of Japan, had taken part in the liberation of Malaya and Singapore and received the surrender of the Japanese at Kuala Lumpur. Furthermore, the AOC at that time had been Air Vice-Marshal The Earl of Bandon who was now back in Singapore as the C-in-C FEAF.

Kuala Lumpur eventually became the last RAF station in Malaya and it was finally handed over to the newly formed Royal Malayan Air Force (RMAF) on 1 April 1959, whereupon HQ 224 Group moved back to Singapore to concentrate upon the primary tasks of the RAF in the Far East. Subject to a number of minor internal changes, this was the command organisation to the end of the Emergency.

Offensive Air Support Operations

After the intensive and widespread combined operations of 1954 and 1955, in which the strike squadrons had played a major part, it was not surprising that the targets offered by the greatly reduced and widely scattered terrorist gangs in subsequent years were few and even more difficult to locate than before. Offensive air support was reduced to a minimum, enabling the squadrons not only to conserve weapons but also to concentrate on training for their primary roles which had been sadly neglected while the Emergency was at its height. 1956, it must be remembered, was the year of the Suez crisis and Bomber Command detachments to Malaya were reduced as the attention of the RAF at home became focussed on the Middle East.

Strict selection and careful categorization of targets submitted by the ground forces was exercised and full air support was provided only if there was a reasonable chance of furthering their aims and a high probability that terrorists were present. This reduction of effort continued through 1957 and into 1958 when Sunderlands were employed for the last time. No 205/209 Squadron was then rearmed with the Shackleton, after which it concentrated solely on maritime reconnaissance and rescue. Also in 1958 the medium bomber commitment ceased with the return of 1(RAAF) Squadron, equipped with Lincolns, to Australia. It had made a great contribution to FIREDOG operations for almost eight years and its departure from Tengah was viewed with much regret.

Many more changes took place in the order of battle because 1958 also saw the formation in Malaya of a Commonwealth Strategic Reserve which contained, inter alia, two RAAF Canberra squadrons. The RAAF element of this force was concentrated at Butterworth which then became a Royal Australian Air Force station. Its squadrons remained available for FIREDOG operations but the reduced tempo required little effort from them. However, their presence in Northern Malaya ensured that a rapid response could always be guaranteed should the need arise. The Australian takeover at Butterworth freed 45 Squadron to move down to Tengah where it relinquished its Venoms in favour of the Canberra B2.

For the next year very few air strikes were required and squadrons were gradually released from the commitment. No 60 Squadron which had started the Emergency with its Spitfires in 1948 and participated throughout, rearming successively with Vampires and Venoms, was the last to be released when it changed its role to that of a night fighter squadron equipped with the Meteor NF14. By that time the offensive support role of the air forces had ended.

A particular feature of the later years of the campaign was the superiority in this particular type of operation of the piston-engined aircraft over the jets which superseded them. The Lincoln, with its long endurance, huge bomb load, night capability and relatively slow speed, could 'loiter' in a target area for hours, dropping bombs at irregular intervals in a harassing type of attack. Its replacement, the Canberra, on the other hand, possessed relatively short endurance, particularly if flown at low altitudes, and could not maintain a lengthy presence in a target area. Furthermore, until Godfrey cockpit coolers were fitted, the intense heat and humidity affected Canberra aicrcrews seriously. The same problems existed for the smaller strike aircraft; Vampires and Venoms were at a disadvantage compared with their predecessors, Tempests, Hornets and Brigands. In addition to their operational shortcomings, most of the jet replacements created greater maintenance problems with consequential reductions in serviceability.

Air Transport Operations

If the intensity of offensive air support fell away during the last few years of the Emergency, this was certainly not the case with the support given by the transport squadrons. During 1956 and 1957 the amount of freight carried by the Valettas of the Medium Transport Force increased to nearly three times that which had been carried during the previous two years, but the number of passengers declined as the areas freed from Emergency restrictions expanded and troops were concentrated in the north and south of the Federation to mop up the remaining pockets of resistance. Communications flights between the major airfields were similarly reduced, which was fortunate as Valetta serviceability began to give some cause for concern. Although a good aircraft in most respects it lacked the rugged simplicity of its predecessor, the Dakota, and required many more hours of maintenance in the harsh Malayan climate and operating conditions. One could not visualise a Valetta surviving after being accidentally double loaded as had happened with more than one Dakota as already mentioned.

Nevertheless the squadrons, based at Changi and detached in rotation to Kuala Lumpur, fulfilled their air supply, paratrooping and communications tasks to the end. The gradual withdrawal of troops from the last operational areas in 1960 necessitated a large number of special trooping flights which brought the total of passengers and equipment carried during the last year of the campaign to double that of 1956 when the operations had been at their height.

Similarly the Austers, Pioneers and latterly Pembrokes of the Short Range Transport Force were fully occupied during the final years and, had it not been for a considerable build up of the helicopter force, of which more anon, they would have been hard pressed to serve the jungle patrols, police forts and the mass of airstrips which had sprung up throughout the operational areas. Their task was facilitated by the expansion of the Royal Malayan Air Force. This small force was gradually equipped with twin-engined Pioneers, permitting some of the light freight and passenger sorties to be handed over to them. In July 1959, as an example, Pioneers of the RMAF transported 15,372 lbs of freight and 122 passengers. During the final twelve months more Pioneers, both single and twin-engined, were allotted to the force, so that by the end of the Emergency the RMAF was sharing the light transport tasks almost equally with the RAF Pioneer squadron.

The Significance of the Helicopter

The part played by helicopters throughout the Emergency has been touched upon in this narrative, but so important was their role that they deserve a special section devoted entirely to their development and operational techniques. Shortage of space precludes more than a summary of the work they carried out from 1950 to the end of the campaign. This summary is largely based upon the great experience and knowledge of Wing Commander J R Dowling MBE DFC AFC, who was one of the first helicopter pilots to operate in Malaya.

The requirement to use helicopters operationally originated in the Far East, and the rapid development of successive types and their introduction into RAF service can be credited to the Malayan Emergency and, in particular, the need to evacuate casualties rapidly from deep jungle locations. After a great deal of controversy between various Government departments in London and HQ FEAF in Singapore it was decided to form the Casualty Air Evacuation Flight at Changi, with three Dragonflys, in May 1950. The performance of the Dragonfly in tropical conditions was quite unknown and, furthermore, there seemed to be some failure in the Ministry of Supply to appreciate that Malaya had a tropical and extremely humid climate. Nevertheless the unit was formed with several pilots whose helicopter experience was rudimentary and who had to assimilate the tricky flying of the Dragonfly 'on the job'. It was a resounding success and the CAEF operated for 20 months before losing one of its helicopters— a casualty of the 'not so neutral jungle'. The fillip to the morale of troops, whose great fear was to be injured in some isolated and inaccessible clearing, was immense and a great economy as men no longer had to be diverted from a patrol to accompany an injured comrade to safety.

Austers of 656 Squadron played an important role in ensuring the success of these early Dragonfly operations. They could accompany a helicopter, guide it to a suitable pick up point and provide the essential communications between air and ground. Without their help and the expert local knowledge of their Army pilots, the casualty evacuation sorties would have been extremely hazardous if not impossible in the majority of cases. It must also be mentioned that the Dragonfly had no instrument flying capability, could not fly at night and had to avoid flying in heavy rain because of the risk of damage to its wooden ribbed, fabric covered rotor blades. There were many other severe limitations but these few aircraft established the need for helicopters and proved to be the forerunners of a most valuable force.

Initially patients could only be carried externally in a stretcher pannier, with perspex panels at the head, which gave the injured man a terrifying view of the whirling rotor hub. He was exposed to a great deal of vibration and, in all respects, it was an unnerving experience. It was, however, a life saver and that was all important. Eventually the engineering staff was able to design an internal fitting without modifying the Dragonfly and patients were then protected at least from the worst of the discomfort.

The success of these initial casualty flights persuaded the authorities to expand the CAEF with the result that during 1953 several more Dragonflys were shipped out to Singapore and the Flight was upgraded to become 194 (Helicopter) Squadron. More trained pilots arrived and it was then possible to maintain a detachment at Kuala Lumpur which greatly facilitated the work of these very short range aircraft. Unhappily, January of this year brought the first fatality when a rotor blade fractured at the hub with the Dragonfly at 3,000 feet. It fell to the ground, disintegrating on the way, and the pilot, a senior policeman and an Army officer were killed.

When 194 Squadron was formed, the CAEF had been in existence for two years and four months, had evacuated 265 casualties and had pioneered operational helicopter techniques in support of ground forces under most difficult conditions with grossly underpowered aircraft, but with only one major accident due to an error by an inexperienced pilot. It could truly be said that the foundations for future helicopter operations had been well laid.

As 194 Squadron slowly built up to its full establishment of 12 Dragonflys, reinforcement came in the form of 848 Squadron (Royal Navy) on 8 January 1953. This unit was equipped with ten American built S-55s and, with 194 Squadron, formed 303 Wing at Sembawang in Singapore. The S-55 could carry five fully armed troops into and out of large clearings and four where the clearing was of Dragonfly standard. For casualty evacuation three stretcher cases and two walking patients could be loaded which gave the small force a sudden and most welcome increase in capability. Perhaps the most important development stemming from 848 Squadron's arrival was the ability to handle the tactical movement of troops in respectable numbers which had not previously been practicable. It became essential to be able to deplane troops from a hovering position to avoid dependence upon a firm clearing in the jungle. True to naval tradition, 848 Squadron experimented with scrambling nets but these became caught up in the many protuberances on a fully equipped soldier, often resulting in the most appalling entanglements at the most crucial moments. After a few fruitless experiments with the nets, the alternative of providing a knotted rope became standard practice for descents from the hover.

The next generation of helicopters to reach FEAF comprised the Sycamore and the Whirlwind, the latter being a British adaptation of the American S-55 in service with the Royal Navy. The Sycamore was subjected to lengthy trials in Malaya and initially had considerable trouble with cracking and swelling of the wooden members of the rotor blades due to the climatic conditions. However, these troubles were overcome after some delay and when it eventually superseded the Dragonfly in 194 Squadron it was greeted with enthusiasm because of its greater cabin size and better performance, its positive handling characteristics, larger control margins and, in particular, its excellent serviceability rate. If it had a drawback, it was the low height of the rotor blades which made it dangerous for inexperienced passengers to leave the cabin while the blades were in motion, and also disadvantageous in jungle clearings with tall scrub and bushes. Sensible precautions by the pilot could, however, minimize this shortcoming and, when 194 Squadron received its full complement in July 1956, it proved to be an excellent replacement for the Dragonfly.

On the other hand, early versions of the Whirlwind, which had been eagerly awaited as it was regarded as the first real troop carrying helicopter, were disappointing. Although it had a spacious cabin for ten passengers, its early performance in Malaya was so poor that it could often carry no more than two. Here was another example of grave underestimation of the effects on aircraft performance of the Malayan conditions. The Whirlwind Mark 2 was five per cent heavier than its American predecessor, the S-55—a small increase it may be thought, but quite enough to reduce its comparable performance drastically. There was great pressure to introduce the Whirlwind because the S-55s of 848 Squadron, which had given sterling operational service, were fast approaching the end of their useful lives, and were heavily dependent upon a dwindling stock of American spares.

A Mark 4 version of the Whirlwind had a somewhat better performance but still remained far from satisfactory even after efforts had been made to reduce its weight by the removal of various items of equipment for specific operations. A new squadron—No 155— was formed around the Whirlwind force and this reached its full strength with Mark 4 aircraft by late 1955. This allowed 848 Squadron, which had been held in Malaya far beyond its original commitment of one year, to be released to return to its NATO role although its S-55s were in poor shape after four years of sustained and most valuable support to the ground forces.

In spite of all the technical troubles which afflicted 155 and 194 Squadrons, the multifarious tasks of the small helicopter force were met satisfactorily. It was fortunate that the demand for this type of support began to fall away in 1957 as the situation improved—a decline which coincided with the increasing technical problems of the Whirlwind.

As the Emergency approached its conclusion it was decided that the Far East helicopter force could be reduced to meet demands elsewhere, notably in the Middle East. The Sycamore had now achieved an excellent reputation and its capability was little less than that of the Whirlwind. FEAF recommended that, when Kuala Lumpur was handed over to the RMAF towards the end of 1959, the whole of the remaining helicopter commitment could be achieved by one squadron of 12 Sycamores operating from Butterworth. Unhappily before this reorganisation could be carried out the second of two fatal Sycamore crashes occurred, caused by the main rotor blades disintegrating. The whole force had to be grounded and some Whirlwinds had of necessity to be retained in the Command. Nos 194 and 155 Squadrons were disbanded at Kuala Lumpur in June 1959 and together re-formed as 110 Squadron with five Whirlwinds at Butterworth.

By this time anti-terrorist operations were virtually confined to the Thai border and 110 Squadron carried on with troop lifting and casualty evacuation in that area until the end of the campaign. Butterworth, beside the sea, was a much more congenial location for the squadron than the humid claustrophobic atmosphere of Kuala Lumpur and the flat open paddy fields were a welcome relief, after the sinister jungle. Most of the families lived across the water on Penang Island and the squadron was able to enjoy a period of relative peace after years of hazardous operations.

It would be all too easy to criticise the policy which resulted in helicopters being sent out to Malaya without adequate testing and development under the conditions in which they were required to operate. It must always be remembered, however, that the pressure to use this type of aircraft, which was very much in its infancy, was immense and difficult to resist when it was known that the effect on the morale of the troops in the jungle would be immensely heightened by the assurance that there was a means of evacuating them if they were injured. The risk of technical difficulties was, therefore, accepted and there can be no doubt that the early introduction of helicopters into the campaign not only facilitated its progress to a successful conclusion but also gave an impetus to helicopter development which was later to pay great dividends. Without them the Emergency would probably have been prolonged and would certainly have resulted in many more casualties among the Security Forces.

The End of the Emergency

There was no sudden end to the Emergency comparable, for example, to the war against Japan in 1945. It would be true to say that it petered out and its conclusion can only be identified by the lifting of the Emergency regulations on 31 July 1960. The MRLA never surrendered. As the campaign officially ended, there remained about 500 terrorists who had withdrawn to the relative sanctuary of the Betong salient, strategically situated just outside Malay territory between Kedah and Northern Perak. Here, under their leader Chin Peng, they were to be kept together as a continuing threat to the security of Malaya, to await the day when political and racial difficulties, fostered by subversion, would create conditions under which the armed conflict could be renewed. As it was clear to the Federal authorities that this residual threat could not be overcome by military means alone, but only by an enlightened administration, informed public opinion and increased prosperity, they considered that these desiderata could best be assured by lifting the Emergency regulations. It must be said that it was the opening up of the jungle forts in hitherto inaccessible areas of the country which enabled the 'enlightened administration' to function in spite of the terrorists. The cost of the campaign was formidable. From 1948 until Malayan independence in 1957 it has been estimated that the total cost exceeded £700,000,000, of which £525,000,000 was provided by the United Kingdom. At the end of the 12 years nearly 7,000 communists had been killed and 4,000 had surrendered or been captured. But also more than 2,000 civilians had lost their lives as had over 1,000 Malayan police and 500 British, Malayan, Gurkha, Australian, New Zealand, Fijian and East African Servicemen. The advance of communism in South-East Asia had been halted—but at a great price.

The role of the Royal Air Force and its Commonwealth partners
had always been in support of the ground forces. No more than a
handful of squadrons had participated at any one time but their work
had been vital to the success of the operations. Without that support
the campaign would have been even more protracted or even lost,
many more lives would certainly have been lost and the cost would
have escalated.

13

South-East Asia Treaty Organisation

British Defence Policy

The decade following the end of World War II saw a radical development in Britain's defence policy which affected the overseas RAF commands, the Far East being no exception. A number of factors contributed to this change, notably the threat posed by the intransigence of the Soviet Union in Europe which resulted in increasing the gravity of the cold war following the Blockade of Berlin in 1948–49. In addition, the growth of communism in the Middle and Far East threatened many countries which were either British Commonwealth or colonial territories, or which were gaining their independence from British rule. Britain was not only physically and economically exhausted as the result of her war effort, but was losing much of the hitherto reliable support from her former possessions as one by one they gained their freedom, developed their own national policies and no longer needed the assistance of Britain's armed forces.

Consideration of all these factors led the British Government and the Chiefs of Staff to the inevitable conclusion that Britain would no longer be able to embark upon a major war on her own. The rapid development of air power had produced a situation of great potential danger to the British Isles and, although in 1946 the United States alone possessed nuclear weapons, it was clear that not many years would pass before Russia would have developed similar weapons, and the danger to Britain would be even greater. It had, therefore, become virtually imperative for Britain to join with her allies to combat the cold war in Europe and the insidious spread of communism elsewhere.

It was under these depressing circumstances that the North Atlantic Treaty Organisation (NATO) was born, due largely to the foresight and initiative of Winston Churchill and President Truman of the United States. Britain was thus a founder member of an alliance which in due course comprised fifteen nations, and was able to shelter under the umbrella of the American nuclear deterrent with her European colleagues while she rapidly developed her own nuclear capability.

A second international alliance, the South-East Asia Treaty Organisation, and the one with which this narrative is mainly concerned, was designed to protect the area of South-East Asia and the Western Pacific against further communist infiltration as a result of Mao Tse-tung's takeover in China and communist influence elsewhere. Finally, Britain was a founder member of a third alliance, originally entitled the Baghdad Pact[1], which was formed in the Middle East to bolster up the southern flank of NATO which was exposed to the threat of Russian expansionism towards the Eastern Mediterranean, Turkey and the Gulf States.

The Origins of SEATO

By 1951 the increasing threat from Russian and Chinese sponsored communism to the nations of South-East Asia and the Western Pacific area was viewed with grave concern, and Britain, Australia, New Zealand, France and the United States maintained close military liaison regarding action to be taken in the event of aggression. The desire for more specific guarantees of mutual assistance in the area grew as the threats to Korea and Indo-China materialised. During 1953 the French, who were by then being extremely hard pressed in Indo-China, showed distinct signs of a willingness to consider a negotiated peace—an attitude which was strengthened by the disaster at Dien-Bien-Phu, when 15 French battalions were encircled and, after a bitter struggle, overwhelmed by Viet Minh forces.

A conference under United Nations auspices, which was held in Geneva in July 1954, failed to find a satisfactory solution to the intractable problem of Vietnam and in particular the lack of viability of South Vietnam owing to opposition from the Eastern bloc countries. It was then clear that a pressing need had arisen for the establishment of a collective defence organisation in South-East Asia in accordance with "the purpose and principles of the Charter of the United Nations".

Events moved rapidly and like-minded nations met in Manila on 6 September 1954. Eight nations were represented, namely, Australia,

---

[1] Later renamed the Central Treaty Organisation.

Britain, France, New Zealand, Pakistan, the Philippine Republic, Thailand and the United States. At the conclusion of the conference the eight Powers signed a South-East Asia Collective Defence Treaty (which came into force on 19 February 1955, after due ratification by all the signatories).

Under the terms of this Manila Treaty nations agreed "separately and jointly, by means of continuous and effective self help and mutual aid, to maintain and develop their individual and collective capacity to resist armed attack and to prevent any counter subversive activities directed against their territorial integrity and political stability"[2]. The Charter of the Treaty ran to 11 Articles but the agreement quoted above is the nub of the Treaty from the military standpoint. One important qualification which should perhaps be mentioned is that 'aggression' referred only to communist aggression.

How SEATO was Organised

Within a short time of the signing of the Treaty the permanent headquarters of SEATO was established in Bangkok. The choice of the capital of Thailand was an eminently sensible one. Not only was Thailand a stable kingdom but it lay in the centre of the area covered by the Treaty and, more important, it was close to the region where the dangers of communist aggression were greatest, ie, Vietnam, Laos and Cambodia. It was thus hoped that the presence of the headquarters in Bangkok would act as some deterrent to Chinese communist aspirations and give some added protection to Thailand and Malaya.

The governing body of SEATO, the Council of Ministers, consisted of the Foreign Ministers of member countries. They met once a year and were permanently represented in Bangkok by the ambassadors to Thailand. A Secretary-General and a permanent headquarters staff were provided by the nations concerned, divided into working groups specialising in such matters as Budget Control, Intelligence and Military Planning. It is with the last of these that this narrative is mainly concerned.

RAF staff officers, usually of group captain or wing commander rank, held a number of appointments in the Military Advisers Group, drawing their briefs etiher direct from the Chiefs of Staff Secretariat in the Ministry of Defence, or more often from FEAF where the

---

[2] Article 2 of the Manila Treaty

Commander-in-Chief maintained a watching brief over RAF affairs in SEATO on behalf of the Chief of the Air Staff.

There is an important distinction to be drawn between SEATO and its European counterpart, NATO. The latter contained large contingents of forces provided by each member nation and placed under the command of a Supreme Commander. Thus the RAF 2nd Tactical Air Force in Germany was commanded and operationally controlled by SACEUR, and other forces were 'assigned' to NATO to be placed under command in specific circumstances. In SEATO, on the other hand, there was no permanent command structure and no standing forces were allocated to the Organisation. It was merely a framework for the production of plans into which member nations were committed to place appropriate forces if and when a particular plan had to be implemented. In this respect SEATO had much in common with the Central Treaty Organisation (CENTO) with its headquarters in Ankara.

It would be inaccurate and unjust, however, to regard SEATO as a mere 'paper tiger'. It has to be remembered that all its member nations possessed large scale sea, land and air forces within its boundaries. Many, such as Pakistan, Thailand and the Philippines for example, were indigenous to the theatre and maintained all of their armed forces on their home territory. Others, such as Britain and the United States, had significant forces stationed within the theatre and also the ability to reinforce them rapidly by air if the need should arise.

It had to be assumed, as in any alliance, that the political will to stand by the guarantees enshrined in the Articles of the Treaty would be forthcoming if the need to implement a military plan arose. The greatest responsiblity of the planning staffs was to ensure, not only that their contingency plans were kept up-to-date and realistic in the light of current intelligence, but also that the command structure and forces required could be assembled efficiently and rapidly.

SEATO Exercises

No plans are of great value unless they can be tested from time to time and their weaknesses exposed and subsequently rectified. During the first eight years of its life 27 SEATO exercises were held, in all of which FEAF squadrons, often reinforced by detachments from the home commands, took part. One of the largest of these exercises, code named LITGAS, simulated a full-scale amphibious assault on the

Philippine island of Mindoro with the participation of 20,000 men, 75 ships and 300 aircraft. Lasting four weeks this proved to be an arduous and highly realistic exercise in which all the member nations of the Treaty took part. As in the case of NATO exercises, it was found that the standardisation of equipment and procedures needed to be greatly improved. It was imperative, for example, that aircraft of one SEATO nation could refuel on an airfield of another without the need to bring their own ground handling paraphernalia. Standardisation therefore played a large part in the work of the SEATO staff. Some progress was made but many differences in radio equipment, frequencies, voltages, aircraft starting and refuelling equipment, etc, persisted. The problem was somewhat eased in that the majority of aircraft were either American or British—it would have been far worse had there been aircraft built by many different nations.

RAF and Commonwealth Participation

Within the overall area covered by SEATO, Britain had entered into various defence agreements with her Commonwealth partners, namely, Australia, New Zealand and Malaya. In October 1957, Malaya, which was not a member of SEATO and had just become an independent nation within the Commonwealth, signed a mutual defence and assistance agreement with Britain which provided, inter alia, that the British Government might maintain naval, land and air forces in the Federation. This gave rise to the formation of a Commonwealth Strategic Reserve and it was under this agreement that Australia assumed command of Butterworth for the location of Sabre and Canberra squadrons. The RAF squadrons on the Singapore airfields formed part of this Reserve, all of which could, when required, be used in support of SEATO.

In addition, the RAF was at this time reorganising its main strategic air route to the Far East consequent upon various overflying limitations in the Middle East, and to avoid the need to overfly India, Burma and Ceylon. Fortuitously the period also coincided with the development of larger and longer range transport aircraft such as the Britannia and later the Comet, Beverley, Argosy and Belfast. The greatly increased airlift capability of Transport Command enabled Britain to develop a policy of rapid reinforcement of SEATO from Strategic Reserve land forces based in the United Kingdom and Kenya. Mobile squadrons of close support aircraft in 38 Group formed an essential element of this Reserve and were also available to move to the Far East at short notice. No longer was Britain so dependent upon the maintenance of costly garrisons overseas. Rapid improvements in the techniques of in-flight refuelling were proving an additional benefit to rapid reinforcement, enabling fighters and other short range aircraft to avoid any embarrassing need to stage through countries where sensitivity to Britain's plans might exist.

Thus, although the air forces immediately available in the theatre were modest, the SEATO plans were largely based upon a rapid build-up of units from outside. It was a policy which applied not only to SEATO, but to CENTO and NATO as well, and had the great advantage of allowing the RAF to maintain a larger force more economically at home than would have been possible in widely scattered overseas bases.

Later Stages of the Treaty

SEATO continued in existence for 22 years, well beyond the period with which this book is concerned. The flags of seven of the eight member nations were finally hauled down from the Headquarters building in Bangkok at sunset on 30 June 1977. On the following morning only the flag of Thailand was hoisted, a lonely symbol of what had been an alliance of eight nations.

Whether the Treaty can be described as a success or failure is a matter for debate. Circumstances in South-East Asia changed so markedly during the final 10 years, notably with the invasion of South Vietnam by the communist North Vietnamese, that the Treaty became largely inoperable and its eventual demise was in fact proposed by two of the regional members, Thailand and the Philippines.

On the debit side the unsatisfactory involvement of SEATO Powers led by the United States in Vietnam must be regarded as a failure. But there is a credit side. As Sir David Lee Cole, the British Ambassador to Thailand, said at the time,[3]

"I do not think it can be disputed that its existence bought time, over 20 years of comparative peace for the regional members in South-East Asia. Given the fate of some of their near neighbours, that is no small achievement."

Nor can the effectiveness of SEATO be judged on political and military performance alone. In the civil field, it achieved much by bringing greater economic efficiency, immense improvements in

---

[3] Diplomatic Report No 248/77

health, agriculture and technology to the vast under-developed areas of South-East Asia, and did much to repair the ravages of the Japanese occupation.

There is no doubt that the skilfully handled 'cold war' which the Soviets pursued relentlessly in Europe, the Middle East and South-East Asia, always stopping short of the direct military action which might have brought the nuclear deterrent into effect, posed most difficult problems for the members of all the international defensive alliances. And so, like CENTO, SEATO outlived its usefulness, its existence rendered anomalous by the march of events, but that is not to say that during its lifetime it did not bring its members into closer harmony and was able to record many successes. To quote finally from the British Ambassador.[4] "A necessary creation of the cold war, SEATO lived rather too long and lasted into times for which it was unsuited."

---

[4] Diplomatic Report No 248/77

14

An Island Staging Post

From the earliest days of aviation until the end of World War II it had been possible to fly an 'all red' air route from the United Kingdom to Australasia, and even short range aircraft rarely had to land at an airfield which did not either lie in British territory or belong to a close friend of Britain. Bulk supplies were invariably transported by sea, usually through the Suez Canal and across the Indian Ocean. Movement throughout the British Empire therefore posed few problems, but that situation changed radically during the years following the end of the war.

The independence of India and Burma, followed some years later by that of Ceylon, created some problems for Britain in maintaining a strategic air reinforcement route from the United Kingdom to the Far East and the Antipodes. It was not that these newly independent nations forbade normal overflying and staging by RAF aircraft, but the risk always existed that some international political development might cause them to object to a British reinforcement operation and impose a ban at an embarrassing moment.

It must be remembered that denial of overflying rights became a political weapon of considerable potency during the 1950s, particularly in the Middle East, and Britain understandably did not wish to be faced with such a development on her vital air route to the Far East where there were long oversea stages and relatively few diversionary or alternative airfields.

Although transport aircraft such as the Hastings, Britannia and Comet were able to fly increasingly long stage lengths and the development of in-flight refuelling was steadily increasing the flexibility of fighter aircraft, the avoidance of India, Pakistan and Ceylon would leave an unbridgeable gap between Aden or Bahrein and Singapore. It was therefore advocated by the Chiefs of Staff that this gap must be filled by a suitable staging airfield somewhere in the

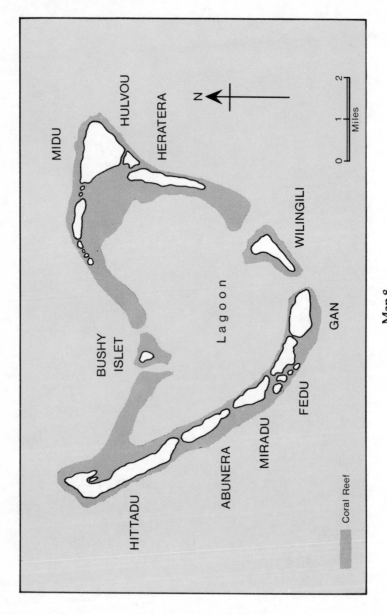

Map 8
Addu Atoll showing position of Gan and Hittadu

central Indian Ocean area. This would still permit diversions in emergency either to Masirah Island, where the RAF had a small base, or to one of the airfields in Pakistan, India or Ceylon. The choice of a suitable location was extremely limited and almost automatically fell upon Addu Atoll in the Maldive Islands which already had a small airstrip.

Addu Atoll and Gan

The Maldives are a group of coral islands situated some 400 miles to the south-west of Sri Lanka. Malé, the capital, lies about 415 miles from Colombo and the King of the Maldives rules over two hundred inhabited islands and an unknown number of uninhabited islands, variously estimated from 2,000 to 12,000, the former figure probably being the more accurate. In the Maldivian language the King has a grandiose title which, freely translated, means 'Sultan King of Thirteen Provinces and 12,000 Islands'.

Addu Atoll is the most southerly of the Maldive Group, 40 miles south of the Equator, and consists of a circlet of small islands enclosing a lagoon measuring 10 miles from east to west and six and a half miles from north to south (see Map 8). The islands are flat and low lying being rarely more than five feet above sea level and are composed of a coral base overlaid with sandy humus soil from decayed vegetation. The lagoon is a magnificent natural harbour and anchorage at all seasons of the year and, with a depth varying from 20 to 40 fathoms and one excellent entrance, is capable of accepting the largest ships. *RMS Queen Mary* is the biggest ship ever to use the lagoon and is known to have anchored in it at some time during 1942. Addu Atoll comprises 25 named islands fringing the lagoon, of which five are inhabited by a total population of about 6,700 who eke out a precarious existence by fishing, harvesting coconuts and growing vegetables. Being 350 miles from Malé they are visited infrequently by local sailing boats which take their harvest of copra but otherwise leave them virtually undisturbed.

Gan lies at the southern extremity of the atoll, bordering the main deep water entry to the lagoon (see Map 8). Although one of the smaller islands measuring only $1\frac{3}{4}$ miles $\times \frac{3}{4}$ mile, it was nevertheless the most suitable for airfield development, being less densely covered by trees and vegetation than its neighbours and with excellent unobstructed approaches over the open sea. This narrative is primarily concerned with the RAF development of Gan, but a great deal of

clearance had already been carried out and a wartime airstrip constructed in 1942 when Addu Atoll was used as an advanced operational
base by the Royal Navy. It had been intended to provide facilities
for two Fleet Air Arm squadrons when temporarily disembarked but,
in the event, the airstrip was used only spasmodically and was
eventually abandoned.

The Building of RAF Gan

The development of Gan into a first class airfield capable of accepting
the largest and heaviest aircraft dates from January 1957. Supervision
of the arduous construction work was in the hands of officials of the
Air Ministry Directorate-General of Works who drew up plans for a
single runway utilising the full length of the island together with a
domestic camp and technical facilities for about 500 airmen, which
was expected to be the ultimate strength of the station. A civilian
contract was let to Messrs Richard Costain and the advance party
was commanded by an officer of 5001 Airfield Construction Squadron
which reached Gan on 30 January accompanied by the Prime Minister
of the Maldives whose task was to inform the islanders of the project.

A small village of some 200 dwellings existed at the western end of
the island in a position which would have caused an obstruction to
aircraft approaching the runway. One of the first tasks, therefore, was
to rehouse the villagers and this was done on the neighbouring island
of Fedu (see Map 8). Although some objections were raised, the
Prime Minister managed to convince the headman that his people
would be better housed and would undoubtedly benefit from the
move. This turned out to be correct as over the years the Adduans
gained immeasurably in their very low standard of living, in health
and in social development.

The island was completely ringed with coconut palms to a depth
of one hundred to four hundred yards inland, but part of the central
area consisted of grass and low scrub where the vegetation had
originally been cleared for the wartime airstrip. An initial survey
revealed that upwards of 11,000 trees would have to be felled.
After various experiments with mechanical saws, hand digging and
explosives, it was found that the quickest and most efficient method
of felling the trees, which had relatively shallow roots, was to push
them over with bulldozers. Another problem was that certain areas
of swamp required filling, but coral was easily obtained for this
purpose from the offshore coral reefs. Of course no loading facilities

existed and before heavy machinery could be brought in, a 400 foot jetty had to be constructed from the shore to the edge of the reef. As soon as that was completed, work went ahead rapidly with a labour force which eventually exceeded 2,000 men including 1,300 Pakistanis, 600 Maldivians and 120 Europeans. It was a difficult and exacting piece of construction as eight inches of rain would sometimes fall in one day, the average day temperature was always in the 80s and the living conditions were primitive. However, two years saw the main construction completed at a cost of £4,000,000.

In order to facilitate the supply of the island while construction was in progress, the original airstrip was quickly refurbished and the first aircraft to land on it was a Bristol Freighter of the RNZAF on 30 August 1957. Until then a twice weekly service of Sunderlands from 205/209 Squadron at Seletar had brought in food, mail and personnel, alighting in the lagoon. Moorings had originally been laid down off the island of Hittadu and these were improved to give the Sunderlands refuelling and rudimentary servicing facilities. Once again the versatile Sunderland proved its great value in these circumstances. Shipping could obviously not have been laid on with twice weekly frequency and the airmen and civilians owed much to 205/209 Squadron's punctual and frequent arrival with their creature comforts in the months before landplane facilities could be provided. From 2 September a Valetta service operating from Ceylon was inaugurated and it was thenceforward possible to reduce the long Sunderland flights from Singapore.

Owing to the need to locate radio transmitters some distance from the receivers and also to avoid creating a flying obstruction with high transmission aerials and masts, it was not possible for all radio facilities to be built on Gan itself. It was therefore decided to construct the transmitting station on the site of the wartime radar installation on the island of Hittadu at the north-west corner of the lagoon, alongside the original flying boat anchorage.

Movement around the perimeter of the lagoon was made much easier when a coral causeway was built linking Gan to Hittadu and the other islands on the western side of the lagoon. It was not an easy task and, even when finished, the narrow causeway was frequently damaged and on at least one occasion broken by storm and tide. However, the task was completed and the causeway was improved over the years making communication between the islands much easier than by boat. The causeway also made it possible for some of the islanders who no longer lived on Gan to be employed by the RAF and to 'commute' to work on foot. The majority, however, continued with their old habit of commuting by boat.

Command and Control

During the early construction of RAF Gan it was appropriate for the station to be controlled by the nearest RAF formation, namely, AHQ Ceylon. The Sunderlands which provided the air support until the airfield was suitable for landplanes often staged through Ceylon from Singapore and were thus able to take on board the immediate needs in supplies and personnel which had been radioed across to the AHQ. As soon as the airfield became operational permitting trunk route staging through Ceylon to be discontinued, control by AHQ Ceylon became inappropriate and thus, on 1 November 1957, it was transferred to HQ FEAF. The Command Headquarters then controlled the whole of the southern part of the strategic air reinforcement route from the Indian Ocean to the south-west Pacific and China Sea—from Gan to Christmas Island. This situation continued for as long as FEAF existed but further changes in control were necessary as the RAF withdrew from the Far East in the early 1970s. For the sake of the record it should be stated that control of Gan was assumed by Air Support Command for a brief period from 1 September 1972, but was handed on to HQ Near East Air Force (NEAF) on 1 April 1973, where it remained until the island staging post finally closed down on 29 March 1976.

As the station developed in size and importance the rank of the Commanding Officer was upgraded. Flight Lieutenant G M McNeil was the first commander and he handed over to a squadron leader four months later as the personnel strength mounted. By June 1958 the appointment rose to wing commander rank and, finally in August 1971, to that of group captain where it remained until the last Commanding Officer, Group Captain W Edwards AFC, closed down the station in 1976. Some 550 airmen was the peak establishment, making Gan a full sized operational station. During the 19 years of activation by the Royal Air Force, Gan had 21 Commanding Officers, all of whom enjoyed the unique experience of command offered by this remote tropical island.

Operational Activity

The flow of air traffic through the station was carefully geared to the development of the facilities available and increased steadily over the years until between 6,000 and 7,000 passengers in transit were being handled every month, and correspondingly large tonnages of cargo. Most of the passengers comprised Servicemen and families en route to and from Singapore who were on the island for a mere one and a half hours. Nevertheless accommodation had always to be available for an overnight stay in the infrequent event of some aircraft unserviceability and this necessitated the building of a transit hotel.

The traffic was not, however, confined to transport aircraft. Many operational aircraft from the home commands, notably 'V' bombers, Shackletons and Canberras, used Gan on their way to exercise in or to reinforce FEAF. In later years Victor tankers from Strike Command frequently used the airfield as a base from which to refuel fighters over the Indian Ocean on their way to and from Singapore. Gan was a welcome sight to the single seaters on their long open sea crossings and a comforting diversion if in any difficulty. Thus Gan had to be prepared to service almost every type of aircraft in operational use with the result that its airmen accumulated a great deal of technical skill.

The isolation of the island called for the highest degree of efficiency from its signals staff, as navigation aids and ground to air communications generally were vital to the safety of aircraft. Sudden short but severe storms which were prevalent in the Maldives could create serious problems in locating the tiny atoll if homing and approach equipment and procedures were less than first class. Fortunately the standards were very high and it was exceptional for a diversion to Ceylon to be necessary.

During the last few years of the station's life, upwards of 350 aircraft movements a month were being recorded. At 12 per day this cannot be described as dense traffic but when it is remembered that most of these were large four-engined aircraft usually carrying a hundred or more passengers and requiring very large quantities of fuel, frequently in the middle of the night, the work load for a small station was heavy and continuous.

The need for rescue services was fortunately small but, nevertheless, they had to be present and ever ready. A Britannia or a VC10 going into the sea on the approach or take off with a full load of passengers would have been a major disaster. With this eventuality always in mind, one or two Shackletons of 205 Squadron were usually maintained at Gan for rescue duties over the whole central area of the Indian Ocean and controlled from a well equipped Rescue Coordination Centre on the station. In addition, for local use, a comprehensive Marine Craft section was maintained with craft, vehicles and life rafts ready to carry out any rescue in proximity to the airfield. Rescue facilities for more than 100 people could be brought into operation within minutes. The fact that no serious accident occurred during the occupation of Gan by the RAF is a great tribute not only to the efficiency of the services provided by the station, but also to the standards of flying by the RAF crews who passed through it.

Owing to the spasmodic arrival and departure of aircraft, a three shift day had always to be worked, and for seven days a week. This presented no particular hardship as the establishment of airmen and civilian staff was geared to a three shift system and so excessive hours of work were not required. It so happened that the majority of scheduled services tended to pass through Gan at night—in many respects an advantage as the night air was always cool and fresh whereas high day temperatures could create discomfort for servicing crews and passengers alike. Transport Command aircraft which represented the bulk of the traffic were scheduled to pass through Gan at suitable intervals to prevent overloading of the facilities but plenty of excess capacity existed to deal with unforeseen contingencies.

Living and Working Conditions

A one year unaccompanied tour was the rule for all officers and airmen as it was clearly impracticable to accommodate families and all that would have entailed on the island. In that respect Gan was similar to the small RAF stations on the Arabian Peninsula, Masirah, Salalah and Riyan, but conditions were generally superior. The climate has been described as 'tropical oceanic' which, in simple terms, means hot and humid but relieved by sea breezes. There are no seasons in the accepted meaning, daytime temperatures averaging 87°F and nights which rarely fall below 70°F. Little variation from these levels is experienced throughout the year but frequent showers and occasional storms do tend to lower the temperature briefly.

At one time Addu Atoll was said to be unhealthy, but this was probably due to the luxuriant vegetation and swampland and also to the complete lack of hygiene and medical facilities. Occupation of

Gan by the RAF cured that. The clearance of trees and scrub, the elimination of swamps and other mosquito breeding areas, and the introduction of medical facilities made the island as healthy as any other similarly situated RAF station. With sensible anti-malarial precautions and strict attention to personal hygiene the incidence of sickness was very low and no healthier looking body of airmen could be found anywhere. The climate was such that air conditioning was necessary only in certain technical buildings, such as signals cabins. Fans only were provided in messes and living quarters and were found to be quite adequate.

Prefabricated bungalow type quarters were provided for all personnel, officers and senior NCOs being allocated single rooms and corporals and airmen in rooms accommodating four. Immense trouble was taken to provide a full range of recreational and sporting facilities and, in this respect, no station in the RAF was better equipped. In addition to the natural delight of excellent swimming, fishing and sailing offered by the lagoon, there were ample opportunities for other sports such as football and hockey, and education and cultural activities such as music and drama flourished. The station's own radio programme was broadcast throughout the day and the airmen even constructed their own 18 hole golf course which, with a par of 68, was a considerable challenge in a temperature in the high 80s.

As the station was so close to the Equator darkness fell early and particular attention was therefore paid to the provision of evening entertainment. A cinema functioned each evening with four changes of film each week. NAAFI set up an excellent club with restaurant on the shores of the lagoon which had magnificent views across to the island of Fedu. As all commodities were duty free, prices were low and there was little excuse for failing to save money and live well. Gan was one of the few places where tonic cost more than gin!

To the passenger in transit Gan appeared idyllic and indeed to some airmen it was—but not to all. It could be a lonely tour of duty for those who had family problems at home. The constant passage of Servicemen and their families on their way home from the Far East was a regular reminder of the isolation of Gan. Nevertheless, morale was always very high and the staging post was regarded throughout its life as a happy and efficient station; there was never any shortage of volunteers to serve there for twelve months and thus 'notch up' a full overseas tour.

Working conditions varied considerably for the various tradesmen. No hangars were ever erected and all aircraft servicing had to be carried out in the open air. Fitters, riggers, armourers, electricians and other engineering trades often had to work in extreme temperatures on difficult and delicate tasks. Many cold drinks and salt tablets were consumed if, for example, the station was unlucky enough to have to change an engine—fortunately a rare occurrence. Even so, high standards were maintained. For example, the scheduled stop for a VC10 was one and a half hours, but the duty shift always reckoned to turn a VC10 round in 50 minutes and it was usually the passengers rather than the servicing crew who imposed any delay on its departure.

Rebellion

The Maldivians have always been a gentle and peace loving people, devout Muslims and content to pursue their fishing and agricultural activities with little interest in the political life of the islands centred in Malé, far to the north of Addu Atoll. Relationships between the Adduans and the RAF were excellent, particularly when the development of Gan brought more work and greater prosperity to the islanders as well as medical care and other benefits which they had never previously experienced. It therefore came as something of a shock when they rebelled against their own Government on 1 January 1959. A new Government had taken office a year earlier and wished to renegotiate its Agreement with Britain in spite of the fact that the islanders themselves were perfectly content with the existing arrangements.

Several Maldivian Government officials were forced to seek protection from the RAF as the Adduans became hostile and threatening towards them. The situation was awkward as Britain had undertaken to defend the Maldives but not to interfere in internal affairs in any way. The Government wished work on Gan to cease while the Agreement was being re-negotiated, a request which was quite unacceptable at that stage of construction. Certain islands to the north of Addu joined the rebellion but their intransigence collapsed after the Government had re-established its authority in the islands of Huvadu and Malake in July 1959. At this point the British Government offered its good offices to bring about a peaceful settlement with Addu. The ploy worked. Early in the following year the Minister of State at the Commonwealth Relations Office, Mr (later Lord) Alport, visited Malé and signed a new Protection Agreement. The terms were much as before but the British Government gave an assurance that it would do all in its power to bring about an early reconciliation between the Maldivian Government and its Adduan subjects. Some little time later a reconciliation was achieved and the rebellion collapsed. The Adduans obtained the modest improvements which they had sought and relations with the RAF were even better than they had been before the rebellion. The whole episode was something of a storm in a tea cup but had nevertheless caused both the British Government and the RAF on Gan considerable embarrassment. Fortuitously there had been no violence, sabotage or incidents directed against RAF personnel and the work of the station had continued normally, but with a little extra vigilance.

The Last Years

During the 1960s the staging post prospered. No basic changes were made but improvements in its facilities and amenities continued to be made and the traffic reached a peak with the introduction of the VC10 and Belfast. Much larger than any aircraft in previous RAF service they tested the capacity of Gan to its limits but, by this time, the station had worked up to a high pitch of efficiency and coped admirably.

When British defence policy heralded withdrawal from the Far East in the late 1960s, it was clear that there would be an uncertain future for Gan. Questions were raised as to whether its facilities would be needed after the large scale movement between the United Kingdom and Singapore was reduced. The answer came in the 1975 Defence White Paper which revealed an intention to withdraw from Gan by 1 April 1976. Traffic decreased rapidly after the last troops left Singapore and the station started to run down during 1975 leaving only the basic staging post and communications for a further few months.

The first three months of 1976 were spent in back loading sea and air freight and handing over many of the installations to Maldivian officials who were anxious to maintain the airfield for civil purposes. There was heartfelt regret on the part of the Adduans who continued to give their unstinted support to the end. For almost 20 years the relationships had been warm and cordial and one cannot do better than quote from an article in Air Clues of September 1976, in conclusion:

"There is an enduring memory of an island of matchless natural beauty and of a remarkable spirit in community among the island's airmen, soldiers and civilian staff."

A small monument constructed by the Department of the Environment and set up near the former Station Headquarters now commemorates the former RAF presence. The inscription reads:

"Royal Air Force Gan, 1956–1976."

15

A Few Quiet Years

There were few periods during the turbulent history of the Royal Air Force in the Far East when FEAF squadrons were not engaged in active operations somewhere in the theatre. One such short period followed the Malayan Emergency which finally petered out in 1960 after twelve years of continuous jungle operations. It proved to be a valuable breathing space before the Command was again plunged into operations in December 1962—on this occasion in confrontation with Indonesia.

This chapter is designed to take advantage of that brief lull of little more than three years in order to describe the life and work of RAF personnel and their families in Singapore and elsewhere in the early 1960s, a time when reconstruction following the devastation wrought by World War II had been virtually completed and the future disengagement of Britain from the Far East was no more than a discernible possibility.

Life in Singapore

Singapore has always had the reputation of being one of the most cosmopolitan cities in the world, a crossroads of international commerce and shipping and latterly an important junction of the air routes between east and west. Little did Sir Stamford Raffles imagine, when he established his trading post on that flat, swampy and not too healthy island in 1819, that it would become the thriving centre of trade, commerce and communications which Servicemen knew in the 1950s and 60s.

The standard tour of duty for the majority of RAF personnel had been stabilised at two and a half years on a fully accompanied basis. The Army, on the other hand, carried out a three year tour of duty and this difference created a bone of contention largely because the three year tour qualified personnel for a 'change of air' holiday at public expense whereas the two and a half year tour did not. Accommodation, living conditions and climate were all conducive to family life and, unlike their less fortunate colleagues in parts of the Middle East, married airmen did not have to suffer unaccompanied tours. Many hundreds of married quarters had been, and continued to be built on or adjacent to the three main stations on the island. For those—and there were many—who could not immediately move into quarters, there was no great shortage of rented accommodation or 'hirings' within easy reach of the stations. In spite of being over 7,000 miles from home and very close to the Equator, a posting to Singapore was regarded by the majority of officers and airmen, but not by all, as a highlight in their careers. WRAF personnel were equally happy with the opportunity to experience life on this pleasant and comfortable island.

On so many overseas RAF stations opportunities for entertainment and off duty pursuits existed only on the stations themselves, which could be a considerable restriction. Not so in Singapore where the city—never more than a few miles from any RAF unit—offered a fascinating variety of leisure activities, far too numerous to mention in detail. Singapore has always been a duty free port where goods ranging from motor cars and photographic equipment to jewellery and clothing could be bought for incredibly cheap prices after 'suitable negotiations' on the usual eastern pattern. Shopping was, therefore, one of the most attractive family occupations, and a time-consuming business if the best bargains were to be obtained. Every individual had his own favourite shops, ranging from C K Tang's in Orchard Road where the most exclusive and delicate art works were to be found, to the Thieves Market where it was said that you could buy back your own property stolen earlier from you!

Second only to shopping came 'eating out'. How many thousands of airmen tasted their first Chinese meal in Singapore and experimented with chopsticks? This experience undoubtedly contributed to the popularity of the Chinese 'take away' at home. By the 1960s the standards of hygiene and cleanliness in restaurants had risen to high standards, thanks to Government regulations, one great asset of Singapore being that the natural water was sweet and pure, and quite fit to drink from the tap without the need to take precautions. The range and variety of restaurants and eating houses was unlimited, specialising in Chinese, Indian, Malay, Indonesian, European and many other national dishes. At the old Kallang Airport restaurant below the

Control Tower, for example, one could obtain excellent Sydney Bay oysters, removed from their shells, packed in barrels and flown in from Australia and served in 'phoney' shells at absurdly cheap prices. If so disposed, even a lowly paid Leading Aircraftman could afford half a dozen oysters during an evening out from Changi or Tengah.

The skill of the Chinese as tailors and the speed with which they could run up garments became legendary. It was possible to order and be measured for a lightweight dacron khaki uniform in, say, Changi Village in the evening and collect the finished garments the following morning. It was a waste of time and money for officers and airmen to buy their tropical kit in the UK before setting out for Singapore, the usual practice being to travel out from the UK in plain clothes and then to equip fully on arrival. Many passengers passing through Changi in Transport Command aircraft could, while staying overnight in the Transit Hotel in Changi Village, have items of uniform and civilian clothes made and fitted before their departure.

Nowhere in the Royal Air Force were there better opportunities and facilities for sport. In addition to the usual facilities for tennis, football, cricket and even rugby, swimming and sailing were understandably extremely popular pastimes in a climate which varied little throughout the year—hot and humid days with temperatures in the high 80s or low 90s during the day, falling to about 75° at night. In addition to station swimming pools, the Singapore Swimming Club and Changi beach offered some variety to swimmers and the two sailing clubs at Seletar and Changi were always well supported. Dinghy sailing in the Johore Strait with its strong currents and the hazards of fast moving shipping required both skill and caution and a helmsman's certificate was not easy to obtain and was the mark of a competent sailor.

As the heat of the day diminished and early darkness fell at about 6.30 pm all the year round, the shorts and open shirts gave way to long sleeves and slacks to ward off such mosquitos as had escaped the strict DDT spraying and other anti-malarial precautions. This was a delightful time of day when Tiger or Anchor beer in the station Malcolm Club or NAAFI restaurant gave promise of a pleasant evening. Changi and Seletar were perhaps favoured in this respect as, being situated on the Strait, a breeze off the water usually helped to cool down the heat of the day. Tengah, being in the centre of the island, retained the daytime temperature and humidity longer but was nevertheless a thoroughly comfortable and well equipped station for leisure activities. Despite the compelling attractions of the night life of the city, every station abounded with evening leisure activities in the form of a cinema and a wide variety of clubs which catered for a wide range of hobbies.

One reason why it was so essential for the three stations to have a wide range of recreational facilities was that the opportunities for families and single airmen and airwomen to take local leave were relatively few. It was possible to travel up country to Fraser's Hill, the Cameron Highlands and even to Penang but such excursions were not cheap and, apart from some relief from the heat, the advantages were not great. Consequently the majority tended to spend periods of local leave on the island and enjoy more of its undoubted attractions than was possible during working days. Expeditions further afield to Kota Tinggi or the east coast beaches added some variety to local leave. The incentives to get away for a break were not as pressing as they were in places such as Aden, Bahrein or Sharjah.

It would be wrong to omit from this description of life in Singapore the importance to the families of servicemen of medical, dental and educational amenities. With regard to the former, the RAF hospital at Changi was first class. Accommodated in part of the original Army barrack blocks alongside Headquarters FEAF, it was spacious and airy with modern equipment and facilities. The maternity wards were, in particular, excellently laid out and equipped and many hundreds of RAF children first saw daylight streaming in across the Johore Strait. In the education field the RAF administered both primary and secondary schools on all the stations, staffed with UK-based teachers augmented by locally engaged teachers, mainly drawn from Service wives. In 1960 there were, for example, 3,430 children of school age in FEAF and this figure had risen to 6,511 by 1966. Most of these children were educated in RAF administered schools and the remainder in Army schools.

This formidable list of amenities and social facilities provided in Singapore illustrates the immense administrative responsibilities which the presence of families impose upon a RAF overseas command. Not only did FEAF have to provide and run the various domestic activities on the spot, but also organise the movement of wives and children to and from the UK, deal with the many legal problems which arise in a large community, and instruct and guide families on their relationships with local communities. Many of the families had never previously been abroad and Singapore provided a strange environment and an unusual climate for them. It is all too easy to think of FEAF merely in terms of a Command concerned with the deployment and operation of aircraft whereas its administrative and logistic burdens were immense.

This account of life in Singapore for Service men and women has probably given the impression that a posting to FEAF was idyllic. Attractive though it undoubtedly was for leisure and recreation, working conditions were often difficult and exhausting, taking some of the gilt off the gingerbread. Working hours varied, but in general were between 7.30 am and 4.30 pm, hours which were dictated by the Singapore Government's regulations for civilian employees. These hours may sound satisfactory but it has to be remembered that technical work could be most exhausting in the heat of the day. In other tropical theatres it was often found desirable to start work earlier and discontinue during the afternoon.

Technical facilities had been vastly improved by the early 1960s but it was still necessary to carry out most of the servicing work on aircraft in the open. In many respects that was preferable to working in the stifling conditions of a hangar and advantage could be taken of any breeze that was available. Engineering and armament tradesmen probably had the most trying time although electrical and instrument fitters, working in confined spaces inside aircraft, suffered greatly from the heat and humidity. The high humidity caused rapid corrosion which was exacerbated by the frequent heavy rainstorms producing a constant wetting and drying process in salt-laden sea air, the perfect conditions in which corrosion of so many parts of an aircraft's structure thrive. Fortunately the heavy rainfall prevented that additional enemy—blowing sand which was such an unpleasant feature of many Middle East airfields—and ensured that aircraft were frequently washed down with fresh water.

Despite the tropical trials to which all new aircraft were subjected before entering RAF service, the conditions under which they had to operate in the Far East revealed many weaknesses which had failed to come to light in pre-production trials. Maintenance of aircraft and equipment generally was, therefore, much more difficult and time-consuming than in temperate climates, and there is no better example than the problem posed by the Mosquito which has been mentioned earlier. These local factors made the assessment and provision of spares a difficult problem. Spares for a newly introduced type tended to be based upon European experience and this was often highly inappropriate. Failure of particular items in FEAF bore little relation to the failure rate in, say, the UK or Germany, with the result that it could take many months for an adequate flow of certain items to the Far East. Initiative and improvisation were required and, indeed, were displayed to a high degree throughout the Command in an effort to maintain acceptable rates of serviceability. Cannibalisation of one aircraft or vehicle to provide spares for another is a highly undesirable policy but it was often essential to keep at least part of a squadron or unit operating. The fact that Singapore was on the main strategic air route from the UK undoubtedly facilitated the speedy arrival of urgently demanded items from manufacturers or UK Maintenance Units but this was fortuitous and not an entirely satisfactory alternative to the holding of adequate stocks in the Maintenance Units at Seletar.

If working conditions and problems for ground personnel were often difficult, they were scarcely less so for the aircrew. Until the advent of jet aircraft with integral cockpit cooling systems such as the Godfrey cooling equipment in the Canberra, aircrew suffered considerably from heat, humidity and often extreme turbulence. The crews of piston-engined aircraft fared particularly badly. Lincolns, Shackletons and the lighter aircraft types were generally compelled either by the nature of their tasks or by weather conditions to fly at relatively low altitudes where turbulence in monsoon weather could be most uncomfortable and even dangerous. When to this were added temperatures and humidity always present at such heights, a sortie of several hours' duration could leave a crew soaked with sweat and exhausted. Fortunately judgement seemed to be little affected and aircrew became acclimatised within a few months and accepted the discomforts, usually losing any surplus weight in the process. It was always noticeable that the resident aircrew stood up to peculiar flying conditions far better than those who were on short detachments from the home commands.

For all these reasons acclimatisation is a most important factor in determining the ideal length of tour in various overseas localities. Two and a half years was probably ideal for FEAF. A very short tour would have given inadequate time for personnel to settle down physically and build up to a peak of efficiency in the equatorial climate, whereas a long tour of, say, five years would probably have pushed them beyond the peak into a period of increasing weariness and its attendant ills. This had been particularly noticeable in prewar days in India where the standard tour length was five years. Sickness, both physical and mental, tended to increase during the latter part of a tour when Europeans began to lose their initial resistance to disease. Strict anti-malarial precautions and the regular intake of salt tablets were insisted upon throughout FEAF. If these sensible measures were meticulously followed, airmen and airwomen generally remained very healthy during their Far East tour.

The Operational Scene

After the vicissitudes of the postwar years, the rehabilitation of South-East Asia was virtually completed by 1960. The Korean War and the Malayan Emergency had come and gone, independence of most of the countries in the theatre had been achieved and the South-East Asia Treaty Organisation together with some lesser defence treaties had been established. FEAF appeared to have entered a period of some stability although the problems of South Vietnam were steadily increasing. The Viet Cong were continuing to develop their guerilla tactics and the United States forces were becoming more and more involved. The danger that the communist pressure might spread further south towards Malaya and Singapore was ever present and gave added purpose to our presence in the Far East.

For a few years at least, however, FEAF squadrons were able to concentrate upon training and combined exercises designed to raise their operational standards to a level which the constant interruptions of recent years had made it difficult to sustain. The years 1962 and 1963 provided a welcome breathing space and full advantage was taken of it to tune up the Command as a whole and to prepare for the introduction of the 'unified' Far East Command organisation which came into being on 1 January 1963 (See Chapter 7).

Subsequent to the independence of Malaya the Royal Air Force had gradually withdrawn from its airfields on the mainland and concentrated a compact and well balanced force on its three Singapore stations. Butterworth, it will be recalled, had been handed over to Australian command and housed 78 Wing and three RAAF squadrons, two mounted on Sabres and one on the Canberra B2. This valuable contribution to the Far East Strategic Reserve and to SEATO held a watching brief over the northern frontier of Malaya where the remnants of the MRLA terrorists still lurked as a potential menace. The RAAF contingent was strengthened at Butterworth by the Sycamores of 110 Squadron RAF and Valettas of 52 Squadron, which moved there from Kuala Lumpur in 1960.

Kuala Lumpur had, for some years, been the centre of the expanding Royal Malayan Air Force which was now slowly gaining in size and experience under its Royal Air Force commander. Under the impetus of independence, and strongly supported by RAF logistic and technical backing, the small force made rapid progress and was able to take over most of the routine internal security tasks in the peninsula.

RAF Tengah

Work on modernizing Tengah had been progressing steadily for a number of years and by 1962 it was virtually complete. It was busy and crowded with no less than five operational squadrons in residence for most of the time. All were mounted on jet aircraft making a homogeneous pattern which facilitated air traffic control, an important consideration when the level of movements was high.

No 60 Squadron, the oldest resident unit, had exchanged its Venoms for the Javelin 9, thus altering its role from that of Day Fighter/ Ground Attack to All Weather Fighter with a good night capability. The Javelin had shown itself to be an exceptionally rugged and efficient air defence fighter in both the UK and Germany and so was well proven by the time it reached Tengah. Armed with air-to-air missiles and sophisticated radar it was one of the earliest aircraft which could be genuinely regarded as a 'weapons system'—a term which was beginning to be increasingly used to describe the latest generation of jet aircraft.

The Day Fighter/Ground Attack role at Tengah was now filled by 20 Squadron. This famous old squadron, which had spent most of its pre-war years on the North West Frontier of India, had latterly been in the Second Tactical Air Force in Germany. It was disbanded there in 1961 and the number plate transferred to the Far East. On 1 September of that year the squadron began to rearm with the Hunter GA9, another aircraft well proven in Fighter Command, in Germany and in the Middle East. The Hunter in various roles was one of the great post-war successes and remained in service for more than 20 years. Although subsonic in level flight, it was cleared for supersonic flight in a shallow dive, was easy to fly, had good firepower and was an excellent steady platform for both cannon and rocket projectiles. With pylon-mounted long range tanks or a choice of weapons, the Hunter was extremely versatile, and versatility counted for a great deal in a theatre with such a wide variety of tasks to be fulfilled by relatively few squadrons.

The light bomber, a category which had been absent from FEAF for some years, reappeared in the form of the Canberra B2 which had already served with distinction in Bomber Command since 1952. No 45 Squadron received this version of the Canberra after moving down to Singapore from Butterworth where it had spent some years on Venoms as the resident air defence squadron. The Canberra at last brought some stability to this Squadron which had been somewhat unfortunate in being equipped with six different aircraft types within ten years, and also having an unfair proportion of moves within the Command. The fourth squadron at Tengah was 75 RNZAF Squadron, part of New Zealand's contribution to SEATO and the Strategic Reserve. It too was armed with the Canberra B2 and completed a balanced force of one day fighter/ground attack, one all-weather fighter and two light bomber squadrons.

This left 81 Squadron, the sole photographic reconnaissance unit which had served in the Command since the end of World War II, and provided all the survey and tactical photography for the Command throughout the succeeding years. After a few years on the Meteor 10, the squadron received the Canberra PR7, a much longer range aircraft which could complete many of the squadron's tasks in a fraction of the time taken by its predecessors. The badge of 81 Squadron has an interesting history. It depicts a red five pointed star, or 'mullet' in heraldic phraseology, with a sword in the foreground. This badge is based on that of the First Russian Army and commemorates the time spent by the squadron in Russia during World War II.

RAF Changi

Changi, like Tengah, had been modernised and improved out of all recognition during the decade up to 1962 and, with its new runway capable of accepting the largest and heaviest aircraft, and with excellent technical facilities, had achieved international airport standards. Since the prewar days of Army occupation the domestic accommodation standing high above the airfield on well wooded slopes leading up to Fairy Point had always been comfortable and attractive. With the addition of further married quarters, a hospital, schools, clubs and sports facilities, Changi had developed into one of the most pleasant stations on which to serve anywhere in the Royal Air Force. Being situated at the easternmost point of the island, surrounded on three sides by the Johore Strait, Changi had the benefit of whatever breeze was blowing which lowered the humidity and gave welcome relief, particularly at night, from the discomforts associated with the centre of the island and Singapore City.

It had always been the policy to concentrate FEAF's transport squadrons at Changi, and in this there was no change. No 48 Squadron, a long time resident on the airfield, had changed its twin-engined Valettas for the four-engined Hastings and carried out the bulk of the scheduled services within the Command, supplemented occasionally by aircraft of the Far East Communications Squadron, also housed on the airfield.

All of Transport Command's scheduled services to the Far East either terminated at Changi or passed through on their way to Hong Kong or Australia, where the rocket range at Woomera was largely maintained by a mixture of RAF and civil aircraft. Trooping by sea had virtually disappeared and at this time most of the personnel trooping for all three Services between the UK and the Far East was handled by Transport Command. Although the rapid transfer of personnel from the temperate European climate to the tropics created acclimatisation problems which had not existed in the days of the troopship, the time saved was measured in weeks and even months. The greatest disadvantage of trooping by air was that families were separated from their heavy luggage for many weeks, but as most of them went straight into fully furnished quarters or hirings, this presented no great hardship. The transport terminal and Movements Section at Changi were, therefore, constantly humming with activity as Britannias, Comets and Hastings, together with a good mixture of civil aircraft, passed through by day and night.

A newcomer to Changi was 205 Squadron. It will be recalled that this squadron, linked with 209 Squadron, had retained the Sunderland base at Seletar long after this famous flying boat had disappeared from RAF service elsewhere. It could not, however, be kept beyond 1958 and, during that year, 205 Squadron was re-equipped with the Shackleton Mark I and II. This heralded the end of the flying boat base at Seletar which had been the scene of the arrival of the first RAF aircraft to reach Singapore in 1924. Many felt that a four-engined landplane could not adequately replace the flying boat in this theatre with so much open sea space, but this was probably a nostalgic rather than a practical view. So many airfields had been developed in the Far East that areas such as Borneo, which had earlier been suitable only for flying boats or light aircraft, could now be visited by large landplanes. The superior performance of the Shackleton enabled it to carry out all Maritime Reconnaissance and Anti-Submarine tasks with greater speed and efficiency, and so it became the natural successor to the Sunderland throughout the RAF.

No 205 Squadron moved to Changi during 1958 and took its place alongside the transport squadrons. One of the squadron's subsidiary but extremely important roles was that of Search and Rescue over the whole area of the southern Indian Ocean. The ability to carry and drop an airborne lifeboat in addition to all the usual survival gear gave the Shackleton a particular value in this role along the strategic air route flown constantly by the large transport aircraft. As already mentioned (Chapter 14) one or more aircraft from 205 Squadron were kept permanently on detachment at Gan to cover the most distant parts of the Ocean. Finally, one must not fail to mention 41 RNZAF Squadron, equipped with Bristol Freighters, which had operated from Changi for several years during the Emergency, and which continued to be located there as a valuable part of the FEAF transport force.

Headquarters FEAF remained at Changi; surely the only Command Staff ever to be housed in partitioned barrack blocks. Nevertheless those spacious and lofty buildings had proved highly suitable and staff officers gained the benefit of light, airy offices with wide and open verandahs, catching all the available breeze. Air conditioning was unnecessary in such conditions. Changi had undoubtedly been well planned and built originally, and in a sense it was fortunate for the RAF that the Japanese and their prisoners had constructed the airfield, thus making a cast iron case for it to be taken over from the Army after the re-occupation.

RAF Seletar

This, the original RAF station on the island, had always been something of a problem largely due to the impossibility of extending the airfield to take the fast and heavy aircraft of the post-war years. When such aircraft had to be flown into or out of Seletar's single inadequate runway for servicing or repair at one of the station's two Maintenance Units, they had to be lightly loaded and flown by experienced pilots in daytime only. Many of the technical facilities, such as hangars, were so good, however, that the fullest possible use had to be made of them with the result that the station tended to house a very mixed collection of the less demanding types of aircraft and also the main storage, heavy maintenance and repair units for the whole Command. Nos 389 and 390 Maintenance Units occupied much of the accommodation and they needed a great deal of space. The distance of Singapore from the main sources of all supplies in the UK necessitated holding unusually large reserves of aircraft, MT vehicles, technical spares, barrack equipment and clothing. In the humid conditions which prevailed, covered storage was essential and, even then, there were immense problems in combating corrosion and deterioration of sensitive equipment.

In addition to its heavy support commitments room could still be found at Seletar for three squadrons. The largest of these was 34 Squadron which was equipped with that great load carrier the Beverley, at the time the largest aircraft in service with the RAF. Slow and ponderous though it was the Beverley was an immensely useful aircraft capable of carrying 3 ton trucks, Ferret armoured cars and a variety of vehicles and large stores which no other aircraft could take. Many derogatory comments have been made about it, some referred to it as "a loosely assembled collection of spare parts," and some as "the furniture van". Invariably these remarks were made with affection as nobody underrated its value, particularly in the overseas commands where land and sea communications were usually slow and difficult. For example, 34 Squadron could ferry a replacement fire tender to Labuan in Borneo or a helicopter to Brunei in half a day where other means of transportation might have taken weeks. No 34 Squadron, therefore, complemented the other transport squadrons at Changi and Butterworth.

When 209 Squadron severed its link with 205 Squadron and relinquished its Sunderlands, it changed its role to that of a Light Transport Squadron, being equipped with a mixture of Single and Twin Pioneers which were used mainly for communications duties up-country in Malaya and later in Borneo. Their short take off and landing characteristics suited Seletar where they could use the original grass surface and occupied little space.

The third squadron was equipped with the relatively new twin-rotor helicopter, the Belvedere. No 66 Squadron reached Seletar from an initial short stay in Butterworth in July 1962. The Belvedere was a complex heavy lift helicopter, greatly welcomed by the Army in view of its capability to transport heavy and awkward loads into and out of inaccessible sites. A 5.5 inch howitzer could, for example, be slung under the fuselage and positioned accurately upon a firing point, thus saving a great deal of manhandling by the gun crew. The Belvedere had its teething troubles like most new designs and it was appropriate that 66 Squadron should be based at Seletar where the best servicing and repair facilities existed. The initial problems were eventually eradicated and 66 Squadron went on to give sterling service in Borneo from 1963 onwards. (See Chapter 16).

Seletar was also the home of Headquarters, 224 Group when it moved down from Kuala Lumpur shortly after the independence of Malaya. This Group, commanded in 1962 by Air Vice-Marshal F Headlam CBE, of the Royal Australian Air Force, controlled all the operational squadrons in FEAF, including those of the RAAF at Butterworth. A number of distinguished RAAF officers had shared this appointment with their RAF colleagues, an arrangement which had worked well and which fostered close harmony among the Commonwealth contributions to SEATO. AVM Headlam took full advantage of this relatively quiet period in FEAF's history to bring the training of his units up to a high standard, as is shown by the unusually large number of SEATO, inter-Service and purely unit exercises which were arranged. Operational interruptions had prevented some squadrons from obtaining as much armament practice camp training with live weapons as was desirable and every opportunity was now taken to rectify this deficiency.

RAF Kai Tak

It will be recalled that Hong Kong had been extremely busy during the Korean campaign in providing the base support for the British naval and RAF units participating. This period followed the communists takeover in China and there had been well justified fears that Mao Tse-tung would set his sights on Hong Kong. Although the Colony had always been regarded as virtually indefensible against a major attack, two fighter squadrons and a large force of infantry were maintained there against any possible Chinese incursions. In the event, however, the new regime in China clearly decided that Hong Kong was of considerable value as a trading port and a link with the Western Powers. The military effort which would have been needed to capture it, and the world wide reactions which would inevitably follow were not thought to justify upsetting the status quo, and no hostile action developed.

No 28 Squadron had for many years provided the air element of Hong Kong's defence, and the squadron remained, but in a much emasculated form. It exchanged its Venoms, which had given excellent service, for the Hunter GA9 and, by 1962, the establishment had been cut right down to three aircraft. This was regarded as enough—but only just enough—to show the flag, to maintain a visible presence and to assist the Army units in monitoring the frontier over which illegal refugees from China crossed in increasingly embarrassing numbers. In the unlikely event of a serious Chinese threat to the security of Hong Kong materialising, Kai Tak could rapidly be reinforced by one or more FEAF squadrons and plans for such a contingency were kept up-to-date. For example, Hunters of 20 Squadron or Javelins of 60 Squadron, supported by transport aircraft from Changi could at anytime strengthen Hong Kong's air defences within a day. Such plans were frequently practised and a constant stream of aircraft moved between Singapore and Kai Tak. Within the narrow confines of the colony, Kai Tak had always been an extremely congested airfield, a situation which was further exacerbated by the increased demands made by civil aviation. In consequence, it made good sense to maintain the resident RAF force at the lowest level compatible with security.

The RAF Regiment

Only an occasional mention has been made in this narrative of the part played by the squadrons of the RAF Regiment in the Far East. In the early postwar years they played an important part, mainly in their primary role of airfield defence when the various countries within SEAC were being re-occupied. As this phase was completed the strength of the Regiment was progressively reduced and the formation of the RAF Regiment (Malaya) was initiated using experienced RAF Regiment personnel as instructors. Gradually these indigenous Regiment squadrons were able, particularly in Malaya, to assume full responsibility for airfield defence and other internal security duties, releasing their RAF mentors. By 1962 the purely RAF squadrons had been reduced to three in number, 15 and 63 Squadrons being deployed at Changi and Tengah respectively and 1 Squadron up-country at Butterworth for airfield defence duties with the RAAF Fighter Wing. All of these were Field Squadrons and at this time no Anti-Aircraft Squadrons of the Regiment were deployed in FEAF.

The Quiet is Disturbed

Before the end of 1962 shadows of conflict were once again becoming visible in the Far East, not on this occasion from communist activity to the north of Singapore but from the direction of British Borneo. The events which developed will be described in the next chapter. FEAF, like other RAF commands overseas, was destined throughout its life to experience almost continuous political turbulence, inspired either by communist ideological pressure or by the pressures of nationalism.

However, FEAF had been granted a few quiet years in which to consolidate, to bring its largely re-equipped squadrons up to a high state of training and operational efficiency and generally to put its house in order after the long and wearisome Malayan Emergency. Appropriately during this period the Command was presented with the Queen's Colour, an honour normally bestowed after 25 years of service. The Colour was presented on 13 January 1961, by the Earl of Selkirk GCMG CBE AFC, the United Kingdom High Commissioner for Singapore. The colour bears the symbol of a Chinese junk and the motto 'Eastward' which has been taken as the title of this book.

16

Indonesian Confrontation — I

FEAF had taken full advantage of the few quiet years following the satisfactory conclusion of the Malayan Emergency. By the end of 1962 all the squadrons, including those of Australia and New Zealand, were well equipped and trained up to a high pitch of operational efficiency, the Royal Malayan Air Force had grown steadily in size and skill, and the nations of SEATO had conducted many combined exercises planned by the Treaty's international staff centred in Bangkok.

Preparations were in hand, sponsored by Great Britain, to bring a greater degree of independence to the remaining British territories in South-East Asia. This was to be achieved by incorporating British North Borneo and Singapore Island into the concept of a Greater Malaysia within the Commonwealth, based upon the now fully independent Malaya. It was the knowledge of this concept which aroused fierce opposition from Indonesia whose President Soekarno and his nation of 100 million people saw their dream of total domination of the whole of Borneo in particular in danger of slipping away from their grasp. Although their aspirations also encompassed Malaya and Singapore, the focal point of their hostility lay in Borneo, and it was in this vast and underdeveloped island that the first signs of what came to be termed 'Confrontation' became evident towards the end of 1962. In order to understand the events of the next three years, some description of the geography, terrain and climate of this little known island is essential.

A Brief Description of Borneo

One of the largest islands in the world, Borneo measured some 800 miles from north to south and 600 miles at its widest point from east to west. In spite of its great size it was sparsely populated and largely covered by dense and impenetrable jungle. Little attempt had been

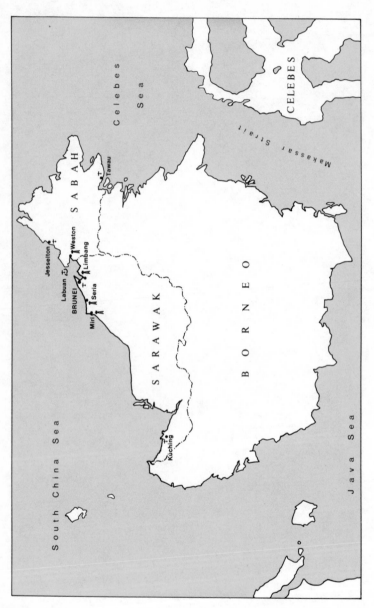

Map 9
Sketch map of Borneo

made through the ages to develop the interior which remained much as it had been for centuries, the main centres of population being on the coastal fringes.

The four States into which Borneo was divided were Kalimantan, Sarawak, Sabah and Brunei (see Map 9). Of these Kalimantan was by far the largest, occupying three quarters of the island, but it was also the most underdeveloped. Much of its dense jungle remained unexplored as movement through it was virtually impossible except by river or uncharted native tracks. Until 1949 Kalimantan had been part of the Dutch East Indies, but was then transferred to Indonesia as part of the independence agreement.

Next in size was Sarawak covering an area of 48,000 square miles with its capital at Kuching. Like its Indonesian neighbour Sarawak was largely undeveloped except for a small area around the capital. Communications were conducted along the wide, fast-flowing rivers, and by air to the scattered jungle air strips which had been constructed chiefly by timber firms and missionaries. The Ibans or 'Sea Dyaks' inhabited the interior, living in the celebrated 'long houses'. It was not uncommon for the whole population of one village to live in a communal 'long house', each family having its own rooms but sharing a common verandah. The Ibans were the original head-hunters of Borneo and many shrunken skulls could still be seen hanging in little wicker baskets in the 'long houses'. The last known head-hunting orgy took place in 1945 when many Japanese heads were added to previous collections.

North Borneo, or Sabah, as it was known, lay to the north of Sarawak, the two together forming the original Crown Colony of British North Borneo. Sabah was approximately half the size of Sarawak with an attractive coastal capital at Jesselton. Like its neighbours the interior was largely undeveloped but, unlike Sarawak, extended right across the island to the east coast where the port of Tawau provided a second main entry to the state.

Lastly there was the small, but wealthy independent state of Brunei, sandwiched between Sabah and Sarawak. Covering a mere 2,500 square miles with a population of 84,000, it derived a rich income from its oilfields at Seria. Brunei was ruled by its Sultan who firmly resisted any proposals to join with his neighbours for fear of dissipating the oil revenues.

Mention must also be made of the important island of Labuan, situated 20 miles off the coast. Originally part of Brunei, it was later transferred to the province of Sabah. Labuan was used as a Royal Air Force staging post, fluctuating in size depending upon the commitments in Borneo of the Singapore-based squadrons. It was manned by detachments from Changi and, like the islands of Gan and Masirah in the Indian Ocean, was ideally situated and secure from the troubles which so often affect mainland airfields. Labuan was to become extremely important during the years of Confrontation.

Borneo's climate was not unlike that of Malaya but the dense jungle seemed to attract even heavier and more frequent rain. Heat and humidity were the main constituents and together these produced a great deal of low lying mist and fog at certain times of the day with a build-up of immense formations of cumulus cloud leading to torrential rain at other times. There were two monsoonal seasons but the impact of these was less well defined than in, say, Burma or Bengal. Although there was some seasonal variation, it would be deceptive to refer to a 'wet' and 'dry' season. As one writer succinctly put it: "during the wet season it rained all day, and during the dry season, every day". The heavy and frequent rainfall tended to keep the daytime temperature within bounds—the middle and high eighties being the average with a humidity of 80% year in and year out. In short, it was an oppressive and exhausting climate for the European, and this needs to be taken very much into account when studying the operations of the RAF in Borneo.

A typical day's weather for the airman started with thick mist until about ten o'clock followed by a clear period of good flying weather lasting for four or five hours. A gradual build-up of convection cloud, developing into massive cumulo-nimbus then took place resulting in torrential rainstorms accompanied by violent turbulence and severe downdraughts in the mountainous regions. There might then be a brief period of clearance before darkness fell all the year round at about seven o'clock. It will be clear from this somewhat daunting description that tactical air operations had to be confined to several hours in the middle of the day. Night operations in proximity to the mountains were impracticable, not only from the point of view of the hazards involved but also because of the difficulty of locating targets.

In this respect air operations in Borneo were similar to those in Malaya but, if anything, more difficult. Until Confrontation started the mapping and survey of Borneo was virtually non-existent and such maps as existed were of small scale and little value for tactical purposes. This deficiency added to the prevailing weather pattern created immense problems for aircrew trained with modern navigation equipment. Even a return to the art of map reading was unsatisfactory as no reliance could be placed upon the only maps available. As will be seen pilots and navigators were compelled to adopt a form of navigation to a target area which depended heavily upon personal knowledge and experience of the features of the terrain such as ridges, rivers, valleys, outcrops of stone and 'long houses' buried in deep jungle, accompanied by stopwatch timed runs on specific compass headings. Under these conditions experience counted for everything and it was clearly unwise to replace aircrew earlier than was absolutely essential.

Finally, in describing the features of Borneo, distance and the mountainous terrain must not be ignored. A glance at Map 9 will show that the nearest point to Singapore was 400 miles, and Tawau on the eastern seaboard of Sabah some 1,300 miles from the main base of all the aircraft involved. Within Borneo the frontier between Kalimantan and the three British-supported territories was about 900 miles in length, most of it set in dense jungle where infiltration could be effected anywhere, provided of course that the infiltrators were able to penetrate the jungle. Although the coastal fringes were relatively flat and low-lying, there were rugged and mountainous regions in the interior, some of the peaks rising to 13,000 feet and frequently obscured in the prevalent mist and low cloud. It is against this background of inhospitable conditions that Confrontation was to be staged.

The Political Situation

The political situation in 1962 has to be viewed with the knowledge that Sarawak and Sabah were British Crown Colonies and Brunei a British Protectorate with an autonomous Ruler in the person of the Sultan. Great Britain was therefore committed to deal with any internal subversion or hostile incursions across the frontiers of any of the three States. She could not stand aloof and her forces based on Singapore were an earnest of her intention to maintain the security of those dependencies within the Commonwealth. Consequently British sea, land and air forces were automatically involved from the first hint of trouble. That hint became apparent during 1962 when certain elements in the three Borneo territories, strongly supported by the Indonesian Republic, objected to the concept of Malaysia, a project which the United Kingdom Government was determined to see accomplished.

Owing to the backward nature of the country, political development had been slow. Sabah possessed five parties in 1961 but these merged a year later into the Sabah Alliance Party. In Sarawak there was a predominantly Chinese grouping which had the reputation of being a front for communist activities and which strongly opposed any suggestion that Sarawak should be included in the proposed Malaysia. Additionally the Colony possessed a powerful underground communist movement.

Political development in Brunei was centred on the Sultan himself. Although enjoying a considerable revenue from oil, the Sultan's rule was autocratic and his administration was hardly of the Western democratic type. Poverty was widespread and, as always, this generated dissatisfaction which led to the formation of a militant political organisation; in this case the Partai Ra'Ayat which possessed a military wing known as the Tentera/Nasional Kalimant Utara (TNKU). This organisation can be likened to a Mau Mau type anti-colonialist movement and was strongly sympathetic to Indonesia. Thus the stage was set for active subversion in all three territories when the proposal to incorporate them into Malaysia became known.

Rebellion in Brunei

The curtain went up on what was to become a Confrontation of almost four years' duration on 8 December 1962 and, not surprisingly, the initial action took place in Brunei. There had been rumours of the existence of a Borneo Liberation Army as early as June of that year and in November the British Resident in the Fifth Division of Sarawak[1] had warned the authorities in Kuching that "some political intrigue seemed to be going on". On 7 December the Commissioner-General for South-East Asia, at the conclusion of a routine visit to Brunei, informed the Commander-in-Chief in Singapore that a rebel attack on either the Sarawak oilfield at Miri or on that belonging to Brunei at Seria was a distinct possibility on the following day. HQ FEAF possessed an up-to-date plan ALE to airlift an infantry company from Singapore to reinforce the Brunei Police, and the appropriate

---

[1] Sarawak was split up into five Divisions for civil administrative purposes, the First Division being the southernmost, in the Kuching area; the remaining four extending progressively northwards.

17. A supply of fuel leaving an Argosy of 215 Squadron in Borneo, 1966

18. The RAF Regiment on jungle patrol in Borneo

19. A Twin Pioneer of 209 Squadron leaving a jungle strip

20. The airmen's swimming pool at Changi with the RAF Hospital in the background

force was brought to immediate readiness. When rebellion broke out as forecast on 8 December the British forces were fully prepared for it and went into action immediately.

The revolt originated not only in Brunei as predicted but also in the Fourth and Fifth Divisions of Sarawak and the rebels belonged to the TNKU which was reported to comprise 15 companies, each of 150 men, armed with shotguns, parangs, axes and spears. The targets were mainly police stations, a number of which were caught by surprise and rapidly overwhelmed.

Plan ALE depended inevitably on the rapidity with which troops could be flown in from Singapore by the Royal Air Force. FEAF was fortunate in having more transport aircraft available on 8 December than had been the case for some weeks, including the bonus of a Transport Command Britannia at Changi which was promptly commandeered for the operations. Twelve Hastings of 48 Squadron, four Beverleys of 34 Squadron and a number of Pioneers of 209 Squadron immediately started the lift of two companies of Gurkha Rifles to Brunei. The Britannia was compelled to land at Labuan which had the only runway capable of accepting it, but the first Beverley was ordered to reconnoitre Brunei civil airfield and discharge its 93 troops there if possible. The pilot, Squadron Leader M G Bennett DFC, heard from Labuan control that the civil airfield had been obstructed but, on inspection, he found that the obstacles had been removed. They had in fact been cleared by the Controller of Civil Aviation in person assisted by the civilian fire brigade. Squadron Leader Bennett landed his aircraft safely and the Gurkhas took over the airfield.

Meanwhile the Britannia had been turned round by the staging post airmen at Labuan in one hour and ten minutes and was able to return to Changi by lunchtime and complete a second round trip during the day. More Beverleys of 34 Squadron carried full loads of troops, vehicles and ordnance from Seletar during the day, one of them continuing after unloading at Brunei to Jesselton, to undertake more ferrying duties.

The situation which met the troops as they landed was extremely confused. In Brunei town the rebels had been driven out of the power station which they had captured earlier in the day and their attacks on the main police station, the Sultan's palace and the Prime Minister's residence had all been repulsed by police with the aid of a platoon of the North Borneo Field Force. These latter troops had been ferried

down from Jesselton in a Twin Pioneer of 209 Squadron which had
been on routine anti-piracy patrols at the time, and by sundry small
civilian aircraft. Elsewhere the situation was more serious. At Tutong
and Muara the unfenced wooden police stations had been captured
and the towns were dominated by the rebels. Similarly the police
station at the important Seria oilfield had fallen and a number of
Europeans were being held as hostages. Using these hostages as
shields, the rebels attacked Panaga police station at the western end
of the oilfield. The attack was repulsed but one hostage was killed
and five injured.

Later in the day the police post at Anduki and the airfield were
captured by rebels, the runway being immediately obstructed with
vehicles. Consequently, with the exception of Brunei town where the
Sultan was protected and the central Government maintained, the
whole State was virtually in rebel hands by mid afternoon on 8
December. In neighbouring Sarawak the position was somewhat less
serious. The town of Limbang was seized and Weston was in danger
of being occupied, but energetic action by police reinforcements
restored the situation by 0630 hours on the following morning.

The Airlift Continues

It was an ugly picture and had it not been for the rapidity and great
efficiency with which plan ALE was activated, it would have been
even more serious. FEAF and its transport squadrons must take most
of the credit for the speed with which the initial troops and their
equipment were flown to Brunei within a few hours of news of the
revolt reaching Singapore. On 8 and 9 December 28 transport aircraft
loads were flown into Brunei including reinforcement for the small
staging post party on the airfield at Labuan who worked round the
clock with remarkable energy and efficiency in deplaning troops,
vehicles and equipment and turning the aircraft round. During the
next eleven days the airlift continued unabated, every available transport aircraft being pressed into service. These included a Bristol
Freighter from the RNZAF, a Hercules of the RAAF, Shackletons of
205 Squadron and a Valetta from 52 Squadron as well as the Britannia
from Transport Command alternately flown by a crew from 99
Squadron and one from 511 Squadron. By the thirteenth day after
the revolt broke out, the airlift had taken into Brunei 3,209 passengers,
113 vehicles, assorted guns and trailers, 13 dogs, two Auster aircraft,
one re-fueller and no less than 624,308 lbs of freight. Fortunately the

well developed facilities at Labuan permitted such an influx. The original plan ALE complement of Gurkhas was considered inadequate to deal with the situation and was reinforced by elements of the 1st Battalion, The Queen's Own Cameron Highlanders under the command of Lieutenant-Colonel W G McHardy MBE MC.

Although heavier equipment, vehicles, ammunition and more troops began to arrive by sea during the latter part of this initial period; the first essential was to get fighting troops into immediate action to isolate and mop up the centres of the revolt before the rebels had time to consolidate their first gains, and before Indonesian sympathisers could cross the border from Kalimantan in significant numbers. In view of the paucity of good airfields in the area, a great strain was placed upon RAF Labuan and it was remarkable that so large a force could be deployed with such rapidity. ALE had indeed been well planned and executed, aided by the few hours of warning which the authorities had received.

A Joint Force Headquarters

Within a few days of the outbreak of trouble it was clear that all three Services would be closely involved and that some form of Joint Force Headquarters would be essential to co-ordinate and control operations. On 15 December an inter-Service team was despatched from Singapore with instructions to find a suitable location and to assess the communications requirements.

Initially the team met with some opposition because the RAF had already established its own control on the airfield at Labuan, whereas the Army had taken over some air-conditioned offices in the Brunei Residency. Neither wished to move and the Navy showed little interest at that time in a Joint Headquarters. As things were developing, however, such a headquarters was obviously essential and, after some reconnaissance and negotiation, a girls' high school in Brunei was selected. This was approved without delay in Singapore and Major-General W C Walker CBE DSO was appointed as Director of Operations; he was later succeeded by Major-General G H Lea DSO MBE.

Within three days the school had been transformed into a Joint Force Headquarters complete with the essential communications back to Singapore and forward to the units in the field. This was a great achievement on the part of the various signals staffs concerned. The three Services moved in and on 24 December the HQ was fully operational with the resounding title of HQ COMBRITBOR (Commander, British Forces, Borneo).

Initial Operations

As soon as the small British and Gurkha force landed at Brunei, the Force Commander decided to give immediate priority to the relief of Seria and the capture of Anduki airstrip. A Twin Pioneer of 209 Squadron reconnoitred both places carrying the Force Commander and the Brunei Police Commissioner. Although rebel flags were seen to be flying over most of the area, landing at both places appeared to be possible and a bold plan was conceived to land troops simultaneously at Seria and Anduki.

The troops involved practised rapid deplaning and the exit doors of the aircraft detailed for the operation were removed. At 1245 on 10 December five Twin Pioneers of 209 Squadron carrying 60 men, an Army Air Corps Beaver with the Force Commander and a 34 Squadron Beverley with 110 men took off. With considerable skill and no little hazard the Twin Pioneers with Wing Commander Graves, the CO of Labuan, in the leading aircraft landed successfully on a rough, grassy and extremely soft area to the west of the Seria oilfield complex. The first Pioneer came in over high trees and pulled up within 10 yards of a road ditch facing a 'Halt Major Road Ahead' sign. The other four Pioneers were ordered to land in the opposite direction which entailed brushing through a tree with their port wing tips. One aircraft was bogged during this tricky landing but the troops deplaned rapidly and doubled two miles to their objective, Panaga Police Station, which they speedily relieved without opposition.

Meanwhile the Beverley pilot faced a particularly hazardous landing at Anduki. He concentrated all his passengers on the lower deck, approached low along the coast line to avoid detection, climbed over trees at the last moment and braked hard on landing using only a quarter of the runway length. The troops leaped out in full battle order and the Beverley executed a short field take off in the same direction, 1 minute, 48 seconds after landing. Even so the aircraft received two hits in the rear fuselage and tail unit from a light automatic weapon fired by a rebel in the control tower. There were, however, no casualties and the attacking party split up and soon captured the airfield and its buildings.

Slowly but steadily the Army units consolidated their hold on Seria and Anduki and the insurgents were forced to surrender or withdraw.

On the following day, 11 December, the weather deteriorated but both Pioneers and Beverleys flew reinforcements into Anduki in torrential rain, an operation which reflected great credit on the aircrew.

An episode which qualifies as a piece of military bluff was enacted during this operation, and it involved a Canberra of 45 Squadron based at Tengah but temporarily detached to Labuan. Before the leading troops flew into Seria the rebels telephoned the Shell Petroleum Company and threatened to attack Panaga Police Station using their hostages as a screen. During this conversation the Canberra pilot flew low over Seria and made a number of dummy attacks. A second rebel's voice interrupted the conversation to say that the hostages would not be harmed. A similar ploy was used two days later when four Hunters of 20 Squadron staged a mock attack on Seria Police Station, one aircraft firing its guns over the building and into the sea. This was followed by a broadcast from a 209 Squadron 'Voice' Pioneer, calling upon the rebels to surrender. Immediately after the broadcast a British platoon stormed the Police Station and rescued 48 European hostages, 16 of whom had been imprisoned in a one man cell. This very rapid and, for the rebels, quite devastating onslaught on two of their major prizes had a demoralising effect with the result that a number of other places which they had occupied including Limbang, Bangar, Bekemi and Niah were recaptured with little difficulty by a Royal Marine Commando and other reinforcements brought in by air and sea.

From 12 December onwards the British forces built up rapidly as the first Royal Navy ships began to arrive from Singapore bringing more infantry, a second Royal Marine Commando with its Brigade Headquarters, Ferret armoured cars and a battery of Royal Artillery. These forces under the overall command of General Walker were more than sufficient to mop up any pockets of resistance from the original revolt and to deploy, albeit thinly, along the vast frontier separating the British territories from Kalimantan.

1963 opened with exceptionally heavy rain and severe flooding throughout Borneo which hampered operations aimed at removing the last traces of the Brunei revolt. The opportunity was taken by General Walker to endeavour to win the hearts and minds of the native population with a series of food drops and evacuation sorties. For example, Beverleys parachuted food supplies to those towns and villages isolated by the floods and were supported by a number of

Royal Navy helicopters which assisted by lifting evacuees from the worst affected areas. This psychological campaign was to assume great importance at a later stage when frontier infiltration by guerillas trained, armed and encouraged in Indonesia began to assume serious proportions. It has to be remembreed that the population of the Borneo territories was polyglot with a predominance of Chinese and Malays. Many of these were pro-communist and, therefore, sympathetic to Indonesian aspirations. The indigenous inhabitants were largely primitive agricultural people concentrated in the 'long houses' and generally disinterested in politics. The problem of maintaining loyalty and security in the face of infiltration was therefore considerable.

Infiltration Increases

The initial and localised revolt could be said to have been crushed within the first two months of 1963 but it was the signal for a steady increase in raids across the border from Kalimantan. Although the frontier had been thinly screened with Gurkhas and troopers of 22 Special Air Service Regiment (SAS), they were insufficient to prevent an Indonesian raid on the Tebedu Police Station south of Kuching on 12 April 1963. This was followed by a raid on Seng in Sarawak in August. These and other raids were repulsed with little difficulty but the pattern had become clear and what had started as a local and internal revolt had degenerated into Confrontation with the neighbouring state of Indonesia, which meant that trouble was liable to occur at almost any point along the immensely long frontier.

The Indonesian Government came out into the open with various inflammatory statements such as "we have given our sympathies to the people of North Kalimantan (North Borneo) struggling for their freedom". Later the Indonesian Army Chief of Staff announced that the Army was awaiting the order to move in support of the people of North Borneo, and that he had two divisions of volunteers trained and ready to enter the territory. It was also stated that Indonesia had helped to train 6,000 anti-British, anti-Malayan rebels from the North Borneo area.

British Government Reactions

The deteriorating situation was well understood in London as revealed in a telegram from Lord Selkirk in Kuala Lumpur to the Colonial Office which contained the words, "it would be rash to assume that the emergency in Brunei is over .... The situation will continue to be precarious". Later in 1963 Mr R A Butler, the British Foreign Secretary, said—"we hope that Indonesia will realize our sense of purpose... come what may, we intend to support Malaya in her struggle for independence and success. I hope this will not mean any Confrontation with Indonesia... but nothing will prevent us from backing the growth and independence of Malaya".

Not only had it been made crystal clear that Britain intended to support the project for establishing a Greater Malaysia with any armed force which Indonesia's attitude might necessitate, but that quelling the Brunei revolt would not permit the release of forces from the North Borneo territories for as long as the threat continued to exist.

Proclamation of Malaysia

This then was the situation when Malaysia came into existence on 16 September 1963, with the full support of the British Government, Singapore, Sarawak and Sabah. Its formation was also approved by the United Nations whose Secretary-General, U Thant, affirmed that the peoples of North Borneo wished to join Malaysia.

Indonesia immediately broke off diplomatic relations with the new State of Malaysia whose Government responded by breaking off its relations with both Indonesia and the Philippines, the latter country being hostile to the inclusion of North Borneo in the new state.

Brunei alone remained as an independent state outside Malaysia and under the protection of Britain. It may seem surprising that this small state, which had been the scene of the original revolt, should wish to stand alone but it has to be remembered that its autocratic Ruler had treasured his independence for many years and was concerned lest his considerable oil revenues should be swallowed up by covetous neighbours in any amalgamation with them. This attitude was well known to the authorities and no great pressure was placed upon the Sultan of Brunei to alter the status quo.

Sarawak and Sabah were jointly given the title of Eastern Malaysia while Malaya and Singapore formed Western Malaysia. It was quite clear that the proclamation of 16 September had greatly increased the dangers of Confrontation with Indonesia not only on the borders of Eastern Malaysia but also along the shores of Malaya and Singapore. A state of undeclared war existed and the events which followed will be dealt with in the next chapter.

17

Indonesian Confrontation — II

It was fully expected that Indonesian raids across the Kalimantan frontier with the North Borneo territories would be stepped up after the September proclamation of Malaysia, but the intensity of the reaction throughout Indonesia was much more violent than had been thought likely. So intense was it that there was considerable fear for the lives of British residents in that country. When it became clear within three days of the inauguration of Malaysia that the Indonesian Government was either unwilling or unable to ensure their safety, it was decided to evacuate to Singapore all those British personnel who wished to leave.

Fortunately an additional transport squadron had been formed in FEAF during August to reinforce the transport force which was heavily committed to supporting the forces in Borneo. No 215 Squadron, which had been disbanded in the UK in 1957, was re-formed at Changi and equipped with the Armstrong Whitworth Argosy C Mark I, a four-engined turbo-prop transport powered by Rolls-Royce Dart engines. Already proven in UK service this aircraft was a valuable general purpose addition to the FEAF fleet and the aircraft were flown out from Benson by their crews to form 215 Squadron on 1 August 1963.

On 19 September three Argosies, and one Hastings of 48 Squadron, flew to Djakarta under a guarantee of non-interference and a substantial proportion of the British community was evacuated to Singapore. Over a period of a few days more than 400 people were flown out. Thereafter any overflying of Indonesian territory was prohibited which was a considerable inconvenience to the RAF as it entailed re-routeing all Transport Command scheduled services to Australia to avoid Indonesian airspace. It did not, however, prevent Indonesian Air Force aircraft from flying frequently over Malaysian territory and nine such incursions were recorded in November alone. Four of these were identified as B25 Mitchell bombers escorted by P51 Mustang fighters.

Intense diplomatic activity followed this development, involving the USA, the Philippines and Siam, and resulted in a totally ineffectual cease-fire in Borneo being announced. The incursions into Malaysian air space continued as before and it became necessary for FEAF to establish an Air Defence Identification Zone (ADIZ) around ·the borders of Sabah and Sarawak which extended to three miles offshore.

In order to police this ADIZ, which added considerably to the RAF commitments, and to protect the area from aircraft committing hostile acts, eight Hunters were despatched from 20 Squadron to Borneo. Four were positioned at Labuan and four at Kuching. Additionally 60 Squadron deployed two Javelins at each of these airfields, thus giving Eastern Malaysia a permanent day and night, all-weather air defence system. The Rules of Engagement applying to interceptions were amended to give pilots the authority to engage and destroy Indonesian aircraft overflying the ADIZ without first obtaining authority from the ground after a sighting. This additional commitment gave 60 Squadron, the only all-weather fighter squadron in the Command, an operational area some 1,600 miles in length extending from Butterworth in the west to Kuching and Labuan in the east. Although this was an impossibly long frontier for a single squadron to patrol, the addition of Mark 9R Javelins carrying long range fuel tanks and Firestreak air-to-air missiles with crews who had completed two or three tours on Javelins, made the squadron a force to be reckoned with. Whether this strengthening of the fighter defences or the continuation of high level diplomatic talks in Tokyo was the reason, there was a temporary but distinct reduction in the number of violations of Malaysian air space during the early part of 1964.

Increasing Guerilla Activity

In Borneo, however, the inauguration of Malaysia was the signal for the stepping up of raids into Sarawak and Sabah by bands of guerillas from across the Kalimantan border. Most of these bands comprised local Kalimantan Indonesians with a proportion of Sarawak Chinese. It was estimated that some 1,500 of the latter had been trained in Kalimantan·with the primary object of terrorising the locals in order to destroy their will to support the Security Forces. In many respects it was a repetition of the terrorist tactics used in Malaya some years earlier. At this stage in the Confrontation few, if any, Indonesian regular troops participated in the raids but their support was ever present behind the scenes.

The Security Forces were faced with the problem of maintaining internal law and order throughout North Borneo whilst watching the 800 mile frontier and endeavouring to intercept the raiders. The problem was solved by deploying the forces in a series of 'forts' and strong points located behind an outpost frontier screen or picquet line. The immense length of the frontier and the relatively few troops available caused units to become fragmented, thus creating difficulties in command and control. However, the very nature of the country proved something of an asset. There was a strictly limited number of well defined crossing places which tended to confine infiltrators to specific avenues of approach, and any attempt to disperse was severely hampered by the terrain. Full advantage was taken of these limitations in deploying the British and Gurkha troops who depended largely upon supply by air from the Beverleys, Hastings, Argosies and Pioneers, and upon helicopters for communication between outposts, casualty evacuation and local reinforcement. The invaluable part played by helicopters which were now more numerous and more versatile than had been the case during the Malayan Emergency will become evident as this narrative continues. As long as Indonesian regular forces, with their air support which was known to exist, did not participate in any strength, the Security Forces were able to contain this situation, albeit with great difficulty and discomfort.

1963 gave way to 1964 but the long expected introduction of Indonesia's regular troops did not materialise. The RAF squadrons maintained a heavy programme of ferrying, air supply, casualty evacuation and search and rescue among the units scattered along the frontier. The helicopter force was greatly strengthened by the arrival of reinforcements from the United Kingdom. SPINEFORCE, as these reinforcements were codenamed, comprised 225 Squadron, equipped with Whirlwind 10s, and four Belvederes of 26 Squadron. All of these, based at Odiham, had been taking part in a Middle East exercise TRIPLEX WEST and were hurriedly directed from El Adem to Kuching by sea, where they joined the resident force made up of detachments from 110, 66, and 103 Squadrons in Singapore. Thus the helicopter force available to General Walker virtually doubled overnight, bringing immense relief to the overworked detachments.

The photographic work of the Canberra PR7s of 81 Squadron proved to be a vital asset to the troops on the frontier at this stage of

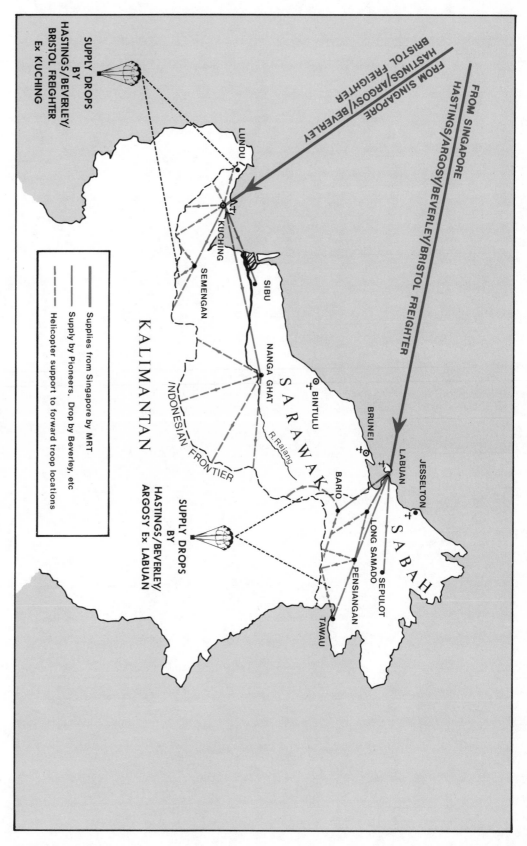

Figure V
Diagram of method of air supply in Borneo

operations. As mentioned earlier, huge areas of Borneo were virtually unmapped, certainly to the large scale required for tactical operations. Flying from Tengah and using Labuan as an advanced base, the squadron met the heavy demands for tactical photography along the length of the frontier, producing prints of a quality which clearly identified frontier crossing points, jungle tracks and isolated 'longhouses'. At this stage of Confrontation penetration beyond the Kalimantan border was strictly prohibited in view of the risk that the Security Forces might be branded as aggressors, a development of which Indonesian sympathisers in the United Nations would have been quick to take advantage. Although frustrating to troops pursuing infiltrators, the prohibition was no great handicap at this time as it was known that no Indonesian concentrations of ground forces, no large supply or ammunition depots and no airfields existed in the dense jungle through which the frontier ran.

The range and endurance of the Canberra was so much superior to any previous PR aircraft in the squadron that not only could a great deal of work be completed during each sortie but the high speed of the aircraft permitted the results to be processed and issued to those requiring the information with the minimum loss of time. Tactical intelligence could not have been gained or updated in any way other than by aerial photography and, although other aircraft than the Canberra carried cameras for specific purposes, the contribution of 81 Squadron was even greater than it had been during the earlier operations in Malaya.

Method of Air Supply

As guerilla incursions increased, so did the mobility and flexibility of the Security Forces and certain tactics were developed to achieve this improvement. As already stated, all supply to the troops in forward locations had to be by air and a diagram at Figure V shows, in somewhat over-simplified form, how the air supply was organised and built up over a period of many months. Labuan and Kuching were the two forward airheads into which bulk supplies and personnel flowed from the Singapore main base. A daily stream of Hastings, Argosies, Beverleys and RNZAF Bristol Freighters flew into these two airfields carrying the more urgently needed supplies, equipment and personnel, leaving bulk supplies of food, ammunition and heavy machinery to be carried by sea. A number of forward airstrips were constructed, usually by Royal Engineers assisted by men of the Airfield Construction Branch of the RAF and by the fighting troops themselves. Many of these are shown in Figure V at Lundu (First Division of Sarawak), Semengan (Second Division), Nanga Ghat (Third Division), Long Samado and Bario (Fifth Division), and Sepulot and Tawau (Sabah).

These and other forward airstrips were kept supplied from Kuching and Labuan in a variety of ways depending upon the nature of the airstrip. Wherever possible supplies were landed by Twin and Single Pioneers of 209 Squadron and the RMAF and occasionally it was possible to land a Beverley or Valetta under favourable conditions. When conditions were unsuitable for fixed wing aircraft, helicopters had to be used, the Belvederes of 66 Squadron being particularly valuable on this leg of the supply system with their load carrying capability and their ability to lift heavy and awkward pieces of equipment and machinery.

There could be no particular standard of construction for a forward airstrip: advantage could sometimes be taken of a clear area on a river bank to carve out a reasonably level runway with good approaches, but many of them were rough, short in length and with approaches requiring considerable skill on the part of pilots. These strips formed the forward bases from which the ground force units carried out their frontier patrols, each patrol remaining in the jungle for about four days before returning to the forward base. These units, often of battalion strength, defended and maintained the airstrips and assisted with the unloading and handling of the supply aircraft.

Detachments of helicopters were maintained at some of the forward airstrips to save transit time from Kuching or Labuan, and these were the means of supplying the day to day needs of the troops on patrol along the border. It was essential for the patrols to be lightly loaded and equipped and therein lay considerable danger to the troops. Movement was inevitably slow and exhausting and the risk of becoming disorientated and lost in the dense undergrowth was considerable. Each man's load had to be a careful compromise between adequate weapons and ammunition with which to fight and sufficient food and water on which to survive.

As even tracked vehicles were useless and totally unable to reach the locations to which patrols were required to go, supply by air was essential and its regularity vital if troops were not to be exposed to even greater danger and discomfort than necessary. RAF and RN helicopters provided the bulk of this tactical air supply and even they were frequently unable to find clearings in which to land. On such

21. The RAF Station on Gan Island in the Maldives with the lagoon in the background

22. The RAF Station and runway at Kai Tak, Hong Kong

23. A Wessex helicopter of 28 Squadron Kai Tak, lowering a Hong Kong policeman during an exercise in the Colony

24. RAF marine craft at speed in Hong Kong harbour in 1966

occasions it was usual for supplies to be winched down into the forest while any passengers had to descend on a knotted rope or abseil—a technique developed earlier in Malaya. Parachutes, whether for supplies or men, were little used in these circumstances as the risk of being caught up in the 200 foot trees was unacceptable.

During the border patrols the morale of the ground forces was greatly strengthened by the knowledge that any casualties could be rapidly evacuated by helicopter. Although the risk of being wounded in an ambush or skirmish was ever present, the danger of a soldier being injured, bitten or suffering from heat exhaustion or other sickness was even greater under the difficult conditions in which the troops had to operate. It was, therefore, a great comfort to know that a Sycamore or a Whirlwind, carrying a stretcher, could be called upon within a very short time should an injury or sickness occur. The helicopter crews were all trained in first aid and had become expert at handling medical cases, flying them back to a forward airstrip or, if necessary, continuing to Labuan or Kuching with particularly serious cases.

Tactical air support in all its forms gave the Security Forces an immense advantage over an enemy who not only did not enjoy such support, but was not infrequently left literally to starve in the jungle if injured or otherwise unable to return to his base. In certain other respects, however, the Security Forces were at a disadvantage. So sensitive was the political situation in this undeclared war that the frontier had to be scrupulously respected, not always easy when it was only defined as a map reference of dubious accuracy in dense jungle. This limitation prevented any follow up of guerillas retreating across the border after an incursion and it certainly put out of the question any 'hot pursuit' or air offensive action by the RAF against camps, bases or other interdiction targets in Kalimantan.

Very few targets for air attack were thus offered or taken on. Nevertheless the known presence of Canberras, Hunters and Javelins acted as a valuable deterrent to large scale incursions into more open country where the intruders would immediately have been heavily attacked and probably destroyed. At this stage of Confrontation, namely during the early part of 1964, action was confined to frequent but small scale guerilla raids without any form of Indonesian air support. Many of these were intercepted and dispersed before they could achieve their object of terrorising the native population. It was a period of small scale activity which gave the Security Forces the opportunity to improve their forward deployment, construct airstrips and develop operating techniques which made the fullest use of the available tactical air support.

This lull in hostile activity was undoubtedly due to knowledge of a forthcoming high level international conference which was to take place in Tokyo in June 1964 and to be attended by the Prime Ministers of Malaysia, Indonesia and the Philippines in an endeavour to resolve the problem of Confrontation. In the event, however, the complete breakdown of the talks was the signal for Indonesia to change her tactics and intensify her effort. Incursions by guerillas on the accustomed pattern were now supplemented by the much more serious challenge of regular Indonesian troops, typified by an attack on the 1st Battalion, 6th Gurkha Rifles at Rasau in Sarawak. This was the first occasion on which regular troops had appeared and the attack took place within 24 hours of the breakdown of the Tokyo talks. The Gurkhas lost five killed and had five wounded, an outcome which they regarded as a severe reversal, if not a defeat, although it was in the face of an exceedingly professional attack.

It was obvious to General Walker that Confrontation had entered a new phase and that new methods were needed to counter the greatly increased threat. Accordingly infantry companies were ordered to operate from permanent, heavily defended bases or forts with full artillery and air support. During the month of July no less than 34 attacks on the pattern of the first took place, but the lesson had been learned at considerable cost to the courageous Gurkhas and further casualties were minimal. It was now abundantly clear that, although war had not been declared, the situation had deteriorated far beyond mere confrontation with bands of guerillas.

Hostilities Spread to Western Malaysia

Until August 1964, operations were confined to Borneo but in that month a more sinister threat emerged. On 17 August approximately 100 armed Indonesian regular troops went ashore at three separate points in Johore on the west coast of the Malay peninsula. These incursions were followed ten days later by an attack on the Esso Island bunkering station off Singapore and upon a Malaysian patrol craft by an Indonesian flotilla. On 2 September 96 Indonesian paratroopers were dropped from a C130 Hercules near Labis in North Central Johore. Although not intercepted, it was thought that the Hercules crashed during its return flight to Indonesia.

The impact of these events on HQ 224 Group was considerable and the implications serious. It had always been extremely difficult to control the movement of small craft and native boats in the narrow straits of the Malay peninsula, but it was the bold infringement of Malaysian airspace by the Hercules which dropped the paratroopers that offered a strong challenge to the RAF. If a transport aircraft could approach and complete such a mission, it followed that the strike aircraft with which the Indonesian Air Force was known to be equipped posed a deadly threat to the RAF stations on Singapore Island and to the RAAF station at Butterworth.

HQ FEAF reacted immediately by calling all its strike/attack aircraft to alert states, a procedure which involved 60 Squadron Javelins, 20 Squadron Hunters, the RAAF Sabres at Butterworth and even the ageing Meteor 8s of 1574 Target Towing Flight at Changi. After several false alarms and many hours of standby duty 20 Squadron was ordered to carry out a series of strikes in support of the ground forces engaged in fighting the Indonesian paratroopers who had landed in Johore. Fourteen sorties were flown by the Hunters, each armed with 16×3 inch rocket projectiles with 60 lb semi-armour piercing heads and a full load of 30 mm Aden gun ammunition. A thousand square yards of jungle known to contain the enemy was not the most satisfying target from the pilots' point of view but they were able to use a line of discarded enemy parachutes as an aiming point in the hope of destroying their supplies. It was a lengthy and difficult but successful operation for the ground forces: all but ten of the enemy paratroopers had been eliminated by the end of September. The Indonesians who had been landed from boats on the coast near Pontian proved less easy to liquidate, but with strong helicopter and Pioneer support, this was eventually achieved by the end of October.

A certain Lieutenant Sukitno, who was taken prisoner shortly after landing by parachute during the Labis operation, was sufficiently disillusioned to write a pamphlet bearing his own picture and telling his fellow soldiers of the futility of infiltration. At the request of the Malaysian Prime Minister a million copies of this pamphlet were dropped over Indonesian territory by Hastings and Argosies. It failed, however, to deter subsequent landings which continued on an increasing scale. Between 17 August 1964 and 29 March 1965 there were 41 incidents of landings, attempted landings and sabotage in Western Malaysia. Indonesian personnel who are known to have participated totalled 740 of whom 451 actually landed. One hundred and forty-two were killed and 309 were captured.

One of the most serious incursions occurred on 23 December 1964 in Johore and this generated an RAF air strike codenamed BIRDSONG. Real and simulated attacks were carried out by Hunters of 20 Squadron and, for the first time, by Canberras of 45 Squadron, in an effort to demoralise the infiltrators and compel them to split into small groups. The attacks were repeated on Christmas Eve and again on Boxing Day under the control of a Forward Air Controller (FAC) flying in a Whirlwind of 103 Squadron. Belvederes and Whirlwinds helped to maintain the mobility of the ground forces with the result that BIRDSONG was judged to be a highly successful operation and the infiltrators were eliminated.

Improvements in Air Defence

In addition to his close involvement with infiltration, the Commander-in-Chief, Far East, was painfully aware of the danger of hostile air strikes against military and civilian targets in Singapore and the Malayan peninsula. Some of the incidents which had already taken place were within 12 miles of the city and these had demonstrated the area's vulnerability to intrusion by low flying aircraft taking advantage of a gap between the radar cover of Bukit Gombak and Butterworth. In order to close this gap the County Class cruiser *HMS Kent* was despatched to the Malacca Strait in an air defence role and Royal Navy Gannets, disembarked from *HMS Victorious*, were tasked with patrolling the air space in conjunction with RAF aircraft. The air defences were further strengthened by the arrival at Tengah in September of eight Javelins of 64 Squadron from the United Kingdom, a most welcome reinforcement for the hard-pressed Javelins of 60 Squadron which still maintained its detachment in Borneo in addition to the increased burden of defending Western Malaysia.

These were not the only additions to the air defence forces. A Light Air Defence Regiment RA was hastily drafted from Germany and a number of 20 mm guns were transferred from naval reserve stocks to the Singapore airfields where they were deployed and manned by the RAF Regiment. Some indication of the seriousness with which the threat was regarded was the order issued to 65 (SAM) Squadron on 14 September 1964. This unit, armed with Bloodhound Mk II SAMs, had been engaged in tropical trials at Seletar for the previous six months but was now told to bring one of its missile sections to immediate operational readiness and prepare to defend Singapore. Yet another deterrent to Indonesian air strikes was the presence of a number of 'V' bombers at Tengah. Several Victors of 57 Squadron, Bomber Command, were retained beyond the normal period of their detachment. Their potential was well known to Indonesia and their presence did not pass unnoticed.

On 28 October 1964, a full scale air defence exercise was held when all passive defence measures were brought into action and 50 RAF, RN and RAAF aircraft took part. These aircraft were all seen over Singapore City as an indication to the people of the Island that this was the sort of response there would be to any Indonesian air attack. While the sight of 50 aircraft flying over their city probably cheered its inhabitants, it did not prevent more landings, attempted landings, and sabotage. These posed considerable problems for the Security Forces, and RAF aircraft and the civilian airlines were given an additional worry when, on 29 March 1965, Indonesian anti-aircraft guns on the Riau islands to the south began to fire indiscriminately on aircraft approaching and leaving Singapore. Although all aircraft were immediately ordered to avoid these islands, the firing continued at intervals and, up to the end of 1965, a total of 59 firings had been reported. In addition Indonesia placed a total ban on flying over two of her islands, namely Bintam and Batam, with a threat to shoot down without warning any aircraft ignoring the ban. As a result the airway over the Riau islands to Djakarta and Australasia became unusable and an alternative route had to be devised. This in itself was not too difficult but perhaps the most serious effect of the firing was the deterioration of the already strained relations between Indonesia and Australia.

During the first half of 1965 pressure on Western Malaysia continued and the RAF was continually involved in reconnaissance and close support of the ground forces mopping up the small pockets of infiltrators. Fortunately the visible strength of the air defences acted as a satisfactory deterrent to Indonesian air strikes, and no attacks were made on the Singapore airfields. Nevertheless, there remained a serious threat and no relaxation of defensive measures was possible.

One example of a raid which took place on 30–31 May 1965 serves to illustrate the determination of Indonesia to create the maximum amount of dislocation on the peninsula. A party of 25 regular troops landed on the south coast of East Johore near Tanjong Pen-Gelih, and only seven miles due east of Changi. They left their boats on the shore and occupied some old World War II Japanese fortifications. Their aim was to establish a firm base, await the arrival of reinforcements and then to move to Kelantan to train 'dissident groups'. After a platoon of the Singapore Infantry Regiment had suffered heavy casualties, the 4th Malay Regiment and a Police Company were despatched to the scene and succeeded in killing one infiltrator on the morning of 31 May. As the position which the Indonesians had taken up was reasonably secure against ground attack, it was decided to use four Hunters of 20 Squadron to dislodge them. These aircraft, under the control of an FAC, set up a textbook pattern of firing rockets at the enemy emplacements followed by intensive cannon attacks. No Indonesians were killed in these attacks but they were driven out of the fortifications. During the next night the ground forces captured 13 of the raiding party and by 12 June all had been accounted for; one killed, 18 captured and six surrendered.

None of these raids caused any serious damage but they were a great irritant, locking up many troops and police during the lengthy and widespread mopping up operations, causing considerable anxiety to the population of Malaya and Singapore and keeping the RAF and other air defence forces on high alert states. They also distracted attention from the operations in Borneo which remained the scene of the main Confrontation and where Indonesian activity continued to escalate.

This description of the effects of Confrontation on Western Malaysia would not be complete without some mention of the problems faced by the community in Singapore. In view of the risk of air raids, at one point plans were considered for setting up an Air Raid Warden scheme along World War II lines, using UK-based civilians. There was also the threat of sabotage—a bomb exploded, for example, in the technical area at Changi in May 1964—and on several occasions there were riots in Singapore City that caused curfew restrictions to be imposed. The need for such measures placed an additional burden on all uniformed personnel who were already stretched operationally but morale remained very high and all ranks made a willing contribution in their efforts to ensure that families and the civilian population were kept well informed and safeguarded.

A Politico-Military Dilemma

This increase in activity in Borneo accompanied by a much greater participation in cross border raids by regular Indonesian troops created many difficulties for the Security Forces. Although the strict prohibition on hot pursuit into Kalimantan had not greatly inconvenienced them in the early stages of the campaign, it was now denying them many opportunities to follow up and destroy raiding parties. In addition, certain Indonesian bases had now been established close to the border which served as safe harbours for the retreating infiltrators. It had become increasingly clear that ground and air attacks on these bases and on the many transverse tracks which ran close to, and parallel with, the border would be of immense value.

Admiral Begg, the Commander-in-Chief Far East, made repeated requests to London for authority to extend his harassing attacks across the border with the result that a small concession was made during 1964, permitting him to carry out hot pursuit to a depth of 3,000 yards into Kalimantan, and allowing him to open fire against hostile mortar batteries, but only in self defence. Furthermore, such operations were to be undertaken on a 'deniable' basis only—a term which meant that they left no evidence, such as civilian casualties or damage which might support a charge of aggression being levelled against the Security Forces.

This limited extension of authority gave some assistance to the border patrols, but it did not prevent Indonesian raids from being mounted on an ever increasing scale with the inclusion of more regular forces and occasional hit and run attacks by aircraft. So fleeting were the latter that there was little or no chance for the RAF Javelins and Hunters to intercept them, operating from their bases at Kuching and Labuan.

By the end of 1964 it was apparent that there was virtually no prospect of a negotiated peace as conference after conference failed to make progress. The British Government and those Commonwealth Governments involved had continued to reinforce the Security Forces without notable success, and they were all greatly concerned at the continuing drain on their defence resources. Consequently, on 13 January 1965, the British Government authorised a further extension of cross border retaliatory action with the expressed intention of minimising the effects of the Indonesian build-up. The C-in-C Far East was instructed to carry out offensive patrol operations across the border to a depth of 10,000 yards and to attack any suitable targets found in that area. All necessary precautions were to be taken to avoid inflicting civilian casualties and damage, and also to prevent news of the operations becoming generally known.

Open and declared warfare was the last thing that Britain wanted as was the case with Australia, New Zealand, Malaysia and the Philippines, all of whom wished to maintain relations with the huge and widespread Indonesian Empire on their doorsteps. Nevertheless, provocation had reached a level at which an entirely non-retaliatory policy was no longer acceptable, and strictly controlled counter offensive measures were deemed necessary, not only to discourage further infiltration but to maintain the morale of the Security Forces whose tolerance had been beyond praise. The politico-military dilemma was acute, but the modest relaxation of the original non-violation policy approved by Governments showed considerable wisdom, judgment, and understanding of the intensely frustrating situation which the Security Forces were compelled to endure.

Confrontation continues in Borneo

The sporadic raids and frequent violations of the air space in Western Malaysia in no way reduced the level of Confrontation in Eastern Malaysia. Indonesian activity across the Kalimantan border steadily increased throughout 1965, regular forces participating in large scale raids and the Indonesian Air Force showing a greater tendency to penetrate into Sarawak and Sabah, although it must be said that its forays showed little determination in the face of the known RAF air defence. Many violations were reported but so fleeting were most of them that the Hunters and Javelins could rarely reach the reported position of a violation in time to intercept. On only one recorded occasion did a Javelin meet an Indonesian C-130 Hercules head on in a valley close to the border. The two aircraft passed within 100 feet of each other and the Javelin pilot clearly saw the horrified faces of the Indonesian crew in the cockpit. By the time he was able to turn round and give chase the Hercules had fled back across the border. Nevertheless the detachments of Javelins and Hunters at Labuan responded by scrambling to every reported violation, both by day and night, and this rapid reaction undoubtedly had the desired effect of deterring the Indonesian Air Force from making deep penetrations.

Similarly, constant maritime patrols by the Shackletons caused many Indonesian naval vessels to retire back into international waters, notably in the area around Tawau which Indonesia clearly regarded as one of the more favourable areas for infiltration.

RAF Labuan

The importance and growth of the RAF station on Labuan Island deserves particular mention. It will be recalled that, when Confrontation started in December 1962, Labuan was a small staging post, housing a detachment of no more than 78 airmen from Changi. However, it had an excellent runway capable of accepting the largest aircraft and the security advantage of being an offshore island. When Confrontation came, it was therefore the obvious, and indeed the only choice for the main RAF base in Borneo.

Under the initial command of Wing Commander W E Thomas AFC the station was rapidly developed and an intensive building programme of largely prefabricated hutted construction carried out. By May 1964 the station strength had risen to about 500 airmen and a year later to over 1000, a rate of expansion with which the building programme could not keep pace, and a good deal of tentage had to be used, an uncomfortable alternative in the prevailing conditions of heavy rain and high humidity. But this had to be accepted in view of the operational importance of Labuan. As the strength grew, it was no longer appropriate for the station to continue as a satellite of Changi and it became a fully independent, self-accounting unit with the resident airmen completing a one year unaccompanied tour instead of the previous short detachments from Singapore. Until early in 1965 the majority of the aircrew with their aircraft served in detachment from the Singapore squadrons, the length of these detachments varying considerably from a few days to several months depending on the operational requirements.

With as many as 30 aircraft of nine different types operating from the station at any one time, it could probably claim to be more versatile than any other station in the RAF. Being at the centre of the ADIZ, air defence figured largely among the station's commitments. Hunters from 20 Squadron and Javelins from 60 and later 64 Squadrons maintained high states of readiness by day and night, scrambling whenever a suspicious aircraft was sighted or heard within the protected air space. Complementing the air defence role was that of maritime reconnaissance and 205 Squadron usually maintained two Shackletons at Labuan to liaise with RN ships and keep a constant watch on the waters around Borneo. This constant vigilance was a time consuming and often deadly boring task, and particularly so because the majority of reports and sightings tended to be of little or no significance.

In the medium range transport role the station could always count on having at least two Beverleys of 34 Squadron and usually one or two Argosies of 215 Squadron. These, supplemented by the occasional Hastings or Valetta, carried out the main supply drops to the forward air strips, ferried the troops from Singapore to and from Labuan and Kuching when battalions were replaced after four months in the jungle and performed a multitude of heavy lift duties, some of which will be described later.

Twin Pioneers of 209 Squadron and the RMAF, and Whirlwind and Belvedere helicopters of 103, 110 and 66 Squadrons, supplemented on occasion by Fleet Air Arm Whirlwinds, formed the short range transport force. This force provided the life lines to the patrols in the most forward positions supplying their every need from ammunition to toilet paper. With their squadron headquarters back in Singapore it was not easy to control these Borneo detachments and it was, therefore, with some relief that Labuan received its first resident squadron when, on 2 March 1965, 12 Whirlwind 10s of 230 Squadron arrived from the UK aboard *HMS Bulwark* and were flown ashore.

By the middle of 1965 Labuan was a crowded and extremely busy station, working round the clock for seven days a week. Some indication of the growth of air traffic can be gleaned from the fact that movements, which had amounted to less than one hundred per month prior to Confrontation, had risen to 2,500 per month by the middle of 1965. The supplies dropped by the Beverleys and Argosies alone reached one million pounds per month in November and December 1964, and continued to increase sharply thereafter. In this connection it is interesting, and somewhat surprising, to find that the station possessed no facilities for repacking the hundreds of supply dropping parachutes used, all of which had to be rescued from the jungle and flown back to Singapore for drying, inspection and repacking.

Confrontation Continues to Intensify

RAF activity at the beginning of 1965 continued to be primarily concerned with the ground forces' logistic requirements. Indonesia was clearly seen to be increasing her forces in Kalimantan and correspondingly the Director of Operations received two additional infantry battalions which he allotted to the First Division of Sarawak. At the same time the Australian and New Zealand Governments authorised their combat units to be deployed in Eastern Malaysia, and a battalion of the Royal Australian Regiment with the 1st

(Australian) SAS Squadron and the 1st (New Zealand) Ranger Squadron were added to the reinforcements. This was the point at which, as already mentioned, 230 Squadron was sent to Labuan from the UK to assist with the helicopter supply lift.

This influx of additional ground forces to meet the increasing infiltration of Indonesian regular troops placed a much greater load on the system for changing over battalions and other units in the forward defence locations (FDL). It was essential that there should be no hiatus between the arrival of fresh incoming troops and the departure of those due to be relieved. There was no accommodation for more than one unit in these FDLs and the changeover had, therefore, to be effected instantaneously, the outgoing troops leaving in the helicopters which brought in their replacements. Fixed wing aircraft could not be used for these changeovers as only the most rudimentary helicopter pads existed at FDLs. Similarly Labuan and Kuching could not each accommodate more than one major unit such as a battalion at a time and the most carefully co-ordinated changeover operation was necessary.

Early in the day the fresh battalion or other major unit would be flown into Labuan and/or Kuching by Argosy, Hastings or Beverley and transferred immediately into Belvederes or Whirlwinds. These would fly to the appropriate forward defence location, unload and reload with outgoing troops within a few minutes. On their return to the main airfield, the medium range transports would have been refuelled and prepared to take them back to Singapore. The shuttle service would continue all day as long as the weather held and, all being well, a complete changeover of several hundred troops would be completed in the day. In this way the FDLs were never left unmanned and the frontier was kept constantly patrolled.

The part played by the Belvederes of 66 Squadron, based at Kuching under the command of Wing Commander P D A Austin AFC, and affectionately named by the local Dyaks "flying longhouses" or "silver longhouses", was particularly important, not only during the changeover of troops but in a series of supply tasks calling for a heavy lift helicopter. As the campaign progressed the value of the 105 mm howitzer increased in importance. There was only a limited number of these guns deployed and the ability of the Belvedere to lift a complete gun, followed by a second aircraft lifting the ammunition, equipment and gun crew, permitted the greatest flexibility in the use of the howitzers. They could be lowered into a previously planned firing position, ranged onto a target and fired within minutes, after which they could be transferred to another site several miles away with the helicopters flying at tree top height to escape detection. The impression created was that the ground forces possessed much more artillery support than in fact existed.

In a similar manner the Belvedere was able to lift an anti-mortar radar detector, a useful device which could trace the flight of an enemy 3 inch mortar bomb back to the base plate from which it had been fired. Within seconds, and often while the hostile mortar bomb was still in flight, reciprocal mortar fire could be opened against the enemy firing position. As with the 105 mm howitzer, this radar could be moved to a new location by a single Belvedere within minutes, thus giving the forward troop positions a sense of security and an accurate means of retaliation under mortar fire. Similarly the UPS1 ground radar could be lifted by Belvedere. One problem with this equipment which was ingeniously overcome was caused by its awkward shape. It was housed in a very long, narrow but heavy case. If slung fore and aft under a Belvedere, it upset the longitudinal stability of the aircraft, and if athwartships the lateral stability was adversely affected, causing the Belvedere to pitch and wallow disconcertingly. The solution was to surround the load with a light wood and fabric framework, converting the radar into a six-sided symmetrical package which could gyrate slowly and evenly below the Belvedere. There were countless examples of heavy and awkward loads being carried by these aircraft to locations inaccessible by any other form of transport, not the least being the ability to lift an unserviceable Whirlwind bodily out of the jungle and carry it back to base.

It became apparent during April 1965 that the Indonesians were planning some form of sustained action in furtherance of their cause at the impending Afro-Asian conference then expected to be held in Algiers in June. As an overture a night attack was mounted against the 2nd Battalion, The Parachute Regiment at Plaman Mapu. Whirlwinds of 225 Squadron were immediately tasked with ferrying men and supplies to the area of the incident. Although beaten off, the enemy repeatedly returned to the area throughout the next fortnight, sometimes daily, in parties varying from 30 to 200. They were constantly ambushed by the Security Forces and chased back to the border with support from the ubiquitous helicopters.

Later in the year, a considerable increase in Indonesian air activity was identified notably opposite the Fourth and Fifth Divisions of

Sarawak. For the first time during Confrontation aircraft were used with some effect on the Malaysian side of the border. On 1 September a B-25 Mitchell and an Invader attacked an undefended kampong using 0.5 calibre machine guns to terrorise the villagers. No casualties were inflicted although two 'longhouses' and workers in the fields were raked with gunfire. This type of hit and run raid at low level within a few miles of the border continued during September. As the raiders could be back across the border within minutes they were almost impossible to intercept by fighters located as far away as Labuan and Kuching.

Despite the continuation of these incursions, the second half of 1965 was dominated by political developments. On 9 August Singapore, which had always been an uneasy partner in the Malaysia concept, left the Federation under a Separation Agreement but Singaporean troops continued to serve in Borneo. Singapore appreciated that her secession did not in any way reduce the threat to her installations from Indonesia, and the not unexpected event made no difference to the British airfields and other military installations on the island. An event of more far reaching implications was the Djakarta coup of 30 September when the Indonesian Communist Party attempted to seize power and a number of senior Army officers were killed. A nationwide anti-communist reaction followed and in the associated political turbulence President Soekarno fell from office.

These events in themselves did not reduce Confrontation immediately but it was noticeable that the campaign was not allowed to escalate. The will and intention to mount large scale and determined incursions was lacking, and it is appropriate to quote from a report[1] to the Chief of the Defence Staff in London from the Commander-in-Chief, Far East, then Air Chief Marshal Sir John Grandy.

"I believe this decline in Indonesian activity to be largely due to the following factors:

a. The very real fear of retaliating action which we might take against Indonesian forces should they be ordered to make large scale incursions, particularly against West Malaysia.

b. The effective methods employed against infiltration in both East and West Malaysia.

c. With certain notable exceptions the poor showing of Indonesian forces, both regular and irregular, in operations.

---

[1] C-in-C Far East's Report dated 1 March 1966.

    d. Logistic and maintenance difficulties.

    e. Lack of sympathy with Indonesia among the Malaysian peoples".

As always in these circumstances, reactions from home took a long time to be reflected in the action of front line troops. Consequently the cross border activity continued in Borneo throughout 1965 but without any marked success. The defensive posture of the Security Forces with abundant air support had been so developed that the situation was kept well under control. Increasing casualties were being inflicted on the enemy, the confidence of the population of Sarawak and Sabah was being restored and the hitherto irksome restrictions against crossing the border were no longer important.

Building up this powerful defensive posture had been a long and arduous task. It had taken a full three years from the initial Brunei rebellion of December 1962, and had been extremely expensive both to Britain and her Commonwealth allies at a time when there was a great desire, indeed a pressing financial need, on the part of all the Governments to reduce the escalating costs of their expenditure on defence. However, the implications of the political developments in the Indonesian capital began to filter through and, by the beginning of 1966, the prospects of an early end to Confrontation looked distinctly promising.

18

The End of Confrontation

The pattern of operations in Borneo slowly changed during the early months of 1966. Development of airstrips and as many helicopter landing pads as possible in the forward defence locations was virtually complete. Cross border tracks used by the Indonesians had been identified and were regularly patrolled so that it was no longer easy for infiltration to take place without becoming known to the Security Forces. In this connection 81 Squadron had completed an immense amount of tactical photography and survey work with the result that ground patrols could at last be provided with accurate maps and prints of the areas most favoured by infiltrators. Being well aware of the vigilance of the Hunters and Javelins, there were few violations of the border of any significance by Indonesian aircraft.

Despite the fact that sound defensive positions had been built up, it was not yet possible to reduce the land, sea and air forces in and around Sarawak and Sabah. Cross border activity continued, but instead of constant small scale incursions, Indonesia confined her raids to less frequent but larger scale sorties using a high proportion of regular troops. The increased size of these occasional attacks revealed that she was fully aware of the strength of the opposition they would meet and this engendered fear of the consequences of hastily planned and executed raids by inadequate forces without tactical air support.

There could, under these circumstances, be no relaxation in the frequency and variety of patrols by the Commonwealth forces, and their air supply requirements showed no diminution. For example, the Beverleys of 34 Squadron, operating daily from Labuan, continued to deliver more than one million pounds of supplies to the forward areas each month, and this figure occasionally exceeded one and a half million pounds. Similarly Belvederes, Whirlwinds, naval Wessex and Pioneers continued at an unabated level with tactical supply, the changeover of units in the field, and casualty evacuation.

A position of stalemate would appear to have been reached, but this in fact was not quite true. The Indonesian Government, having walked out of the United Nations, was clearly worried at the increasing hostility of many of her erstwhile colleagues as well as the isolation of her position in international politics. World wide lack of sympathy led the Indonesian Prime Minister to open discussions with the Deputy Prime Minister of Malaysia in May 1966, when a cessation of hostilities was discussed. Although these talks were inconclusive, the desire to end Confrontation was clearly evident. When in June and July there were only five minor contacts on the Kalimantan frontier, it became clear that, in spite of the apparent failure of the many high level conferences which had taken place, their cumulative effect on the Indonesian Government had been considerable and the initial determination to continue with Confrontation by all possible means had waned. Indonesia could not achieve a victorious end to the campaign and she realised it. Consequently, on 11 August 1966 Malaysia and Indonesia signed a peace treaty in Bangkok and, to the relief of all those involved, Confrontation was formally ended, three years and eight months after it had started.

Ironically, even as the announcement was made, ground and air units in Borneo were engaged in repelling a strong band of Indonesian regulars who had crossed the frontier in Sarawak. RAF Labuan was fully committed to a high level of transport support to the battalion engaged. It was a spirited encounter with casualties on both sides, but the raiding force was eventually routed and chased right back to the border with the aid of helicopter reconnaissance and protection. It was perhaps fitting that this, the last encounter on any significant scale, should find the RAF supporting squadrons at their most efficient, displaying airmanship and skill of a very high order.

The Aftermath of Confrontation

Confrontation might be over, but there were still many thousands of Commonwealth troops dispersed throughout the jungle, and the logistic problem of supplying them while they were slowly withdrawn remained a major task for the RAF transport force. Not only was it impossible to withdraw such a large force rapidly with the limited air resources available but it was also unwise to relax vigilance on the frontier too quickly in case violations continued or the peace agreement did not hold. So many negotiations had failed during the previous three years that there was a natural disposition to regard this latest ceasefire with caution.

The peace agreement, however, did hold and a gradual reduction of land and air forces commenced under the code name PLAY BOY. The air defence force of Javelins and Hunters was no longer needed and returned to its parent station at Tengah. It was a relief for the two Javelin squadrons in particular, Nos 60 and 64, as the Javelin had earlier run into technical trouble with structural cracking which involved the incorporation of complicated and lengthy modifications in Singapore. In order to help out the hard pressed Hunters of 20 Squadron, on whom fell the whole onus of air defence during this process, a detachment of Sabres from 78 RAAF Wing at Butterworth was sent to Labuan for several months, and played its part in safeguarding the ADIZ. An additional guarantee of the integrity of the airspace was undertaken at about this time by the deployment to Kuching of one Flight of Bloodhound missiles of 65 (SAM) Squadron based in Singapore.

Withdrawal of these air defence units relieved some of the congestion at Labuan and Kuching and allowed those two stations to concentrate on bringing the ground forces out of the jungle and transferring them and their equipment to ships and aircraft for passage back to Singapore or, in some cases, direct to the United Kingdom. As Operation PLAY BOY progressed it was possible to reduce the helicopter and Pioneer forces. In particular, 230 Squadron, the resident Whirlwind squadron which had come to Labuan from the UK, returned to Odiham, its main base in the UK. The Whirlwind 10s of this squadron were partially dismantled and flown home in Belfasts of Transport Command, some six lifts in all being needed to complete the move. It was the first time that the Belfast, the largest of Transport Command's load carriers, had flown into Labuan and its immense capacity greatly simplified the squadron's return home.

With the departure of 230 Squadron by air and the naval helicopters by sea the gap was filled by 110 Squadron which concentrated its Whirlwinds at Labuan to help with the final stages of troop supply and withdrawal. No 110 Squadron, it will be recalled, was a resident FEAF squadron which would remain in the Command after the reinforcing squadrons had left the theatre. Even at this late stage, the withdrawal was not without its incidents. In mid October a Whirlwind of 110 Squadron flying from Bario to Limbang suffered engine failure over extremely inhospitable country. With considerable skill the pilot managed to land on a river bank but unfortunately the river rose and immersed his aircraft. It was impossible to rectify the subsequent damage on the spot but the ubiquitous Belvederes of 66 Squadron came to the rescue and lifted the Whirlwind bodily from the flood waters, carrying it to Brunei where it was loaded into a Beverley and flown to 390 MU at Seletar. A valuable helicopter was thus saved and was back in service with 110 Squadron in a few weeks.

This incident is described merely as an example of the frequent occurrences with which the helicopter force had to contend. The initiative and improvisation displayed by air and ground crew alike were extraordinary. Another example is that of the Belvedere pilot who, experiencing severe vibration, landed beside a village deep in the jungle and discovered that a rotor blade pocket was lifting. He found the only roll of Scotch tape in the village, bound up the rotor and returned to base. Not infrequently it was necessary to 'semi-hover' on a steep slope with one wheel resting on the ground while the load was discharged, the downhill wheel remaining in the air. It needs little imagination to visualise the difficulty of such a manoeuvre, but these were the conditions under which the helicopter squadrons were called upon to keep the forward troops supplied.

As PLAY BOY progressed and the tasks of the RAF decreased, responsibility began to be transferred to the Royal Malaysian Air Force. Their Pioneers had participated in Borneo for a considerable time, but in no great strength. It was now time for the RMAF to assume control and the work which had hitherto been carried out by Pioneers of 1(RMAF) Squadron was assumed by 8(RMAF) Squadron which was equipped with the Canadian Caribou. This aircraft, which had almost as good a short field performance as the Pioneer, but many times its lifting capacity, was able to take on many tasks which had previously been carried out by RAF aircraft. This transfer of responsibility was in accordance with the Anglo-Malaysian Defence Agreement wherein the RAF was required to transfer all its responsibilities gradually to the RMAF as its personnel and units were equipped, trained and considered capable of assuming the various roles.

In conformity with this policy Labuan was to continue in being as a Royal Air Force station with a much reduced personnel establishment of about 250. (Its strength was some 750 airmen at the end of Confrontation). In addition to reassuming its original role as a staging

25. A Beverley of 34 Squadron loading troops at Seletar for operations in Borneo

26. Rapid turn round of a 20 Squadron Hunter at Tengah

27. RAF Regiment guard the airstrip at Sepulot in Borneo

28. A Belvedere of 66 Squadron lifting a damaged Whirlwind out of the Borneo jungle

post, it would provide such facilities as Air Traffic Control for the RMAF until those responsibilities could be handed over. The end of Confrontation did not, therefore, herald the immediate departure of the RAF from Borneo.

October proved to be an exceptionally busy month. At times Labuan had as many as 50 aircraft on the airfield, all concerned with the evacuation of the British and Commonwealth troops and their replacement by Malaysians wherever it was considered essential to continue to garrison the frontier. Operation PLAY BOY continued smoothly and, by the end of the month, was virtually completed. The Malaysian Army and Air Force had taken over competently and no further signs of infiltration from Kalimantan were identified.

It had been a long and exhausting campaign: admittedly shorter than the 12 years of the Malayan Emergency, but more arduous. Whereas both campaigns took place in impenetrable jungle, the Borneo terrain was far more rugged and mountainous than that of Malaya. The rainfall was heavier and the weather in general much worse. These conditions increased the privation suffered by troops on the ground and greatly increased the hazards for airmen. These hazards had to be accepted and overcome as the lives of patrols in the jungle frequently depended entirely upon RAF supply and support. It is, therefore, fitting to conclude this chapter with a resume of the part played by air power in the campaign as a whole.

The Contribution of Air Power to Confrontation

The Air Officer Commanding 224 Group, Air Vice-Marshal C N Foxley-Norris (later Air Chief Marshal Sir Christopher) stated in an article in Brassey's Annual of 1967:

"The Borneo campaign was a classic example of the lesson that the side which uses air power most effectively to defeat the jungle will also defeat the enemy."

When Confrontation started in 1962 the Royal Air Force already had a long history of conquering the jungle, a history going back to the defeat of the Japanese in Burma during World War II, followed by intensive operations in the Netherlands East Indies in 1945 and 1946, and then the twelve years of jungle warfare in Malaya from 1948 to 1960. All this experience stood the Service in good stead in this latest campaign.

In all 18 squadrons participated in operations in Borneo. These are listed in Appendix D, and most of them were resident FEAF squadrons, already highly trained and experienced in jungle warfare. Indeed, at least one of them, 60 Squadron, had been in the thick of all the campaigns mentioned above and had operated continuously in the South-East Asia theatre since 1941. There was, therefore, a wealth of experience available and this more than anything else proved of great value to the RAF when faced with the extremely difficult flying conditions in Borneo. Without that level of experience there must surely have been many more accidents and casualties than occurred.

The fact that Confrontation did not last much longer than a full tour of duty for RAF personnel in the Far East meant there was not too great a dilution of experience and it was possible to keep air and ground crews together for a large part of the campaign, a most important factor when the need for local knowledge of Sarawak and Sabah is taken into account. Unusual and hazardous conditions always act as a challenge to professional airmen, bringing out the qualities of initiative and improvisation which many of them never knew they possessed, and enabling them to operate their aircraft to their limits and often beyond. They were constantly spurred on by the knowledge that the troops below were entirely dependent upon their skill and airmanship and that any failure on their part would at best increase the hardship suffered by the jungle patrols and at worst cost them their lives.

It was in all respects a strange campaign. Indonesia possessed an air force of some 15–20,000 men and 550 aircraft comprising no less than 30 different types. The offensive element consisted of a few Russian Badgers and US B25 Mitchells, while the air defence force contained a variety of MIG-17s, 19s and 21s together with a few elderly P51 Mustangs. A competent transport force of C130 Hercules, AN12s, Dakotas and some Russian helicopters made up the total. In spite of this not insignificant force, there was little or no air opposition throughout the campaign. There is no record of any aircraft from either side being shot down in combat over either East or West Malaysia. Nevertheless the RAF had to maintain constant vigilance and scramble to investigate countless reports of air space violations, most of which turned out to be either false or so fleeting as to give no chance of interception. It is clear beyond doubt that the knowledge of RAF strength and competence created a wholesome respect among Indonesia's leaders and the deterrent effect of RAF air defence fighters, light bombers, and 'V' bombers on detachment from Bomber Command was absolute. Sneak raids on the Singapore airfields were daily expected but they never came.

The second unusual feature of the campaign was that, after the initial Brunei revolt had been put down, the Commonwealth forces had little or no internal security problem. Airfields and airstrips required little defence and at no time was more than one RAF Regiment squadron deployed in Borneo for its primary role of airfield defence. The enemies of the RAF were almost entirely those of terrain and climate, both of which were successfully conquered. With open skies and no internal security worries, aircraft were able to range at will over the whole area of the campaign and this was an immense advantage.

Strategic and tactical logistic supply were the keynotes of Confrontation. Although freedom of the seas enabled much of the heavy equipment to be transported to Borneo by ship, most of the troops and the more urgently needed supplies were flown in by the MR transport force. From the main airfields of Labuan, Kuching, Brunei and Tawau, everybody and everything was dependent upon the SR transport and helicopter squadrons. These played a dominant part as has been shown. Without them it would have been impossible for the ground forces to prevent wide scale infiltration from Kalimantan. So here again, the deterrent effect of these wide ranging, air supported patrols was sufficient to keep a close control along the 800 mile border.

Another feature of this unusual campaign was the inviolability of the Indonesian border. Under normal circumstances the bands of retreating marauders would have been energetically pursued and probably destroyed. Interdiction targets such as enemy camps, supply and ammunition dumps would have constituted legitimate targets for RAF strike forces as well as the harassment of retreating patrols. Such action might have shortened the conflict but that is by no means certain. It could have had the opposite effect of driving Indonesia to declare war on Malaysia and, in the early days of the campaign, it would certainly have given her grounds for seeking the sympathy of many countries in the forum of the United Nations, sympathy which was never more than thinly disguised. With hindsight, it was probably wise to respect the Kalimantan border, however frustrating it was on many occasions to soldiers and airmen alike.

Many lessons were learned, not least among them being the inter-dependence of the three Services in this type of campaign. It was not a new lesson, but one which needed to be confirmed again and again as there were always elements in each Service who found it difficult to put their trust unreservedly in the hands of another. The essential need for interdependence had been constantly demonstrated during and after World War II, and no better example can be found than in Borneo. From the beginning operations were controlled by one Commander through a joint staff. Under his overall jurisdiction the air effort was controlled by one senior RAF officer, ensuring that the available aircraft, of which there were never enough, were pro-grammed to the best advantage. The specialised knowledge of flying hours, aircraft serviceability and the capability as well as the limi-tations of aircraft types and their crews could be accurately assessed only by an experienced airman. Where control of an operation was decentralised, and at times that was essential, it was effected only as part of a co-ordinated operational policy and then usually for a short period or for some specific purpose. There is no doubt that the chain of joint command, from the Commander-in-Chief, Far East, in Singapore down to brigade and battalion level worked faultlessly and inter-Service co-operation was excellent.

Nowhere was this better demonstrated than in the helicopter force, bearing in mind that helicopters of all three British Services and latterly the RMAF participated throughout. The significance of these rotary wing aircraft in the Malayan Emergency was described in Chapter 12 and it needs to be remembered that in that campaign of the 1950s they were in their infancy as far as military use was concerned. So important were they to those operations that they set the seal on their permanent inclusion in the RAF order of battle. Development, encouraged by the impetus of insistent demand, was rapid with the result that the Whirlwind 10, Wessex and Belvedere of the 1960s were a far cry from the Dragonfly which had appeared initially in Malaya only 10 years previously. It is not belittling the value of the fixed wing aircraft to say that helicopters played the most important role in Borneo. Rarely less than 50 were in use at any one time and double that number could have been used with advantage so valuable were they in sustaining the forward patrols and in transporting heavy and awkward loads to areas unapproachable by any other form of transport.

The helicopter has fragile and complicated mechanism requiring expert maintenance, as failure in many of the situations in which the crews had to operate would have proved disastrous. Failures there were, but they were not as numerous as might have been expected. A high proportion of the forced landings and accidents resulted in the rescue and subsequent repair of the aircraft, sometimes in the jungle, on river banks and on the seashore. The ability of the Belvedere to lift the smaller helicopters bodily saved many which might otherwise have been discarded. Great credit is due to the ground tradesmen of the squadrons involved for overcoming the most severe technical difficulties to keep these aircraft flying. Very little covered working accommodation was available and the difficulty of, for example, changing the engine of a Whirlwind in torrential rain can well be imagined. These airmen, although based for the most part back at Labuan or Kuching, fully understood the dependence of the troops on the frontier upon the quality of their work, and this knowledge acted as a challenge which they readily accepted. It may be thought that too much credit has been given to the helicopter squadrons in these chapters. It was the peculiar nature of Confrontation which dictated the tactics to be adopted by the Commonwealth forces, and these tactics depended upon the unique characteristics of rotary wing aircraft. The fixed wing VTOL aircraft, ie, the Harrier, had not yet appeared in the RAF order of battle. Even if it had been available it could never have supplanted the helicopter in Borneo in the tactical supply role. When all the circumstances are taken into consideration, no apology seems necessary for placing these aircraft on a pedestal.

So, as 1966 drew to a close, the British, Australian and New Zealand forces had all departed from Borneo, leaving the RAF to close down or hand over the airfields from which the withdrawal had been finally carried out. It remained for the RAF to transfer its remaining responsibilities to the RMAF, a process which was to take some time. It was not in fact until 1968 that the final transfer of Labuan took place, largely due to the wish on the part of Malaysia for the RAF to continue to hold many supervisory posts until the rapidly growing RMAF was sufficiently trained and experienced to take them over.

Under the direction of the CAS, Air Vice-Marshal (later Air Chief Marshal Sir Alasdair) Steedman, the RMAF had expanded into a small, but competent air force, and its participation in Confrontation had given its transport squadrons valuable operational experience. However, total responsibility for the security of Eastern Malaysia was too great a commitment in 1966 and the continued backing of the RAF was essential. Labuan in particular had to remain prepared for rapid reinforcement by RAF air defence, strike and maritime aircraft from across the water should the need arise. The relationship which had sprung up between these two air forces was excellent and both instructor and trainee settled down to harmonious control of Eastern Malaysia.

It is appropriate at this point to quote again from the article by the AOC, 224 Group, published in Brassey's Annual of 1967:

"There can be no doubt of the validity of one major lesson learned from Confrontation. Adequate tactical air forces, supported by strategic air power and properly trained, handled and operated in close partnership with the ground forces, are as essential and critical a factor in a successful military campaign to-day as ever before. If our future national policy envisages the conduct of, or participation in such operations in the future, this fact can only be forgotten or ignored at our peril".

In conclusion, there can be little doubt that this campaign not only preserved the independence of Malaysia, but also prevented the spread of communism into Indonesia, with all the consequences for South-East Asia which might have followed. While final judgment on the implications of failure to resist Indonesia must be left to the political historians, it is certainly arguable that the British and Commonwealth effort from 1962 to 1966 was critical in stemming the spread of communism throughout the area.

19
Developments in British Defence Policy

Three and a half years of Confrontation had proved a most unwelcome addition to Britain's world wide commitments which were already heavy elsewhere. Confrontation might well be called the last straw, bearing in mind that her responsibilities under the NATO and CENTO treaties continued to necessitate the deployment of sizable forces in Germany and Cyprus, as did the unstable situation in Aden and the Middle East generally. Unfortunately the British economy was becoming increasingly strained and the desire to reduce the heavy expenditure on defence was paramount. No longer was it considered possible to become involved in a major campaign in a distant overseas theatre and, quite apart from the desire to reduce such commitments, the cost of armaments of all kinds was soaring alarmingly. It was hardly believable, for example, that the cost of the 900 Spitfires and Hurricanes which fought the Battle of Britain would now buy less than a dozen jet fighters.

Defence Review of 1966

In order to get to grips with this problem, a most comprehensive Review of Defence Policy was initiated by the British Government in 1966 as Confrontation entered its final phase. It was heralded as 'a review to end all defence reviews' but most military men were far too cynical to place much credence in that statement. Nevertheless there was some good reason for such a contention in that the relatively recent unification of policy staffs under the Chief of the Defence Staff held out promise of a well co-ordinated review which would be less inhibited by single Service demand and prejudices than in the past. The results were interesting and some fundamental changes in strategy and policy were subsequently announced.

The Berlin Blockade, the Korean Emergency, the unsatisfactory Suez campaign of 1956, the drain on resources in Aden, the Mau

Mau episode, the Malayan Emergency, and lastly Confrontation had all combined since World War II to place an intolerable strain on the nation's resources which were dwindling with the loss of Empire. It was understandable, therefore, that the first and most important decision to come from the Defence Review was that Britain would not willingly become engaged in another major conflict alone. No longer the first class Power she had been during the early part of the century and with much of her strength drained by World War II and subsequent events, further involvement in major campaigns without the strong support of allies would be intolerable.

Britain had joined, and indeed was the only full member, of all three of the great international Pacts which had been established since the end of World War II, namely NATO, CENTO and SEATO. Membership assured her, at least in theory, of the full support of other member nations should she become involved in major conflict in the areas covered by them. Britain retained, of course, certain purely national responsibilities elsewhere, for example in Cyprus, Belize and Rhodesia, but any emergencies that might arise there were likely to be of an internal security nature and restricted in scope. Consequently only relatively small forces would be needed to deal with conflicts in such areas. Thus the principle of major conflict only in conjunction with allies was the cornerstone of Britain's revised policy which emanated from the Defence Review of 1966.

The second decision of great importance was concerned with finance and in particular with overseas expenditure. Maintenance of many thousands of Service personnel in overseas commands inevitably meant that a high proportion of the defence budget was spent abroad in foreign currency to the detriment of the nation's balance of payments. It is true that there was some offset in that West Germany made a Deutschemark contribution to Britain's NATO forces on the continent of Europe and that Hong Kong contributed towards the maintenance of troops in the Colony. These payments, however, constituted a small part of the total overseas defence costs, welcome though they obviously were.

This was not of course a new problem. It had caused concern in Whitehall for some years with the result that a deployment policy had been devised which the Review of 1966 confirmed and strengthened. This policy entailed the retention of a greater proportion of the forces of all three Services in the United Kingdom but with the capability of being rapidly transported to any overseas theatre in which they were needed. A UK Strategic Reserve comprising 3 Division, a supporting air component embodied in 38 Group and a strengthened Transport Command force of Britannias, Comets and Belfasts, subsequently replaced by Hercules and VC10s, had been formed. The capability and readiness of this force was such that at least a brigade group could be deployed to any part of the world within seven days. With this 'fire brigade' force available expensive overseas garrisons could be reduced and foreign currency thereby saved. An early example of the implementation of this rapid reinforcement policy had been seen during the Kuwait crisis of 1961 when part of the force sent to the head of the Gulf had been drawn from the Strategic Reserve.

In line with this policy, the flexibility of short range combat aircraft, such as the Lightning, was significantly improved by a considerable expansion of in-flight refuelling facilities. A number of Victor bombers were converted to the tanker role and, using bases such as Malta, Akrotiri, Masirah and Gan, they were able to refuel fighters all the way along the strategic route from the United Kingdom to Singapore and beyond.

Understandably there was some criticism of the policy from commanders overseas. From their point of view the possession of a sizable garrison air force in a theatre not only revealed to all a positive presence and acted as a deterrent to trouble makers but also provided a fully acclimatised and experienced force under the direct control of the overseas commander. Furthermore he was spared the uncomfortable feeling of being dependent upon a political decision to reinforce him made many thousands of miles away in Whitehall where his local situation might not be fully understood. He probably felt with some justification that a squadron in his command was worth two in the United Kingdom. On the other hand it was clear that the RAF could maintain a greater front line strength and save a great deal of foreign currency if the majority of its units could be concentrated at home.

Defence White Papers of 1967 and 1968

The Defence Review of 1966 had given a clear warning to FEAF that the Royal Air Force in the Far East would have to accept considerable reductions during the following years when the new scheme of mobility and reinforcement was implemented. The reductions effected at the end of Confrontation when certain units, which had gone out to the Far East as reinforcements, returned to the United Kingdom or were disbanded, were obviously going to be increased. FEAF could not, therefore, look forward with confidence to its pre-Confrontation squadrons remaining undisturbed on the Singapore airfields for very long.

The foreboding was greatly heightened when the 1967 White Paper on Defence[1] was published early in that year with a Supplementary Statement on Defence Policy[2] following a few months later. The first of these documents, after mentioning the return to the United Kingdom of about 10,000 Army and RAF personnel at the end of Confrontation, went on to say "...... further reductions will be made in the coming year ......" While this statement came as no great surprise to FEAF, the second document[3] contained the ominous words:

"In the Far East, we have decided to reach a reduction of about half the forces deployed in Singapore and Malaysia during 1969/ 71".

At that time there were some 80,000 Service men and women in the Far East and it was envisaged that this number would be reduced by 1971 to about 40,000, of whom half would be civilians.

Greater shocks, however, were to come. When the 1968 White Paper on Defence appeared, it dealt a shattering blow to all the Services in the Far East, and it is appropriate to quote relevant passages from it:

"We shall accelerate the withdrawal of our forces from Malaysia and Singapore and complete it by the end of 1971. We shall also withdraw from the Persian Gulf by the same date".

"No special capability for use outside Europe will be maintained when our withdrawal from Singapore and Malaysia, and the Persian Gulf, is complete".

"We shall, however, retain a general capability based in Europe, including the United Kingdom, which can be deployed overseas as, in our judgement, circumstances demand, and can support United Nations operations as necessary".

It had, of course, been well known for a considerable time that Britain intended to withdraw from Aden and the Arabian Peninsula,

---

[1] Cmnd 3202
[2] Cmnd 3357
[3] Cmnd 3540

and ultimately from the Persian Gulf. Many in the Far East thought that this withdrawal would increase the importance of maintaining the strategic air route to South-East Asia and Australasia via the Indian Ocean. If that were so, it would be essential to maintain Gan, for example, and appropriate forces in Singapore and Hong Kong. The thinking in Singapore did not, however, coincide with the views and intentions of Whitehall, as was only too evident from the 1968 White Paper.

Three years in which to dismantle the intricate structure of FEAF and to train up and hand over responsibility to the small, inexperienced RMAF and a Singapore Air Force which was in its early formative stage was far too short a period. The war was escalating in neighbouring Vietnam and, although British and Malaysian forces were not actively involved in significant numbers, the proximity of the conflict to the borders of Malaya was a permanent threat. In addition a strong defence had to be maintained against a resurgence of Confrontation should Malaysia's peace agreement with Indonesia break down. It is not surprising, therefore, that British and Commonwealth commanders in Singapore were far from happy with the blunt statement of total withdrawal by the end of 1971.

As will be seen later, it was not in fact the final decision, but the modification which was to follow was not known in 1968, a point at which it is appropriate to pause and return to the end of Confrontation in 1966 in order to follow the fortunes of the RAF while the policy developments described in this chapter were unfolding.

20

Three Anxious Years

In one respect the Royal Air Force had been fortunate during the three and a half years of Confrontation. The beginning of the period had found FEAF well equipped and armed with modern aircraft and weapons, always bearing in mind that such a distant overseas command was bound to find itself well behind the front line force at home in view of the need to prove new aircraft and weapons where the best maintenance and modification facilities existed before they were exposed to the less sophisticated technical facilities and more exacting climatic conditions abroad. In addition it is true to say that the anticipated air opposition in distant theatres was less formidable than that to be expected in Europe. The Hunters, Javelins and Canberras, together with the transport aircraft and helicopters with which FEAF was armed at the end of 1962, were not only fully capable of matching anything that Indonesia could put up in opposition but also had a useful life ahead of them. There was, therefore, little or no re-equipment of squadrons needed before Confrontation ended in 1966, and this proved to be a considerable advantage which avoided the hiatus inevitable in an intensive campaign if a unit has to be withdrawn from the front line to convert to a new aircraft type. But, by the time the FEAF squadrons were once again able to settle down on their base airfields in Singapore, some of them were due for modernisation.

Unfortunately news of the changes in British defence policy which have been described in Chapter 19 soon began to filter through to the Far East and started to cause considerable anxiety as to the future size and equipment of the Command. The first squadron to feel the wind of change was 215 Squadron which, it will be recalled, had been formed at Changi to reinforce the MR transport force as Confrontation gathered momentum. A limited number of Argosies had been purchased and it was planned to form five squadrons from them. By 1967 the world wide Argosy force was suffering from a shortage of aircraft, as the limited build had been completed and production had ceased. No 215 Squadron had given sterling service in FEAF at a time of great need. The capacity and rear loading capability of the Argosy, exceeded only by that of the much slower Beverley, had ensured that supplies to Borneo were fully maintained at the required level. However, it was the only squadron of its type in FEAF, with the technical complications which that involved, and the decision was made to disband 215 Squadron at the end of 1967. Many of its Argosies were flown to the Near East Command and allocated to 70 Squadron at Akrotiri. Its record of serviceability and freedom from accident had been impeccable and FEAF relinquished the squadron with great regret, particularly as it was destined to disappear from the RAF inventory and was not subsequently re-formed.

To some extent this loss was made good by the re-equipment at the same time of 48 Squadron, which exchanged its Hastings for the C-130 Hercules. Some years earlier the RAF had purchased more than 60 of these versatile load carriers from the United States, adapted them to RAF needs and equipped five squadrons. They were a marked improvement on the Hastings which, with its side door loading, was severely limited as to the type of heavy equipment which could be carried. The short landing and take off capability of the Hercules was much better than that of the Argosy and it had already proved to be an exceptionally rugged and reliable maid of all work. Although the Beverleys too were soon to depart, FEAF still retained with its Hercules an excellent heavy lift capability. If the Hercules had a fault it was that it was both noisy and uncomfortable for passengers but these were disadvantages which had to be accepted in the interests of its much greater versatility for the operational tasks required of it.

The Reductions Begin to Bite

1967 and 1968 were peaceful and pleasant years for the RAF in the Far East. In spite of the war in neighbouring Vietnam, Malaysia and Singapore were calm and beginning to prosper in their newly found independence. There was a great sense of relief that relations with Indonesia had been patched up and, if not exactly friendly, had stabilised into a state of mutual tolerance. The contribution made by the RAF during Confrontation and the training which it continued to give to the RMAF and the Singapore Air Force met with great appreciation with the result that airmen and their families were everywhere welcomed by Malays and Chinese alike, both inherently cheerful and hospitable people.

Confrontation had inevitably created much turbulence for RAF personnel as detachments from squadrons and ground units moved constantly backwards and forwards between Western and Eastern Malaysia, sometimes for a few days, sometimes for many months at a time. But that period was over. It had been a successful campaign and it left a feeling of satisfaction among all ranks which was reflected throughout the Singapore stations as they enjoyed the return to stability.

Although individual airmen were not greatly troubled by the announcements of Defence Policy changes, they were concerned at the rumours of large scale redundancies among all ranks which began to reach them. Unfortunately distance exaggerated these rumours and many long service men became worried about their future prospects, feeling frustrated at their inability to obtain accurate information about the scale of RAF reductions. It was true that the new policy would result in redundancies, but not on the scale feared by many, fuelled by gossip and rumour. It was, therefore, with considerable relief that a series of talks by the Air Member for Personnel was listened to with great attention. During a long tour of all the FEAF stations he talked to more than 13,000 personnel in station canteens, cinemas and messes and brought a proper perspective to the problem of redundancy. It was then realised that natural wastage and retirement would absorb a high proportion of the personnel reductions which the slimmer RAF contemplated by the Government would necessitate. This episode was another example of the importance of communication between policy makers at home and the airmen and airwomen in distant overseas commands. This lack of communication was not as serious as it had been in 1945 and 1946 when 'hostilities only' airmen were desperate for demobilisation, but it was a timely reminder of the duty to keep personnel closely informed of the effects of policy changes. The fundamental difference between the 1945 situation and that of 1967 was, somewhat ironically, that in 1945 men were worried because they could not leave the Service whereas in 1967 they were concerned in case they could not remain in it. But in both cases good communication was the key to satisfaction.

The two Javelin squadrons were among the first units to feel the chill blast of the reductions planned for FEAF. After some years of excellent service with 60 and 64 Squadrons the Javelin had run into severe structural problems. Although the modifications and repairs required were not beyond the capability of 390 Maintenance Unit at Seletar, they were extensive and stretched the limited resources of that hard worked unit considerably. It was decided to phase out the Javelin rather than devote an uneconomic effort to its repair.

No 64 Squadron, which had come out from the UK to reinforce FEAF during Confrontation, was disbanded as quickly as possible, any serviceable Javelins being retained for use by 60 Squadron. Within a year, however, it was the turn of 60 Squadron to be wound up—a great blow to FEAF as it was one of the oldest and most respected squadrons in the Command and the one which had borne the brunt of the air defence commitment throughout the postwar years. On 26 April 1968, the squadron mounted a farewell parade and flypast over Singapore. Appropriately for a night fighter squadron, a diamond formation of nine Javelins took off from Tengah at dusk, treated Singapore to a splendid display as darkness rapidly fell and landed back on the Tengah runway in total darkness. The final disbandment ceremony was held on 30 April, and it coincided with the good news that 60 Squadron was to re-form in the European theatre, regrettably not as a fighter squadron but as the communications squadron of the Second Tactical Air Force at Wildenrath in Germany. And so this famous squadron which held a virtually unbroken record of existence since the early days of the First World War, was to continue but in a non-operational role. Most of its Javelins were reduced to scrap, but a few were sent to Seletar to be used to train technicians of the Singapore Air Force on the maintenance of jet aircraft.

Disbandment of 60 and 64 Squadrons would have left Singapore without an air defence squadron as the RAAF Sabre squadrons were far to the north at Butterworth and could only effectively cover the northern part of the peninsula. One of the Fighter Command Lightning squadrons was therefore despatched to Tengah to fill the air defence gap until the Singapore Air Force was capable of assuming the commitment. All Lightning squadrons had been modified for in-flight refuelling by the force of Victor tankers and so it was possible for 74 Squadron, which had been selected for FEAF, to fly its aircraft out to Singapore, an operation which would have been impracticable for such short range fighters in earlier years. The introduction of a new type did not produce any great problems for FEAF. The Lightning was well proven in UK service, had pioneered the route to Singapore via Gan and was no more complex from a servicing point of view than the Javelin. Furthermore, although its performance was greatly superior to its predecessor, the main airfields of Tengah, Changi and Butterworth were fully capable of accepting it.

The year 1968 also saw the disbandment of 34 Squadron which had continued to operate its Beverleys from Seletar when the Borneo commitment ceased. Eight years had passed since the squadron was formed and this, the last of the Beverley units in RAF service, had played an immensely valuable part in Confrontation. No aircraft had had a harder life and the effects of years of exposure to the harsh climate had made it increasingly difficult to combat corrosion. It was reaching the end of its life and the time had clearly come to pension it off. A tragedy marred the last month of 34 Squadron's service. Having lost no aircraft since the formation of the squadron in 1960, a Beverley and its crew, captained by Squadron Leader N Bacon, were lost only 16 days before the disbandment. The aircraft crashed in the hills of Central Malaya in extremely bad weather. There were no survivors and it took a considerable time to locate the wreckage which was completely burnt out. This accident overshadowed the disbandment ceremony at Seletar on 15 January 1968, but nothing could mar the record of this vast, ungainly aircraft which had everywhere been affectionately abused but which had given the RAF the ability to carry and discharge loads for the Army which had previously been considered impossible.

Occasional mention only has been made of Hong Kong in this narrative where the Hunters of 28 Squadron had provided the essential air defence element for some years. During the aftermath of the communist takeover in China and the Korean war, Hong Kong had been stable and peaceful. Vigilance along the frontier in support of the British land forces, co-operation in anti-smuggling operations with the Royal Navy and the reception of many visiting aircraft on exercises and training missions had constituted the main work of RAF Kai Tak.

As the air threat to Hong Kong continued to be minimal, the Hunter was not the most suitable aircraft for the tasks required of the RAF. Consequently, during 1968, 28 Squadron was temporarily withdrawn and its Hunters replaced by Whirlwind 10 helicopters. After conversion to its new aircraft the squadron returned to Kai Tak. By this time the colony was becoming increasingly concerned at the flow of illegal immigrants from across the Chinese frontier, a flow which the police and land forces found difficult to stem. The Whirlwind proved to be a valuable adjunct to border policing, a most useful anti-smuggling instrument and also an effective search and rescue addition to the Colony's resources. In all respects, therefore, the rearming of 28 Squadron was a sound measure in keeping with the changing needs of Hong Kong.

Departure of the RAF from Borneo

The training of Malaysian personnel to take over commitments in Borneo proceeded smoothly throughout 1967. RMAF airmen were hard working and adaptable and it was decided that all responsibility could be transferred to them by mid 1968. Consequently Labuan gradually reduced its RAF strength to one officer and 30 airmen who continued to handle any specialised servicing required by the scheduled Valetta service from Singapore and the few operational aircraft on exercises or survey work. The RMAF took over the refuelling and general handling of all visiting aircraft.

This situation continued until June 1968 and the last RAF airmen left on the 16th of that month, handing over much of the equipment and the buildings to the RMAF, taking back to Singapore only such items as were still needed by the RAF. Much goodwill had been fostered during the transition, particularly with the Labuan town authorities who gave the RAF a farewell party and expressed great regret at the departure. They well remembered the rapidity with which British forces had responded to the Brunei revolt in 1962 and the tenacity with which Confrontation had been opposed. Their gratitude to Squadron Leader W R Roberts and his handful of RAF personnel as they departed on 16 June was heart warming. It was a satisfactory conclusion to many years of occupation of the Labuan island staging post by the Royal Air Force.

The Reductions Continue

Back in Singapore the reductions foreshadowed in the 1967 and 1968 Defence White Papers continued, the next aircraft to be phased out being the Belvederes of 66 Squadron. The only twin rotor heavy lift helicopter in service had performed splendidly once the initial teething troubles of what had been a radical design were eradicated. It was a particularly unwelcome step as far as the Army was concerned as the Belvedere gave unprecedented mobility, particularly to gunners and engineers in its ability to lift and position accurately pieces of artillery, radar equipment and heavy machinery. The loss of 66 Squadron was accentuated by the knowledge that there was to be no equivalent replacement in the RAF. Although many proposals were to be considered in subsequent years for another heavy lift helicopter, it was not until 1980 that the RAF was able to buy the Chinook from the United States after it had proved itself in intensive operational use, notably in Vietnam.

Ironically 66 Squadron completed its service at Seletar with the busiest month in its short history by completing its monthly flying task in only 10 days. Its final demonstration took the form of flying six Belvederes over Singapore City, each carrying a 105 mm gun of 145 Commando Light Battery, RA and parking them neatly on Seletar airfield. The Squadron was finally disbanded on 20 March 1969 and was not re-formed elsewhere. Its aircraft were dismantled and never again used, a fate which was viewed with as much regret in FEAF as had been the demise of the Sunderland flying boat years before.

In general the reduction and disbandment of the operational squadrons only have been mentioned in this narrative. Many other supporting units were similarly treated, the overall policy being to slim down the staffs and to economise in personnel throughout the Command. For example, the RAF Regiment lost one LAA Squadron, namely 26 Squadron from Changi, which left two units on Singapore island, one at Seletar and one at Tengah. All three stations were for the time being retained but it was clear that in due course they would be handed over to the Singapore Air Force.

HQ 224 Group had continued in operational control under FEAF but, by 1968, its responsibilities hardly justified its retention. Since Confrontation the Group had been established on a mobile basis against the need for rapid deployment in either Western or Eastern Malaysia. But that requirement had also faded as the years passed. Consequently the decision was made to disband the Group at the end of September 1968 and to control all remaining units direct from HQ FEAF. The principle of rotating command of the Group between the RAF and RAAF had been followed since the days of the Malayan Emergency, and the last AOC was Air Vice-Marshal B A Eaton CB DSO DFC RAAF. He was then appointed Chief of Staff at HQ FEAF where he was well placed to control the operational activities of the remaining squadrons. This famous Far Eastern Group had thus been formed and disbanded twice during the past 26 years and for a brief period had been designated AHQ Malaya. The names of its commanders throughout that period will be found in Appendix C.

For very good reasons this chapter has been entitled 'Three Anxious Years.' It covers the period 1966 to 1969 when the future of British forces in the Far East hung in the balance. At the end of that period they were still under sentence to withdraw completely from the Far East by 1971, but slight indications were beginning to appear that the finality of the policy enshrined in the 1968 Defence White Paper might be ameliorated. Representations from the SEATO Powers, Malaysia, and from the Singapore Government were not without their effect in Whitehall and these, coupled with the proximity of the savage war in Vietnam, were causing misgivings about the wisdom of abandoning the theatre completely. The outcome of these deliberations and their effect upon FEAF will be dealt with in the next chapter.

21

Departure

The early part of 1970 did little to allay the anxieties of FEAF despite the rumours that the announced policy of total withdrawal from the Far East was meeting with opposition in Whitehall. The withdrawal from Aden had been completed according to plan more than two years earlier, and it was known that departure of British forces from the Gulf was less than two years away.

FEAF's squadrons continued to rundown, 81 Squadron at Tengah being the next one to suffer disbandment. Many allusions have been made in earlier chapters to the vital photographic reconnaissance and survey work of this squadron. It had been the only squadron fulfilling this role since the end of hostilities in the NEI in 1946 and it had surveyed virtually the whole of South-East Asia with its Mosquitos, Meteors and finally Canberras as well as providing millions of tactical photographs for the operational ground forces in Malaya and Borneo. But 16 January 1970 was the day selected for its disbandment at Tengah which had been the squadron's base for many years. An impressive farewell ceremony was held on the airfield, after which most of its aircraft were flown home to be re-distributed among other PR squadrons. The Standard was laid up and the squadron was not reactivated in another theatre, always a matter for intense regret when a squadron has had such a long and distinguished record.

Within a month it was the turn of two more of FEAF's long service squadrons to leave Tengah. As the Lightnings of 74 Squadron had taken over the air defence commitment it was decided to reduce the size of 20 Squadron and to send its surplus Hunters back to the United Kingdom where they could be re-furbished and give valuable service in the training organisation. This process continued until February 1970 when the rump of the squadron was finally disbanded. But there was to be a future for this old squadron which, in its long history, had been disbanded and subsequently re-formed no less than four times. On this occasion it was to re-form some eight months later at Wildenrath as one of 2TAF's Harrier squadrons.

It was also the turn of 45 Squadron to leave the Far East and these two units mounted a joint farewell parade at Tengah on 18 February 1970. After a flypast by 6 Canberras and 6 Hunters at dusk, their two Standards, which had been floodlit during the parade, were marched off into the gathering darkness. No 45 Squadron was subsequently re-formed at West Raynham in 38 Group on Hunter GA9s and thus became one of the Group's mobile ground attack squadrons designed to reinforce any overseas theatre in an emergency. It was a fitting role for a squadron which had provided FEAF's main strike capability for many years. The departure of 81, 20 and 45 Squadrons virtually emptied Tengah in preparation for handing the station over to the Singapore Air Force.

A Significant Change of Policy

The General Election of June 1970 resulted in a change of British Government, and the earlier rumours of opposition to the defence policies of the previous Government were not long in being substantiated. By this time, however, FEAF had been so emasculated that there was little prospect of any increase in its strength. Nevertheless the issue of a Supplementary Statement on Defence was eagerly awaited from the new Government, and it was circulated in October[1]. So important was it that extracts relevant to British forces in the Far East are worth quoting verbatim.

First Extract. Britain has long standing associations with the Commonwealth countries of South-East Asia and she shares their interest in the stability of the area. The Government believes that the total withdrawal of forces planned by the previous Administration would have weakened the security of Malaysia and Singapore; and that a continuing British military presence on the spot will be valuable in helping to preserve confidence in the area. It has therefore proposed to the four Commonwealth governments of Australia, Malaysia, New Zealand and Singapore that Five Power defence arrangements should be established as soon as possible, which would include a contribution of British forces . . . . They would replace the bilateral Anglo-Malaysian Defence Agreement.

---

[1] Command 4521

Second Extract. It is planned that the British contribution, which has been broadly designed to complement the forces of the other four Governments, will comprise

Five frigates or destroyers on station East of Suez (including Hong Kong)

A British battalion group, including an air platoon and an artillery battery

A detachment of Nimrod long range maritime reconnaissance aircraft

A number of Whirlwind helicopters.

Third Extract. There will also be a considerable number of visits by combat units of all three Services for jungle, air and maritime training and exercises in the area.

Far East Defence Pacts

The defence policy amendments published in the above Statement created considerable confusion as far as the existing defence pacts in the theatre were concerned. The South-East Asia Treaty Organisation was still in being, but it was of course a purely planning arrangement, and had no command structure and no specific forces allocated to it. Up to a point it had been successful in bringing operational forces of the member Powers together for numerous exercises and in achieving some degree of standardisation of military procedures. But it had no 'teeth' and, by 1971, its value was in considerable doubt. It did, however, continue in existence for a further six years, after which it was disbanded by mutual consent[2].

The Anglo-Malaysian Defence Agreement, on the other hand, had proved a valuable pact from the time that Malaysia was formed in 1963, and its greatest successes had been seen during the years of Confrontation. Subsequent reductions in British forces and the expectations of total withdrawal had raised anxieties that this Agreement would eventually decay in spite of the increasing strength of the Malaysian and Singaporean forces. Certainly as far as the air was concerned, these were never likely to attain the versatility and striking power of the departing Royal Air Force.

It was clear that some wider ranging defence arrangements for South-East Asia were necessary to replace the Anglo-Malaysian Agreement. The stability of the area was vital to the interests of Australia and

---

[2] SEATO was disbanded on 30 June 1977.

29. Farewell flypast of 66 Squadron Belvederes at Seletar in 1968

30. A Valiant tanker refuelling Javelin F Mark 9s of 64 Squadron, Tengah

31. Classroom in the Infants School at RAF Seletar

32. Commemorative cairn left behind on Gan Island after the departure of the RAF

New Zealand, both of whom declared their intention of maintaining forces in Malaysia and Singapore indefinitely, a step which was warmly welcomed by those two countries, and also by the British Government. It was this situation which led to Five Power defence talks, and which eventually resulted in the Five Power Agreement outlined in the Supplementary Defence Statement of October 1970. Within this Agreement, New Zealand and the United Kingdom co-ordinated their contributions to the security of South-East Asia under a separate pact, commonly known as ANZUK—the initials of the three nations. The ANZUK force was to be concentrated in Singapore under a joint headquarters.

For a modest cost, estimated at no more than £10M a year in foreign currency, Britain had therefore solved her pressing problem of overseas defence costs and, at the same time, agreed to maintain a significant contribution to the security of South-East Asia as well as the ability to reinforce that contribution rapidly in an emergency. Additionally it ensured that areas for jungle training and exercises in the testing environment of the Far East would remain available for the training of all Britain's forces. Five Power planning continued throughout the remainder of 1970 and into 1971 and the arrangements already announced were amplified in Britain's Defence White Paper of 1971.[3] Therein it was stated that Britain's contribution would be deployed during 1971–72 and, furthermore, that detachments of Vulcan medium bombers, Phantoms and Buccaneers would spend several weeks at a time in the Far East to participate in exercises and maintain the strategic reinforcement route. This latter commitment meant that Gan would continue to function as an important Indian Ocean RAF staging post at least for some time to come[4].

The integrated Command devised to control the ANZUK forces was to be headed by an officer of two star rank appointed from any one of the three participating countries, with his headquarters in Singapore. Finally it was announced that many of the facilities hitherto used by the British forces would be transferred free of charge to the local Governments, a gesture which it was calculated would cost about £19 M during the year 1971–72. Thus the future policy was clearly stated, the Anglo-Malaysian Agreement was wound up and, short of any unforeseen emergency, there was no prospect of any

[3] Cmnd 4592
[4] Gan was not closed down until 28 March 1976.

further reprieve for the Royal Air Force in the Far East. Disappointing though these developments were, at least a toe hold had been retained under the Five Power Agreement and the finality of total withdrawal such as had occurred in the Middle East had been avoided. It now remained for the last phase of the rundown to be implemented and the new ANZUK force established.

RAF Contribution to ANZUK

Tengah, which was virtually emptied of RAF squadrons, became the Singapore Armed Forces base and it was here that the RAF force of maritime reconnaissance aircraft and Whirlwind helicopters was deployed. Eleven Mark 10 Whirlwind helicopters of 103 Squadron, which had earlier absorbed the aircraft and crews of 110 Squadron, were moved from Changi to Tengah in September 1971 and took their place alongside the helicopters of the Singapore Air Force. Similarly three Shackletons, with aircrew and ground personnel, were held back from 205 Squadron which disbanded at Changi in October 1971, and not only moved to Tengah but assumed the title of 209 Squadron. This was a temporary measure as the Nimrods promised to ANZUK were not then available. They eventually appeared as a detachment of 206 Squadron early in the following year and so completed the RAF contribution. This was a most important element of the small force as it constituted the only anti-submarine, reconnaissance, and long range air-sea rescue capability among the Five Powers. It also provided an essential link between the RAF units in Gan, Singapore and Hong Kong.

The Closure of Headquarters

The 31st October 1971 is the date which officially marks the end of the Far East Command. On that date not only did HQ Far East Command close down but it also signalled the disbandment of HQ FEAF. It is therefore a notable date in RAF history. The unified Far East Command had been in existence for almost exactly nine years, during which period it had had six Commanders-in-Chief, three from the Royal Navy, two RAF officers and one from the Army. It was the unhappy task of Air Chief Marshal Sir Brian Burnett to preside over the dissolution of the Command, after some eighteen months in the appointment.

Nine years was not a long enough period for this, the second of the unified commands, to complete the unification and integration of all of its component parts bearing in mind that it superseded three entirely independent command structures. It had, however, made much progress and the period of its life was sufficient, particularly when added to the earlier experience of the Middle East Command, for the Chiefs of Staff and the Ministry of Defence to realise that a sound, efficient and economical organisation had been developed. There could be no doubt that, if Britain ever had to deploy a large force of all arms to an overseas theatre again, the unified command structure would provide the most satisfactory organisation.

HQ FEAF, which had changed its title and its location a number of times since it was established in Singapore under Sir Keith Park in 1945, gave up its accommodation at Changi with considerable regret. Changi must undoubtedly be one of the most comfortable and well found stations that the RAF has ever occupied overseas. Perhaps its climate did not quite match up to that of, say, Akrotiri in Cyprus or Eastleigh in Kenya, but it had so many more compensations that it would be difficult to surpass as an enjoyable 'posting'. Air Marshal (later Air Chief Marshal) Sir Neil Wheeler was the last Commander-in-Chief to hold the three star rank. He completed his tour of duty in November 1970, and as the Command was then beginning to reduce, the appointment was held for the last twelve months by Air Vice-Marshal N M Maynard. A complete list of all the RAF officers who held the various senior appointments in command of formations from 1930 to 1971 will be found at Appendix C.

Formation of ANZUK Headquarters

With the dissolution of the various British Headquarters the way was clear for the establishment of the ANZUK Headquarters. This was set up on 1 November 1971 at the Singapore Naval Base on the Johore Strait. The full title of its commander was 'Commander ANZUK Forces in Malaysia and Singapore', usually shortened to the still cumbersome form 'COMANZUKFOR'. The air element was entitled 'Air Component ANZUK Air Headquarters' and under its control came the three Shackletons of 209 Squadron, and the Whirlwinds of 103 Squadron all located at Tengah.

Understandably many more weeks were needed to pack up and ship RAF equipment home, to hand over those items to be left either for the ANZUK force or for Malaysia and Singapore and to move the last personnel and families out by air and sea. By 1972, however, the once powerful RAF in the Far East was reduced to the staging post at Gan, RAF Hong Kong with 28 Squadron at Kai Tak and the contribution to ANZUK in Singapore. It is an appropriate point at which to close this chapter and, apart from drawing some conclusions about the loss of this distant RAF Command in a final chapter, to close the history of the Royal Air Force in the Far East.

The Defence White Paper of 1975 (Cmnd 5976) announced the intention to withdraw the contribution to ANZUK from Singapore by April 1976, but to maintain a small residual contribution to the Integrated Air Defence System. This policy was confirmed in the Defence White Paper of 1976 (Cmnd 6432) and the detachment of Nimrods of 206 Squadron was withdrawn as announced.

22

Postscript

Some twenty-seven years of post-war experience in South-East Asia have been compressed into less than 300 pages in this narrative. It was a period of quite exceptional change for Britain during which she relinquished control of much of her Empire and withdrew her garrison forces, not only from the Far East but from the Middle East and many other parts of the world. Prior to these developments Royal Air Force airmen and airwomen had been able to gain a breadth of experience unmatched by any other air force. With the departure of the bulk of the force from Singapore in 1971, this wide experience was to be denied to future generations except on very few and infrequent occasions, usually of short duration.

It would be wrong to terminate this story abruptly with the closing of HQ FEAF and the ceremonies which preceded the departure of so many squadrons from the Singapore airfields. Some assessment must be made of how much the RAF gained from its Far Eastern sojourn, and to what extent it will suffer in future years from the lack of service in those parts. At most a man serves forty years and the average is less than half of that period. By 1990, therefore, there will be but a handful of airmen still serving who have experienced service in the Far East. Most airmen will be fortunate if they can look back upon one or two tours of duty overseas, and those will probably have been in Germany where conditions are not all that different from the UK, whereas three, four and even more tours were commonplace in earlier years. A similar situation will arise with new generations of aircraft, weapons and equipment. Except for transitory acquaintance-ship they will not have the benefit of operating in the rigorous climatic conditions which can only be found in distant parts.

One of the primary reasons for compiling this history, and its earlier counterpart,[1] is to safeguard for future generations of RAF

---

[1] Flight from the Middle East by the same author.

personnel some at least of the lessons learned and experience gained by their forbears against the time when—perhaps—the RAF may again be required to operate in the jungles, mountains and deserts of South-East Asia and the Middle East.

Flexibility of Air Power

It has taken the Royal Air Force many years to prove to politicians and its sister Services the true flexibility of air power and to persuade them away from the belief in static garrisons or fragmented air components. The concentration of the various elements of Britain's air power into a single independent Royal Air Force in 1918 was met with much opposition which is perhaps understandable when the severe limitations in range, speed, weapon loads and the fragility of the aircraft of that era are considered. The wisdom of that far sighted decision of 1 April 1918 has been demonstrated time and time again, but nowhere more convincingly than in the Far East. The Command, which covered a vast area of land and ocean, never possessed in peacetime more than a handful of squadrons yet was rarely without some form of operational activity within its bounds. Nevertheless its few squadrons were always to be found at the seat of trouble. It would be invidious to select a particular squadron to illustrate this point but it will have become abundantly apparent in the foregoing chapters that certain units operated with equal facility, often at extremely short notice, in Malaya, the NEI, Borneo, Hong Kong, Ceylon and Korea. Always under a single RAF commander they were switched from region to region as the need arose. This is true flexibility.

It is true that hardly ever did two or more emergencies arise at the same time. Had the Malayan Emergency coincided with Confrontation, for example, the Far East Air Force would have been hard pressed and probably needed considerable reinforcement. But it is in the nature of world events short of a universal conflict that emergencies tend to arise singly and in such circumstances a remarkable economy of force can be obtained by the skilful and timely switching of modest air resources. In this respect, therefore, the Far East theatre did much to drive home the lesson that air power, particularly with the advent of high speed, long range aircraft capable of carrying heavy loads and being refuelled in flight, has immense flexibility which must be used to maximum effect.

Operational Flying

It must be a truism that the greater the variety of conditions under which the RAF flies and operates, the more versatile and proficient will be its aircrew. In South-East Asia conditions of climate and terrain are to be found which are unlikely in any other overseas region in which the RAF served. In particular the monsoonal climate produces violent changes of weather in which even the most sophisticated navigation aids cannot always be relied upon, and the basic skills of pilots and navigators are called into play. Even at high altitudes, rapidly growing cumulo-nimbus clouds can be extremely dangerous for the less robust aircraft. Violent turbulence, thunder and lightning are a feature of these cloud formations and nowhere are they more prevalent than in the Far East. At lower altitudes torrential rain and low cloud are features of the monsoon and, as has been shown in Borneo, can restrict tactical operations severely, putting an immense strain on aircrews attempting to locate a target or landing strip. When to these hostile climatic conditions is added the carpet of dense jungle covering much of the region which makes map reading difficult even when good photographs and accurate maps are available, which is not always the case, experience and skill are essential if safety standards are to be high and operations efficient.

Clearly these operational flying conditions can never be created in Europe, which admittedly has its own particular hazards of fog and icing. The loss of tours of duty in the Far East lasting for several years can only deny to future RAF aircrew the opportunity to become conversant with, and experienced in a type of flying which is unique. To that extent the versatility of pilots and navigators must suffer. This is particularly regrettable so far as single seater pilots are concerned as they, more than any aircrew, are dependent upon their own initiative when conditions are unfavourable.

The RAF has always prided itself on the comprehensiveness of its aircrew training but, to maintain its high standards, it must have access to every possible variation of operating condition. That access has been severely restricted since withdrawal not only from the Far East, but also from the Middle East; and some loss of valuable experience is, therefore, inevitable.

Technical Experience

Throughout this narrative there has been evidence of the failure of airframe, engines and components due to the conditions in which aircraft were required to operate and be maintained. The wooden construction of the Mosquito could not endure the high humidity in the Far East: the rotor blades of the earlier helicopters suffered cracking from the same cause: corrosion on the large top surfaces of the Beverley became serious and salt laden sand and dust ingested by engines shortened their life considerably. In addition, it was noticeable that the performance of many aircraft, of which the earlier versions of the Whirlwind are good examples, was markedly inferior to that of their counterparts in Europe.

With engineering skill, improvisation and hard work most of the technical problems which affected FEAF's aircraft, weapons and equipment could be, and were, solved locally. Furthermore the lessons learnt were incorporated in subsequent designs and the experience gained in squadron use was invaluable to designers and manufacturers alike. Tropical trials of aircraft and equipment have always been carried out with new designs, but they have had to be of relatively short duration and usually conducted on well equipped airfields such as Tengah or Changi. Good though such preliminary trials may be, they can never be a substitute for the hard wear and tear of squadron usage over extended periods and often in the most unfavourable conditions.

In general the provision of spare parts, replacement engines and such items as tyres is based upon the principle of 'fair wear and tear', and appropriate scales are drawn up and stocks ordered when new aircraft and equipment come into service. In some cases where a limited build of an aircraft, for example, is decided upon, an attempt is made to provision spares for the expected life of that aircraft. 'Fair wear and tear', however, has little meaning when applied to equipment used in certain overseas areas, and this applied to the Far East. The consumption of certain items which were particularly affected by the harsh climatic conditions was greater by far than would have been the case in the European theatre. Consequently provisioning scales were always difficult to assess with any degree of accuracy: a Javelin could, for example, use twice as many tyres in FEAF as a similar fighter would use in Germany. There were many instances of equipment remaining unserviceable for long periods due to the delay in obtaining replacement parts from the United Kingdom where provisioning had not taken full account of excessive consumption in the Far East. This problem applied particularly to rubber and perspex items, and also to delicate radio and electrical items which deteriorated rapidly in the humidity and salt laden atmosphere. It was not the solution to hold unduly large stocks at, say, Seletar as the task of maintaining a stockpile of sensitive equipment in good order was far too costly and time consuming.

The loss of Far East service to the RAF inevitably means the loss of the opportunity to submit all forms of technical equipment to extreme conditions over extended periods which alone can expose certain weaknesses. It means that tropical trials will either have to be conducted on a much larger and more realistic scale than before, or that the risk will have to be accepted that airframes, engines and equipment may fail in a manner which would have been avoided had the RAF been able to continue to subject them to hard service in extreme conditions. Similarly risks will have to be taken in calculating provisioning scales in the absence of precise knowledge of the performance of items under such conditions. Much can be done, and is done, to simulate these conditions, but nothing can take the place of practical experience in the theatre.

The Effect on RAF Personnel

We have spoken of the loss of technical experience and of flying and operating techniques. To what extent will the loss of tours of duty in the Far East affect the airmen and airwomen, and the families of the Royal Air Force? It must be remembered that this is not the only overseas theatre from which the Service has either withdrawn or has been severely reduced in recent years. No more than one, or perhaps two tours abroad can now be expected in a full length career although there are still opportunities for detachments of relatively short duration. Perhaps the greatest value which a two and a half year tour in the Far East gave to airmen and their families was adaptability and the increased maturity which came from experiencing the unusual climate and style of living which could often be primitive. Living and working in such conditions frequently called for an unusual degree of initiative and improvisation. Junior officers and NCOs were often called upon to accept responsibility beyond that normally required of men and women of their rank at home. Rules and regulations could not be as strictly enforced and much more scope was left to the initiative of the individual whose self confidence was bound to benefit. The loss of so much overseas service must, therefore, be detrimental to the efficiency of the RAF as a whole, if only because it denies to officers and airmen the opportunity to experience life in widely different parts of the world. "Get your knees brown, chum" will no longer be an appropriate comment for a long service NCO to make to an inexperienced colleague.

Singapore was always a popular posting for Service families who not only found the unusual and exotic environment exciting but also found themselves better off financially when the local overseas allowances and duty free advantages were taken into account. With adequate married quarters, extremely good facilities for recreation and leisure, not to mention good schooling and medical attention, the three main stations on the island were as well found as any in the RAF, and better than most. There is little doubt that the standard of living for airmen and their families was higher than at home: the climate, although sometimes trying, was not unhealthy with the result that the majority of Service men and women gained immeasurably from their tour of duty. Even though detachments of various sorts to the Far East continue, they tend to be unaccompanied, with families no longer able to participate in them, which inevitably increases the amount of separation and turbulence which has always been a major cause of complaint among Service personnel.

However many opportunities are taken to participate in exercises, to send out aircraft, weapons and equipment for tropical trials and to arrange training flights, one must conclude that the loss of the Far East station as a major overseas command has been greatly to the disadvantage of the Royal Air Force in its efforts to maintain a widely experienced and fully adaptable component of Britain's Armed Forces.

After reading this Postscript some may feel that, as the circumstances in which the RAF operates in the 1980s have changed fundamentally from the days of Empire, it is unduly nostalgic to emphasise the loss of opportunity to serve in the tropics. The modern RAF is geared to European conditions and its personnel, weapons and equipment are unlikely to be required to operate for any length of time in tropical climates and over jungle and desert. If this is true, and it may well be, the need for extensive tropical trials of weapon systems and their associated equipment, and the acclimatisation of RAF personnel will clearly be unnecessary. Nevertheless, there can be no certainty that some future emergency may not arise in distant parts requiring the participation of the Royal Air Force—it has already happened on a small scale in Belize and this serves to reinforce the general conclusion that, although the Service is now required to apply its skill and efficiency in different conditions, the loss of tropical experience must to some extent affect the versatility of both men and machines.

Appendix A

Hours and Sorties flown and Casualties sustained by the Royal Air Force in the Netherlands East Indies. October 1945 to November 1946

	Sorties	Hours
31 (Dakota) Squadron	11,200	24,436
47 (Mosquito) Squadron Detachment	77	143
60 (Thunderbolt) Squadron	2,429	3,251
81 (Thunderbolt) Squadron	2,018	3,526
681/684 (Spitfire and Mosquito) Squadron Detachments	285	643
84 (Mosquito) Squadron	391	714
110 (Mosquito) Squadron Detachment	18	47
155 (Spitfire) Squadron	815	1,042
656 (Auster) AOP Squadron	2,300	2,310
Totals	19,533	36,112

Air Crashes believed due to Hostile Action		Officers	ORs
1 Mosquito over Batavia—Bandoeng Convoy			
1 Mosquito over Soerabaya	Killed	3	1
1 Thunderbolt at Ambarawa	Injured	–	2
1 Thunderbolt near Soerabaya	Missing	1	–
1 Thunderbolt near Sabang (Sumatra)			

Air Crashes due to other causes		Officers	ORs
1 Dakota near Batavia	Killed	5	10
1 Dakota returning to Batavia	Injured	–	–
Other flying accidents	Missing	–	–

Casualties due to other accidents

	Died	–	3
	Injured	4	14

Casualties from Indonesian
Hostilities

	Killed	5	12
	Injured	2	19
	Missing	–	2

		Officers	ORs
Killed		13	23
Died		–	3
Injured		6	35
Missing		1	2
	Totals	20	63

Appendix B

RAF Squadrons loaned to the Indian Government after the amalgamation of BAFSEA and AHQ India on 1 April 1946

Squadron	Role	Aircraft	Group	Location in India
5	DF/GA	Tempest	225	BHOPAL
30	DF/GA	Tempest	225	BHOPAL
45	L.B.	Mosquito	225	ST THOMAS MOUNT
298	A/B Forces	Halifax	227	SAMUNGLI CHAKLALA (Det)
176	N/F	Mosquito	228	BAIGACHI
658	AOP	Auster	228	CALCUTTA
355	H.B.	Liberator	228	DIGRI
159	H.B.	Liberator	228	SALBANI
353	Trans	Dakota/York	229	PALAM
232	Trans	Liberator	229	PALAM
10	Trans	Dakota	229	POONA
76	Trans	Dakota	229	POONA

Note: These squadrons were gradually reduced in number before the Independence of India on 14 August 1947.

Appendix C

RAF and RAAF Commanders in the Far East

HQ Far East Command[1]
Formed 28.11.62

Air Chief Marshal Sir John Grandy KCB KBE DSO	28.5.65
Air Chief Marshal Sir Brian Burnett GCB DFC AFC ADC BA	29.5.70

Royal Air Force Base, Singapore

Group Captain H M Cave-Brown-Cave CBE	1. 1.30
Group Captain A H Jackson	17.10.30
Group Captain S W Smith OBE	10.11.33
(HEADQUARTERS ROYAL AIR FORCE FAR EAST COMMAND formed on 1 December 1933—Group Captain Smith retained command with the rank of Air Commodore)	
Air Vice-Marshal A W Tedder	11.11.36
Air Vice-Marshal J T Babington CB CBE DSO	10. 9.39
Air Chief Marshal Sir Robert Brooke-Popham GCVO KCB CMG DSO AFC	18.11.40
Air Vice-Marshal C W H Pulford CB OBE	26. 4.41
Air Vice-Marshal P C Maltby CB DSO AFC	5. 2.42

[1] In addition to the Royal Air Force Commanders-in-Chief, the following officers from the Royal Navy and Army also filled the appointment during the lifetime of the Far East Command:

Admiral Sir David Luce GCB DSO OBE	·28.11.62
Admiral Sir Varyl Begg GCB DSO DSC	1. 4.63
General Sir Michael Carver KCB CBE DSO MC	1. 2.67
Admiral Sir Peter Hill-Norton KCB	18. 3.69

With the loss of Malaya and the East Indies, Royal Air Force Far East, or what remained of it, withdrew to India, and was regrouped under AIR HEADQUARTERS, BENGAL, which was commanded as follows:

Air Vice-Marshal D F Stevenson CBE DSO	20. 4.42
Air Vice-Marshal T M Williams CB OBE MC DFC	1. 1.43

AIR COMMAND, SOUTH-EAST ASIA, came into being in November 1943:

Air Chief Marshal Sir Richard E C Pierse KCB DSO AFC	16.11.43
Air Marshal Sir Guy Garrod KCB OBE MC DFC LLD	27.11.44
Air Chief Marshal Sir Keith R Park KBE CB MC DFC	25. 2.45
Air Marshal Sir George C Pirie KBE CB MC DFC	30. 4.46

Renamed AIR COMMAND FAR EAST on 30 November 1946

Air Marshal Sir Hugh P Lloyd KBE CB MC DFC	18.11.47

Renamed FAR EAST AIR FORCE on 30 June 1949

FAR EAST AIR FORCE

Air Marshal Sir Francis J Fogarty KBE CB DFC AFC	26.11.49
Air Marshal Sir Clifford Sanderson CB CBE DFC	11. 6.52
Air Marshal Sir Francis J Fressanges CB	12.11.54
Air Marshal The Earl of Bandon KBE CB CVO DSO	13. 7.57
Air Marshal A D Selway KCB DFC	30. 6.60
Air Marshal Sir Hector McGregor KCB CBE DSO	31. 5.62
Air Marshal Sir Peter Wykeham KCB DSO OBE DFC AFC AFRAeS	10. 6.64
Air Marshal Sir Rochford Hughes KCB CBE AFC FRAeS	8. 8.66
Air Marshal Sir Neil Wheeler KCB CBE DSO DFC AFC	11. 2.69
Air Vice-Marshal N M Maynard CB CBE DFC AFC	1.10.70

NO 224 GROUP

Group Captain S F Vincent DFC AFC	18. 1.42
Air Commodore J L Vachell MC	12. 4.42
Air Commodore G E Wilson OBE	24. 8.42
Air Commodore A Gray MC	2. 1.43
Air Vice-Marshal The Earl of Bandon CB DSO	19. 7.44

Disbanded 30 September 1945

AHQ MALAYA

Air Vice-Marshal J D Breakey CB DFC	1.10.45
Air Vice-Marshal J W Jones CB CBE	8.11.47
Air Vice-Marshal A C Sanderson CB CBE DFC	28. 5.48
Air Vice-Marshal Sir Francis J W Mellersh KBE AFC	13. 5.49
Air Commodore J L F Fuller-Good CBE	24. 8.51
Air Vice-Marshal G H Mills CB DFC	14. 2.52
Air Vice-Marshal F R W Scherger CB CBE DSO AFC	1. 1.53
Air Vice-Marshal W H Kyle CB CBE DSO DFC ADC	14. 1.55
Air Vice-Marshal V E Hancock CBE DFC	11. 6.57

Renamed HQ 224 GROUP 31 August 1957

Air Vice-Marshal R A R Rae CB OBE	15. 6.59
Air Vice-Marshal F Headlam CBE	24. 7.62
Air Vice-Marshal C N Foxley-Norris CB DSO OBE MA	30.11.64
Air Vice-Marshal B A Eaton CB DSO DFC	4. 3.67

Re-titled HQ 224 (MOBILE) GROUP Mid 1967
Disbanded 1 October 1968

Appendix D

RAF Squadrons which participated in the Confrontation with Indonesia

Squadron	Aircraft	Main Base	Detachments	Tasks
20	Hunter GA 9	Tengah	Labuan/Kuching	Air Defence Patrols
60	Javelin F 9	Tengah	Labuan/Kuching	Air Defence Patrols
64	Javelin F 9	Tengah	Labuan/Kuching	Air Defence Patrols
81	Canberra PR7	Tengah	Labuan	Photo Recce
34	Beverley C 1	Seletar	Labuan	Supply to Forward Areas
215	Argosy C 1	Changi	Labuan	Supply to Forward Areas
205	Shackleton MR2	Changi	Labuan	Maritime Recce
209	Pioneer CC1 Twin Pioneer CC1	Seletar	Various Air Strips	Supply to Forward Areas
66	Belvedere HC1	Seletar	Kuching	Heavy Lift Supply to Forward Areas
110	Whirlwind 10 Sycamore 14	Seletar	Various Air Strips	General Helicopter Supply
103	Whirlwind 10	Seletar	Various Air Strips	General Helicopter Supply
225	Whirlwind 10	UK	Various Air Strips	General Helicopter Supply
230	Whirlwind 10	UK	Various Air Strips	General Helicopter Supply
45	Canberra B 15	Tengah	Labuan	Offensive Standby
52	Valetta C 1	Butterworth	Labuan	MR Transport
28	Hunter GA 9	Kai Tak	Labuan/Kuching	Air Defence Patrols
48	Hastings C1/2	Changi	Labuan	MR Transport
65 (SAM)	Bloodhound	Seletar	Kuching	Air Defence

Appendix E

Glossary of Terms and Abbreviations

AFCE	Air Command Far East
ACSEA	Air Command South-East Asia
ADIZ	Air Defence Identification Zone
AFNEI	Allied Forces Netherlands East Indies
AFPFL	Anti-Fascist Peoples Freedom League
AFV	Armoured Fighting Vehicle
ALFSEA	Allied Land Forces South-East Asia
AOA	Air Officer i/c Administration
AOP	Air Observation Post (Squadron)
BAFSEA	Base Air Forces South-East Asia
Birdcage	First phase of RAPWI Operation
Birdsong	RAF strike in Western Malaysia—December 1964
Bithess	Bituminized hessian runway covering
BOAC	British Overseas Airways Corporation
CAEF	Casualty Air Evacuation Flight
CENTO	Central Treaty Organisation
D/F	Direction Finding
DZ	Dropping Zone
FAC	Forward Air Controller
FDL	Forward Defence Location
JOC	Joint Operations Centre
LAA	Light Anti-Aircraft
LCA	Landing Craft Assault
LSI (L)	Landing Ship Infantry (Large)
MAAF	Malayan Auxiliary Air Force
Mastiff	Second phase of RAPWI operation
MCP	Malayan Communist Party
MPAJA	Malayan Peoples Anti-Japanese Army
MRLA	Malayan Races Liberation Army
MSU	Mobile Signals Unit
NATO	North Atlantic Treaty Organisation
NOIC	Naval Officer in Charge
PBF	Patriotic Burmese Forces
PR	Photographic Reconnaissance
PSP	Pierced Steel Planking (for laying on runways)
Python	Scheme for repatriation from SEAC

RA	Royal Artillery	SEAC	South-East Asia Command
RAAF	Royal Australian Air Force	SEATO	South-East Asia Treaty
RAPWI	Recovery of Allied Prisoners		Organisation
	of War and Internees	SOA	Senior Officer i/c
RASC	Royal Army Service Corps		Administration
RIAF	Royal Indian Air Force	Spineforce	RAF reinforcement of
RMAF	Royal Malayan (later		Borneo in 1964
	Malaysian) Air Force	STSO	Senior Technical Staff
RNZAF	Royal New Zealand Air		Officer
	Force	TAF	Tactical Air Force
RM	Royal Marines	TNKU	Tentera Nasional Kalimant
RP	Rocket Projectile		Utara
SACEUR	Supreme Allied Commander		
	Europe	VE Day	Victory in Europe
SACSEA	Supreme Allied Commander	VHF	Very High Frequency
	South-East Asia	VJ Day	Victory over Japan
SAM	Surface to Air Missiles	Zipper	Operation for recapture of
SAS	Special Air Service		Malaya and Singapore in
	(Regiment)		1945
SASO	Senior Air Staff Officer		

Index

Note: The references in this index do not include the Appendices. Ranks used are those current at the time.

Printed in the UK for HMSO
Dd736234 C30 1/84 (1777)